Travelers Within

Journeys Into Being Human and Beyond

(Volume 1 – AwarenesSphere, Emergence, Presence)

Val Jon Farris

Cover Photo - I.R. Bach
Cover Graphics - Aldo Delgado
Interiors Graphics - Courtesy of the Author
Telomere DNA Image - T. Splettstoesser: www.scistyle.com

Book Title: Travelers Within: Journeys Into Being Human and Beyond (Vol1)
Author: Val Jon Farris
ASIN: B07XF7WJMV (eBook – Kindle Edition)
ISBN: 978-0-578-57364-9 (Paperback)

TESTIMONIALS

"If there is one book I've come across over the years I wish I had studied in my twenties, it is Travelers Within. A magical, difficult journey which challenges us to take an indiscriminate look inside at who we are and what propels us forward to take life full-on, guiding us to be the best human being we can be." — Cynthia English

"Travelers Within is a beautiful guidebook to letting go of the decisions that no longer serve your life. Through using the ideas it presents, I came home to loving myself, no matter the circumstances I found myself in, as a steady-state of being." — Elise Von Holten

"Have you ever wondered why you are the way you are, feel the way you feel, act the way you act? Take the journey of Travelers Within and discover how to use everything that has happened in your life to create the Being you were always meant to be. This book changed my life, and it will change your life, too." — Mindy Carson Brundige

"WOW! What a journey and an adventure. Not a rollercoaster for the faint at heart for sure. But if you can find the courage it will be the best ride of your life." — Anna Ebell

"Travelers Within is a guide book to living life free from burdens and past stories and connecting with your greatest life partner, your inner 'Agent of Being.' I got to know myself in a more empowering way and tapped into an extraordinary inner resource I never knew I had." — Susan Cantor

"Whether you are a teacher, student, yogi, practitioner or just beginning the quest of self-inquiry, this book is for you. The author is a wonderful guide for the journey within, using humor, case studies and anecdotal experiences from his own life to bring the reader closer to their deepest essence, on every level of body, mind, and spirit." — Antonio Elugardo

"Travelers Within is a bugle call to anyone who wishes to deeply explore the questions, 'who am I, and why am I here?' It is also a practical guide to consciously experiencing what we all innately know to be true–that we are spiritual beings having a human experience." — Nola Conn

"Fellow Travelers Within, welcome to the first day of the rest of your amazing life. Dive deep, ascend to your summit and beyond. You are in good hands as you will soon find out. How wonderful to discover just how divinely human we can be!" — Candie Smith

DEDICATION

I dedicate this book to all the remarkable souls I've had the privilege of working with over the years in my programs and workshops. Their courage, vulnerability, and dedication to their own growth has profoundly influenced my life and inspired me to share this inner journey work. This book is a testament to their goodness and greatness. I am deeply humbled and eternally grateful to them all.

ACKNOWLEDGMENTS

I want to thank the following individuals for their contributions towards making *Travelers Within* a reality. This book would have not been possible without their extraordinary gift of time, energy, expertise, and care.

Allison Frazier Balser
Mindy Carson Brundige
Susan Cantor
Nola Conn
Elizabeth Davidson
Anna Ebell
Antonio Elugardo
Cynthia English,
Elise Von Holten
Victoria Reynolds
Candie Smith
John Thompson

While the encouragement, content suggestions, research, editing, proofreading and manuscript production details these people provided were absolutely essential, it was the energy of love, care, and devotion that each of them brought forth during every aspect of the production process that made their contributions so special. —Val Jon

CONTENTS

FORWARD

Greetings to you. I am your literary guide, Val Jon Farris. Thank you for being interested in *Travelers Within.* As its author, I can honestly say that this two-volume set is much more than a simple read, it's an entire "life curriculum." As a behaviorist and seasoned personal-growth facilitator for over three decades, I've discovered that the secret to bringing about extraordinary positive change in people's lives is in weaving inspiration and education together into a vibrant tapestry of development. There are four "threads" I use in the tapestry of my work. They are - compelling content, inspiring real-life anecdotes, focused practices and exercises, and a comprehensive question and answer forum that ensures integration and sustained growth. These four threads have been thoughtfully, (and heart-fully) woven into *Travelers Within* and I'm genuinely enthused to share them with you and have you experience both the journey as well as the inspiring destinations you can arrive at within yourself.

Before we venture in, I want to emphasize that this "journey within" is not for beginners or for those who are new to the world of personal growth. It is rather, an advanced curriculum designed specifically for seasoned seekers and experienced facilitators, practitioners, leaders, and teachers. I have been told many times, by many people, that the material I deliver is far more advanced than any self-development offering they've ever come across . . . while at the same time being easily understandable and life-changing. Part of why I believe their assessment has merit is because I've had the privilege of conducting personal and professional-growth programs for over thirty-thousand people from all walks of life, and from all over the world. Being with and working with so many people over the years I have gained extensive insight into the inner workings of the human psyche. Whatever expertise I personally possess, however, belongs to each and every student, attendee and fellow human being I've had the opportunity of sharing the tapestry of my work with.

Writing *Travelers Within* has been a huge team effort. As an author, there is nothing more supportive than having a dedicated manuscript team who not only share a deep passion for the literary genre but are also intent on having their editorial contributions make a difference for the reader. Those who've supported this effort are not only dear friends, (some of whom I've known for many years), they are extraordinary human beings within their own right. The team's scope of experience includes accomplished authors, teachers and practitioners, CEOs and business owners, film producers, community leaders, and devoted family members and parents. They also embody a wide range of faiths and philosophies, including both Western and Eastern Religions, Metaphysics and Spiritualism, as well as Agnosticism, and even a non-spiritual scientific approach to all things infinite and eternal.

Rather than keeping these remarkable people behind the scenes, I've chosen to bring them out into the light by having each of them make their presence known. The literary contributions this group makes through their diverse sharing and thoughtful inquiries are extraordinary, and they bring a warmth and intimacy to this manuscript that could not have come about any other way. I've asked each of them to introduce themselves, share their personal experience of having worked on the project, and to document whatever questions arose for them after reading each chapter. Their deeply reflective questions demanded that I travel even more deeply into myself in order to answer them. I hope this added interaction provides you with greater understanding. So without any further explanation, I invite you to get to know our esteemed *"Travelers Within Book Team."*

My name is Allison Frazier Balser. I graduated from The University of Santa Monica with a Masters in Spiritual Psychology and a certification in Soul-Centered Coaching. I also having been certified as a Conscious Parenting Coach through The Jai Institute. My life has taken many twists and turns, but as a teen, I was sexually violated, and through this trauma, I entered a spiritual path in my search to be healed. This has been a journey to know my true self and not the one existing in the victim stories about my worthiness or lack thereof. My interests have been about the connection between the body, mind, heart, and the divine, it has been about the narrative we've told ourselves and how we can learn to turn the page to a new story that serves us and no longer keeps us in avoidable suffering. There was always something inside of me that kept searching, and now, in working with others on their journey of discovery, life has been radically fulfilling.

Reading *Travelers Within* has been life inspiring, humbling, and an incredibly powerful journey. I am in awe at the work set forth here and in awe of the experiences and capabilities we humans possess. I feel held in a new way by the path of this writing, my *Agent of Being* and by the energy of this group of readers. Every chapter was in perfect timing with my experiences in life, and I know this was meant to be. I was hospitalized at one point in the reading of this work, and through Val Jon's support, I kept going in order to finish the reading and felt so comforted by being a part of this incredible group of readers. For this and for so much more, I am eternally grateful. I feel I now have the signposts and support I need to engage in my life journey through the in-depth work these books provide. I am honored and humbled to have traveled this inner terrain.

My name is Anna Ebell. I am a filmmaker and screenwriter living the dream of what I wanted to do in my life when I was a young woman. I grew up in a physically, mentally and emotionally abusive home, then went on to find myself in a string of abusive relationships. I spent my youth reading books on self-discovery, spirituality, and astrology. I searched for answers as to what was wrong with me, but I could never find the key to unlock the mystery as to why I felt so all alone in this world, and just something to be used and discarded like trash. I met Val Jon at the rise of my career. I was an entrepreneur and had my own business with my husband. He would spend time with us at our home when he came to our city teaching his workshops. Val Jon has always remained dear to my heart. When he asked me to be a part of this project, a series of unfortunate events caused me to sink into a severe depression and social anxiety and it triggered my PTSD to a point I hid myself away until at one point I began to "travel within." In all the self-help, inspirational and metaphysical reading I had done over the decades I still was unable to find what was causing the pain in my soul. The moment I discovered what in this first book is called my *Primary Decision,* my life made immediate and total sense. It changed nothing in the past, as that is what it is, but my future is now filled with new hope and understanding.

My name is Antonio Elugardo. I'm a teacher of yoga, Qigong, meditation, breathwork, sound therapies, and voice activation. From an early age, my desire was to seek something greater than myself which led me to pursue, but not totally identify with Buddhism, Taoism, Hinduism, Tantra, Occultism, Mithraism and other ancient wisdom schools. My religion is love. I love humanity and continue to see the good in all, despite where people's individual choices have led them. To be human is to be "perfectly imperfect" and I accept that, yet continue to strive for goodness and greatness. The mind can be our best friend or our worst enemy, and the heart may be filled with infinite, unconditional love or superficial approximations of love. With these tools Val Jon has shared with us, I'm humbly reminded of how to venture into the vastness of being. With immense, infinite gratitude, I thank him for sharing his wisdom, insight, heartfelt stories, and authenticity with us fellow inner travelers. May we all be so courageous in the journey of self-discovery and beyond!

My name is Cynthia English. I'm a graduate of the Marshall School, University of Southern California, with a degree in International Finance, the Aspen Writers Conference, and Oxford University's School of Continuing Education for Creative Writing, I wrote my first novel which was published in 2010. Today, embracing the human dynamics and cultural riches I have been privileged to know, I persevere through life's lessons to embrace powerful messages of love, acceptance of different and distinct lives, and preservation of free spirit in all humanity, regardless of origin and culture. I do this by leading the non-profit organization, *Global Scribes: Youth Uniting Nations®* by using technology for positive youth impact around the world.

Travelers Within has been a journey over a lifetime, an internal cacophony of sounds, smells, people and places–memories revisited with an entirely new perspective. I realized, among many things that I have traveled with my *Agent of Being* close by my side on and off over the years, and so one of my goals now is to practice staying aware and indeed, inviting more visits and guidance from my inner mentor. If I lose my footing, I will be reaching for Val Jon's rich guidance to understand where I am and return me to my highest and best inner path.

My name is Elise Von Holten. I've had many extraordinary life adventures and spiritual awakenings . . . one of which was attending Val Jon's public workshop over 30 years ago during a crucial time in my life. I'm forever grateful to him for his teachings and for his friendship over the years. I'm filled with humility and wonder through the journeys of "traveling within" and it's been such an extraordinary flowering in my being! I have no fear of death, and no fear of life, even my chronic illness is shifting. I love this journey and the results given to a willing heart, for that is what I have. My empathic nature has blossomed, my boundaries are secure, and my curiosity in venturing into the unknown is fully engaged. *Traveling within* and contributing to others who are on the path has been, and continues to be my life's greatest joy!

My name is Mindy Carson Brundige. I am a Christian, and while I don't necessarily agree with or believe in some of the various philosophies represented in these two books, or by other members of the team, I'm open-minded and eager to learn what other people think and how they feel. Empathic by nature, I hurt when others hurt or feel joy when others are happy. I now understand more fully this deep awareness of others' emotions. I have been blessed with mostly happy moments on this earth, other than some difficult life experiences and career upheavals along my journey. In fact, I was in the midst of a career transition when I started working with the reader team for *Travelers Within*, and my father had just gone through a serious health scare. I'm convinced my involvement in this project led to my discovery of my *Agent of Being,* which has enabled me to focus on prayers for healing for my father as well as intentionally choosing the position which led to a substantial job offer. I am deeply grateful for this experience and it has taken me on an adventure I never would have expected!

My name is Susie Cantor. I've consulted with the Hospitality Business for most of my adult life and love being of service to people. I'm culturally Jewish and love its devotion to making a positive difference in the world. I believe I've had an adventurous life, although after reading *Travelers Within*, I think I really need to up my game. This is one amazing and mind-bending journey! I've experienced a number of breakthroughs that have brought me more peace and ease. I was able to recall my birth experience of being "taken" from my mom's nurturing body and thrust into a loud, scary world without her, while she was under anesthesia. As an adult, this has caused me to "freeze" in loud and scary situations and when debating opposing views. I'm now practicing facing those situations and finding my voice. I also made peace with my father before his death through one of the many useful practices in these books, and can now hold him in a place of unconditional love.

I've also started using a dream journal after not remembering my dreams for years and am learning from them. I was inspired to find that my favorite pursuit - making a difference in other peoples' lives is actually a spiritual path, and I'm now actively pursuing that path. Most intriguing is learning of my inner *Agent of Being.* Although I've heard people talk about "intuition," or asking for guidance and receiving it, I've never experienced this phenomenon personally. Now I feel I have the knowledge and practices needed to engage with this useful inner mentor. These books are a gift that keeps on giving as Val Jon's writing is so "rich" and engaging. There is something new to be experienced with every chapter!

My name is Victoria Reynolds. I was born into a fundamentalist cult where I experienced the greatest depths of Patriarchy and abuse a little girl can experience, driving me to the edge of sanity and suicide. Yet, within it all, I somehow had a gift of "knowing." There was a voice inside of me who taught me spiritual concepts and rescued me from my suicidal plunge. After running away from home as a teenager, I unknowingly began a life-long spiritual journey and love for the adventure that became my life. My inner-voice guided me through travels that have taken me to four continents, homelessness and loss, financial highs and lows that could make any head spin, and love in a way I never imagined possible. Through all of my adventures, my inner self-discovery, and processing of my pain story has been the most challenging and exhilarating. I've been with my husband for twenty-six years and discovered several years ago that he is my greatest trigger and continually provides me with the opportunity to self-assess. Together we are raising two children who are now teenagers, and I'm helping them spread their wings by spreading mine. The more inner-work I do, the more I expand my potential to be of service to the Greatest Good. From the moment I met Val Jon several years ago, I knew I had met a fellow "inner traveler." There are times I wish I could run away and have the kind of adventures he shares in his books, and yet, I know that raising children, navigating a marriage and being an entrepreneur is just as much a spiritual adventure as climbing any mountain. *Travelers Within* has helped remind me of how far I've come, what Spirit means for me, and the deep, rich connection I now have with my Self and the greater All-ness of all that is. I am eternally grateful for this journey into being human and beyond!

INTRODUCTION

The Higher Self And The AwarenesSphere

"An unexamined life is not worth living." — Plato's Apology

I believe with all my heart that we humans possess deep and abiding goodness and even greatness, (albeit these attributes may not be readily accessible to some). While there is much evidence for the fact that we can be self-centered and petty, it is our greater virtues I'll be exploring in this two-volume set. Demonstrating our pettiness is easy as we can do so with little effort, but demonstrating our goodness and greatness is a far more worthy challenge.

These greater virtues reside within what I call our *Higher Self*[1]. This elevated state of consciousness is the sacred aspect of our identity, the inner location where our spiritual nature resides. Our Higher Self is my way of describing our innate virtues of love, compassion, humility, kindness, and truth. It also represents our deep and abiding connection with whatever it is we consider to be divine or universally humbling in our lives.

Stepping back from exalting our greater virtues for a moment, the human psyche actually contains a diverse range of character and behavior traits ranging from greatness to mediocrity to pettiness. How we orchestrate this wide range of attributes, and which behaviors we choose to act on makes a huge difference in the outcomes we experience in our daily lives. And perhaps more important is the degree of awareness and forethought we bring to bear as we draw from this diverse pool of inner resources. For the more we consider the implications of our actions *before* we take them, the greater the chances are that *after* we take them our outcomes will be much more beneficial to everyone involved.

There are numerous ways of going about accessing the innate virtues of our Higher Self. *Character Modeling*[2] or the process of being influenced by mentors and role models is one of the most effective ways. While athletes and movie stars serve as inspirations for motivating many of us to perform at extraordinary levels, the kind of modeling *Travelers Within* is interested in exploring has more to do with character development than with performance enhancement. Often our best character role models are senior family members, religious, spiritual, political figures and change leaders. Extraordinary mentors such as Mother Teresa, Mahatma Gandhi, Martin Luther King, Maya Angelou, and many others serve as powerful role models for those who aspire to the greater virtues residing within the core of humanity.

Character Modeling and mentoring is a profoundly experiential and emotional process instead of a mental exercise having to do with comprehension. Just because we comprehend something doesn't necessarily mean we will apply it in our daily lives. For example, knowing we should take better care of ourselves does absolutely nothing for actually making healthy lifestyle changes. In fact, our mental understanding of it typically devolves into evidence for reinforcing our inabilities rather than our abilities. If we happen to not achieve our goals, it provides our minds with the reasons why we're not healthier, as well as the self-invalidation factor of having failed to keep our promises to ourselves.

The magical aspect of Character Modeling, however, has to do with directly experiencing the inspirational impact of a mentor's superlative behaviors and actions, living demonstrations of human virtues that deeply move us and motivate us to want to become like them. But make no mistake, inspiration alone does not ensure we will actually adopt and apply the virtues we aspire to. The essential element that ensures the mentoring process turns our aspirations into sustained behaviors has to do with our dedication to implementation. For this reason, the most effective mentoring process we can engage in includes being deeply inspired, and initiating long-term practices and lifestyle changes.

While my assertion about the abiding goodness and greatness residing within us and the reality of acting upon them could come across as naive, I have a few of these life-changing mentoring experiences to draw from that give me the confidence to make such a statement. This "greatness" I speak of isn't tied to ego performance, but rather to our Higher Self's virtuous character traits and capabilities. I fully believe we humans possess far greater capabilities than we give ourselves credit for. The human spirit is resilient, and when we need to, we can accomplish great things and overcome huge obstacles. I want to share with you two of my most beloved mentoring experiences that demonstrate this caliber of Character Modeling. The first occurred many years ago with the now-deceased scholar, engineer, and theologian, R. Buckminster Fuller, and the second one more recently with Sir Richard Branson. My personal experiences with these extraordinary mentors highlight the special kind of Character Modeling we've been exploring, as well as validates my point about the "greatness" dwelling within all of us.

Bucky Fuller And The Power of "Trimtabs"

You may know Buckminster Fuller (or "Bucky" as he liked to be called) as the inventor of the geodesic dome. In the early 1980s, before his death, I had the good fortune of working with him for a short time as his event producer. Thousands of people gathered in auditoriums around the country to hear him address the question, *"What can a single individual do to change the world?"* At those events, Bucky told a story of the U.S. Navy commissioning him to solve a critical engineering problem at the height of World War II. As the war between America and Japan raged on the high seas, the Navy needed larger battleships to seize the advantage. As these "great ships of state," as Bucky called them grew in size, their steering mechanisms required more power to turn their rudders than their engines could produce. The challenge was to find a way to steer the gigantic steel hulls with a fraction of the power.

Bucky's brilliant solution not only helped the U.S. win the war, but it also created a new paradigm for understanding and accessing the capabilities associated with our potential greatness. His solution was an ingenious mechanism called a *Trimtab*[3], a six-inch-wide by a twenty-foot long strip of metal attached by hinges to the vertical trailing edge of a ship's rudder. As the engine's hydraulics force the tiny Trimtab into the path of oncoming water, the pressure of the water pushing against it assists the rudder in making its turns. Cupping your hand into the wind while riding in a moving vehicle produces a similar Trimtab effect. A minor change in the angle of your hand will send your entire arm careening up or down with great force. (For you engineers, I realize my explanation does not take into account the pressure differential and equalization of forces that a Trimtab actually operates on, but my explanation is less complicated and makes the point I want to make so please forgive the discrepancy.)

Next, Bucky posed that like the tiny sliver of metal hinged on the trailing edge of a rudder can alter the course of a great ship of state, you and I as little individuals possess the capabilities needed to change the course of humanity. He stressed that seeing ourselves as Trimtabs is the first step towards being able to both transform our own lives and make a positive difference in our world. This can be a difficult concept to grasp, especially for those who have an investment in being powerless. I remember one particular interaction with Bucky just prior to the start of a nine-thousand person event, my biggest production ever. I was in a terrible mood and everything that could go wrong was going wrong. Just before the event's start, Bucky called me into his dressing room so we could have a little chat. I remember vividly blurting out to him as I entered. *"Bucky, I'm failing . . . I just can't do it, it's impossible to manage this event!"* I will never forget his response. *"Yes, indeed you're surely correct that the 'impossible' can't happen, but the 'possible,' now that's a different story." "Let me ask you a question Val Jon, who determines what is possible and what is not?"* After a moment he continued, *"I believe you can and will make today's event a success . . . however, you must believe in yourself in order for it to come to pass."*

Although his mentoring did nothing to lessen my feelings of overwhelm, as I walked out of his dressing room his words had a powerful impact on me. If I kept believing the challenge was impossible for me to handle, I would surely never succeed. Without believing in myself enough to say *"It is possible and I can do it,"* it would never happen. To finish the story, I did say it was possible that day, and it was indeed my best event production ever for Bucky.

This mentoring experience not only taught me that I possess far more capability than I give myself credit for but also a deeper lesson that is important to consider . . . it's not failure we fear most, but rather sustained success. For the more capable we become, and the more in touch we are with our Higher Self's capabilities, the more we must act on those capabilities. And the more we act on them, the more demand there's going to be for us to continue to demonstrate them. Since we will always be challenged by, (and even dominated by) the challenges we face in our daily lives, why not choose the challenges of rising to our potential greatness rather than constantly doing battle with our pettiness? The reality is that one doesn't become a Trimtab overnight, as it's a long and arduous process of self-exploration and devoted practice. However, those who take Plato's quote to heart by *"living an examined life"* realize that accessing their greatness is indeed possible, and they do so in a way that isn't about proving how great they are, but rather how great all of us can be.

Sir Richard Branson: An "Extreme" Mentor

A few years ago I had the good fortune to work with Richard Branson as a senior leadership consultant for his *Extreme Tech Challenge, ("XTC")* competition. *XTC* is an internationally acclaimed startup accelerator for innovative high-tech entrepreneurs that is designed to give new businesses a competitive advantage in the global marketplace. My role was to work with the finalist competitors and help mature their leadership capabilities in a way that would earn them the opportunity of receiving Richard Branson's financial support and personal guidance. Spending time with Sir Richard, working with him and mentoring the world-class entrepreneurs that gravitated to him from all over the world was truly an honor. I had for many years admired his leadership style, business acumen and philosophy of viewing one's "failures" as a necessary part of attaining success.

Just as Bucky Fuller inspired me to access my greatest inner virtues and *"make the possible happen,"* Richard Branson reinforced this wisdom by encouraging me, and everyone he came into contact with, to take risks and be courageous in the face of failure. Richard Branson certainly is a living demonstration of his own philosophy, as he is truly one of the world's most inspiring success stories. I want to share with you an inside example of just how he lives up to his legendary reputation. During one of our evening *XTC* finalist gatherings on his Necker Island home in the British Virgin Islands, he used an impromptu incident as a powerful example of his leadership philosophy. Right in the middle of addressing the contestants, the international press, and all of the global sponsors attending the gala event, one of his many lemurs appeared in the treetops above him. (Sir Richard has over 200 lemurs on the island that he has saved from extinction, some of which are free to roam the grounds.) Swinging back and forth in order to gain momentum to leap to another treetop nearly twenty feet away, Sir Richard interrupted his speech and directed everyone's attention to the lemur. I'm paraphrasing a bit, but he addressed the crowd with the following commentary, *"This is a risk for that lemur . . . he's not tried this big of a jump in the two years he's been here on the island . . . just as I was mentioning that risk-taking is an essential part of being an entrepreneur . . . and that failure is imminent . . . we must still be courageous and willing to swing out . . . so let's see how he does."* In that tense moment, all eyes were on the swinging lemur. In one huge final swing, he sailed across the gap between the treetops, arms stretched wide . . . and . . . he *just barely* clutched onto a skinny branch extending out from the other treetop!

As the attendees cheered, Sir Richard joined in with, *"So, he lives another day as an entrepreneur!"* Then he added, *"Like the lemur, you contestants here tonight must be willing to risk it all . . . swing out and don't hold anything back . . . present your startups with a passion, and live your lives like your life depends on it . . . because your lives DO depend on it!"*

What an *extremely* inspiring leadership message for us all! Thank you, Sir Richard Branson, for being such an extraordinary global mentor. *(A/N: It was just a short time after this event that a hurricane devastated the British Virgin Islands, destroying much of Richard Branson's home as well as many homes and businesses on the other islands in the chain. And true to his extreme spirit, Sir Richard chose to assist with disaster-relief for all those living on the nearby islands before attending to his own devastated island and home.)*

These two extraordinary mentoring examples live inside me as a powerful reminder that if we are willing to be courageous and live our lives as if we *can* make a huge difference, the greatness that dwells with us will find its way into our faculties and empower us to do so. By "swinging out" and taking the initiative to be Trimtabs in the world, we become powerful way-showers of what is possible, and bright lights that faithfully, and joyfully illuminate the way for others to come into accord with their Higher Selves.

Traveling Into The Inner Terrain of Our Psyche

As "travelers without," (those of us who actively explore the outer world), there are a vast number of extraordinary destinations we can visit during the course of our lives. And just like the outer world, there is an "inner" world that contains a myriad of hidden destinations that are every bit as extraordinary. In fact, this *Inner Terrain*[4] as I call it is far more expansive than all the external geography on the surface of the Earth. I will even go as far as to say that our inner terrain is every bit as vast as the entire expanse of the cosmos. While this may sound far-fetched, I ask that you keep an open mind and join me for a series of "expeditions" into this hidden inner world so you have the opportunity to experience its vastness for yourself.

While not everyone may be an experienced *Traveler Within,* everyone has plenty of experience navigating the outer world. "Traveling" is an activity we are constantly engaged in our entire lives because it's a fundamental skill set for us. As life travelers, we start out crawling on our hands and knees, transition into walking on two feet, and if we live long enough, end up shuffling along with the assistance of a walker or wheelchair. The distances and destinations we travel can vary greatly, as some of us are inclined to live our entire lives near a single location, whereas others are compelled to migrate to far-reaching destinations. The good news is that our skills and abilities with respect to "traveling without" are transferable to the challenges of "traveling within." I want to point out that I do not for a moment assume that there is a "right way" to navigate through life. Each of us must follow our own heart and seek our individual path. I do believe, however, that life is a mysterious journey and that we have an extraordinary opportunity to, as Sir Richard so wisely suggested, *swing out* and passionately explore both our outer and inner worlds. The French poet and novelist, Anatole France, beautifully illuminates the spirit of a *Traveler Within* when he said, *"Wandering reestablishes the original harmony which once existed between us and the universe."*

So what is this inner terrain composed of? Just as the external world is made up of the elements of earth, water, air and fire, our inner terrain or *Psyche*[5], is composed of the faculties of thought, emotion, experience, and memory. While this inner world is invisible to our eyes, it makes itself known through our thoughts, feelings, insights, and inspirations. As an example of this, take a moment to examine your right hand. Hold it up in front of you and turn it slowly. Notice the shape of your fingers and thumb and the lines running across your palm. Look at the backside now and observe your knuckles, blood vessels, and fingernails. Now almost close your eyes, (so you can continue reading on) and touch your right hand with the fingers of your left hand. Feel the softness of your palm, the joints of your fingers, their bone structures and the smoothness of your fingernails. Now touch the tips of your fingers and recall who and what those fingers have touched in your lifetime. Notice that some of your inner terrain is made up of images and experiences of joy, while others bring up less joyful experiences? Essentially you are "traveling within" and beginning to experience the hidden terrain residing in your psyche. The act of consciously engaging with your emotions, memories, and thoughts is what this inner journey is all about. And while there isn't necessarily a direct correlation between the inner and outer terrains we might travel to, there are some interesting similarities I'd like to point out. The first similarity is with respect to our responses and reactions to both physical and non-physical stimuli. The emotions of fear and anxiety I might feel if say, I attempt to climb a perilous mountain in the external world would not be much different from those feelings evoked by a nightmare in which I encounter the same mountain, but in the form of a dream time aberration. In other words, what we experience in our outer world and what we conjure up within our inner world can have a very similar impact on us.

The second similarity is more subtle, yet possibly more important to consider. Just as where we travel to within the outer world can influence our sense of equanimity and well-being, (e.g., strolling through a beautiful park in an upscale neighborhood, versus walking down a dark alley in a bad part of town), so too can our sense of inner peace be affected by where we travel to within our inner terrain. It is important to understand that what we feel in any one moment, such as our moods, attitudes, and states of mind, are not arbitrarily generated, or even necessarily the result of actual encounters with our external circumstances. As hard as it may be to believe, our reactions to external input are quite often the result, not of our circumstances, but of where we travel to within the inner terrain of our psyche.

Just as the outer world is made up of physical geographies with differing degrees of safety and danger, so too our inner terrain is made up of psychological and emotional geographies ranging in a variety of abstract forms from crevasses, plains, and summits, to deserts, lagoons, and oases. A "crevasse" located in our psyche might be associated with past abuse or trauma in which hurt or damage was inflicted upon us. Trauma-related to physical and sexual abuse, especially at a young age, can produce "rips in the fabric" of our inner terrain much like the characteristics of a physical crevasse. Having a meltdown, or "falling into a crevasse within" can be triggered either by current-day abuses or by threats similar in nature to those we initially experienced in our childhood.

To add a bit of reassuring perspective here, some meltdowns absolutely have to do with mistreatment by others, and it must also be understood that we can add to the traumatic effects and magnify them when similar childhood abuses already residing within us get triggered. A simple example of this is getting a massage and having the masseuse come upon an already tender spot in our back. They didn't cause our pain, they simply triggered the inflammation that was already there. We must all be watchful of not falling into the trap of unconsciously acting out what I call, "pains just waiting to show up." Being understanding of, and sensitive to, our own past wounds and of the wounds others still carry within them goes a long way in maintaining nurturing relationships.

Another more encouraging and light-hearted example would be a majestic mountain peak rising up high into the heavens which might be associated internally with past victories, high points or elevated self-esteem. The "higher" we are willing to climb within our inner terrain, (the degree to which we love, honor and acknowledge ourselves, as well as demonstrate our greater virtues with others) the more confident and fulfilled we become in our outer world. Just as in the world of real estate it's all about *location, location, location.* While it's not really as simple as that, the key takeaway here is that where we travel to within our psyche directly influences our outer experiences. The implications of this must not be overlooked as it implies that our moment-by-moment well-being, fulfillment and inner peace is tied to how much awareness we bring to the process of navigating our inner terrain. In essence, the better inner traveler we are, the happier and healthier we will be in our outer world.

Being Our Own Wise Travel Guide

Here's something else to reflect on, what if it's not actually true that others can "bring us down," or that our circumstances determine our degree of inner peace or quality of life? What if instead, we actually allow ourselves to be led by others, or by our circumstances to already existing detrimental terrain existing within our psyche, destinations that whenever we go there we get caught in our own negative emotions? Furthermore, what if the way to go about elevating our well-being and quality of life is less about needing to "heal" old wounds and more about constructing fences and warning signs around the detrimental terrain dwelling within us? After all, wouldn't a wise travel guide make sure such precautions were in place and direct his or her travel party around such detrimental terrain?

The idea of elevating our inner guidance capabilities rather than spending huge amounts of energy on processing past wounds is a controversial idea and one we will explore in greater detail. With respect to this point, I'm not suggesting we ignore much-needed healing work, or that we should simply block out the negative experiences from our pasts. Instead, what I'm saying is that once we've done our healing work, we take the extra steps to mark the affected terrain as "danger zones" so we can avoid falling into them, acting them out, or repeating them in the future. Suffice to say for now that I have good reason to believe our ongoing well-being, inner peace and fulfillment can be profoundly enhanced by taking these extra steps.

Human Beings Being Human

Expanding on my expedition metaphor, and directing our focus towards the nature of our Higher Self, *Travelers Within* is a journey into what it means to be human and beyond. The main premise of this two-volume set is based on a simple yet challenging notion; that while we as a race have assumed the title of "Human Beings," it does not necessarily mean we've achieved the full potential of "Being Human." For the curious and adventurous traveler, this reversal of words points to something extraordinary. For just beyond the wordplay lies a hidden reality in which what it means to be human is turned on its head; a destination where the predictable trek of merely living one's life is transformed into a compelling journey of being fully alive.

The first hint of this hidden reality becomes apparent when we recognize a subtle yet sizable error in how we go about defining our fundamental nature. The title "Human Being" incorrectly implies that "Being" is a noun, when in fact it's actually a verb. As a noun, we Human Beings are mere objects or things, distinct quantities of matter existing separate and distinct from other quantities of matter. Clearly, the generative nature of "Being" is not included in the meaning implied by this title. *Being*[6] is defined as an animating force and dynamically existing presence. Unlike a static object whose nature it is to gravitate towards fixation and predictability, Being is a dynamic phenomenon that constantly adapts, evolves and transforms itself. If we Humans are merely static objects, we might as well call ourselves "Human Doing's" or "Human Having's." For such a boring existence is surely devoid of the aliveness, fulfillment, and joy that accompanies engaging in the daily activities associated with Being. It's a sad state of affairs when who we are is determined by what we do or do not do, or what we have or do not have. I firmly believe the cause of most depression, dissatisfaction, and unhappiness in life is the result of misidentifying ourselves as static objects rather than knowing ourselves as what I call our *Agent of Being*[7].

Our Inner Agent of Being

So what exactly is an *Agent of Being?* It's a little known, yet vital aspect of our human nature that serves as a wise inner mentor and guide for us. An "Agent" is our personal representative who acts on our behalf when it comes to making daily choices. Think of your Agent of Being as a kind of invisible benefactor dedicated to providing you with wise guidance and direction as you travel through life . . . and most notably, from a place of *Intentional Choice*[8]. The choices our Agent of Being offers up to us, (if we pay attention and honor them) are intentional in that they have a very specific direction and destination in mind, and if we take these choices to heart and act on them accordingly, they will assist us in our journey towards becoming a fully realized Human Being.

But the question is, Human Being . . . what? The answer is, Being happy, Being inspired, Being enthused, motivated, in gratitude, at peace, in love, or whatever it is we choose to Be. Our Agent of Being's quality of Intentional Choice exists in sharp contrast to living a life of predictable options in which we are constantly at the effect of our circumstances and struggling to avoid exhaustion, overwhelm, dissatisfaction and the all too familiar reductionist mentality of "just getting by in life."

I wholeheartedly believe that the quality of our lives and the degree of aliveness we experience on a daily basis depends on us coming into accord with our Agent of Being. It is the recognition of this extraordinary internal resource and the commitment to gaining insight into utilizing its wisdom that Plato was addressing in his treatise, *"The Apology of Socrates."* While many assume his apology quote, *"An unexamined life is not worth living"* referred to an elite society of intellectuals who considered themselves to be cognitively superior to the masses, I believe Plato was pointing to the extraordinary challenge of coming into accord with our Higher Self and opening to the wisdom of our Agent of Being.

The Higher Faculty of Self-Awareness

How does our Agent of Being reveal itself in our daily life? Through the very specific, yet rarely utilized faculty of *Self-Awareness*[9]. To be aware is to be sentient and capable of reacting to incoming stimuli, but Self-Awareness is a higher faculty in that it pertains not only to possessing awareness but to being aware of the awareness we possess. When we become aware of our awareness it gives us the edge of being able to adapt and change how we perceive and deal with what we are being aware of. Said another way, Self-Awareness enables us to objectively assess life's circumstances and choose our responses thoughtfully rather than from impulsive and often detrimental "knee-jerk" reactions.

Living an *"examined life"* and possessing Self-Awareness means being able to consciously choose our responses and actions at will, and in a manner that optimizes our well-being and enhances the quality of our lives. The power of conscious choice is perhaps the greatest personal skill set we can ever develop. We may not have control over what happens to us in our daily lives, but possessing the faculty of Self-Awareness leads us to our higher inner terrain and enables us to rise above our impulsive reactions. This added reflective capability makes all the difference in terms of our quality of life and in our navigational capabilities as *Travelers Within.*

One does not instantly come into accord with their Agent of Being simply by recognizing its existence. There is no doubt however that recognition is the first step in that just as Bucky Fuller asserted, it's impossible to acquire a capability that one does not believe exists as a possibility. Once recognition is present, the next step requires a great deal of focused personal intention and inner exploration. The only "shortcut" for accessing one's inner Agent of Being that I know of is through experiencing total devastation, great loss, or sorrow. But in my experience, the high price of admission for these venues of access outweighs the expedited deliverance.

The encouraging news is that those who relate to the notion of traveling within have most likely already completed a good deal of the preparation work needed to come into accord with their Agent of Being. To help facilitate the process, in *Volume 1,* I've outlined the key steps in making contact with your inner Agent, charted the development roadmap needed to facilitate your journey along the way, and compiled specific practices, perspectives, and processes that will assist you in establishing a stable relationship with your internal mentor.

Some of the material we will cover may be challenging to understand and digest at first because of the complexity of the human psyche. We are incredibly complicated creatures with many diverse facets and faculties that intertwine with one another. It's impossible to explore a single aspect of our psyche without calling up many other associated aspects. For example, discussing the experience of love can also activate the discordant feelings of loss, grief, and pain. How these conflicting emotions are woven together, and the interdependencies that come about between them plays a vital role in us gaining greater insight into the act of loving, or perhaps more important, loving newly and consistently.

I will do my best to balance the academic complexity needed to clarify the inner terrain with warm-hearted realness that hopefully brings the material to life for you so it is both digestible and useful. Also, while what I've written in this introduction chapter borders on an academic exercise, I want you to know that it's the "realness" of being human that inspires me most and compels me to explore and illuminate this highly complex material. As a devoted *Traveler Within* myself, I am deeply humbled by the opportunity of the journey, and I love to share in the adventures that arise along the way with others. So without further ado allow me to introduce you to what I call the *AwarenesSphere*[10], a comprehensive inner roadmap we *Travelers Within* use to navigate into the extraordinary world of the human psyche.

Mapping The Pathways To Being Fully Human

Experienced life travelers know the best way to navigate to their desired destination and to ensure a rewarding journey is to use the assistance of GPS or at the very least a trusty map. Having landmarks to show us we're headed in the right direction is extremely useful, especially when traveling through unfamiliar terrain. The same goes for traveling into the terrain of our psyche, as it's just as easy to get turned around there as it is in the outer world. In this opening chapter, I'm going to introduce you to a very special map I've designed for navigating into and through the inner terrain of the psyche.

Now that we have a clear understanding that the purpose of our inner journey is to explore the "higher ground" within us and come into accord with our Agent of Being, we can begin our exploration of the *AwarenesSphere.* This inner roadmap illuminates many of the key behaviors, character traits and growth challenges at various stages in our development process as humans. It also illuminates "best practices" for how to traverse into the higher ground of our Self-Awareness and the terrain where our Agent of Being resides. Think of the *AwarenesSphere* as your personal literary travel guide to becoming a more fully realized and capable you.

The *AwarenesSphere Model* came about as the result of working with thousands of participants and clients over a span of three decades. As a public workshop facilitator, life-coach and leadership mentor to Fortune 100's around the world, I've had the privilege of venturing into the most intimate aspects of people's lives. Through my inner travels with so many remarkable individuals, I've learned a great deal about the human psyche and how to work with many of its relationship patterns, emotional dynamics, and behavioral challenges. As a result, I've come to realize that the terrain of the human psyche can indeed be charted, and our evolution as conscious beings can be guided into its full potential with a fair amount of clarity and confidence.

Before we venture into the *AwarenesSphere's* complex structure I want to ask you to keep something in mind and heart. Think of the times in your life when you ventured into a new and unknown destination, you most likely encountered moments of uncertainty in which you got turned around, confused and felt hopeless and frustrated. I suspect the same will happen as you engage in the unfamiliar terrain of your psyche. Keep in mind that if it were an easy trek, it most likely wouldn't be worth the effort. From my perspective, it's only by engaging in extraordinary challenges that we can produce extraordinary outcomes. I do, however, suggest taking frequent breaks so you have the time you need to integrate the concepts, principles, and experiences I introduce.

I suggest reviewing the *AwarenesSphere* material numerous times just the way you would walk up and down an unfamiliar street multiple times until you find your way. While I will present an abbreviated overview before we start exploring its content, the details about each of the aspects of the *AwarenesSphere* will be spelled out in great detail chapter by chapter. Also, as a way to provide you with additional support regarding some of the more challenging or controversial concepts and principles I introduce, I've also included personalized *"Author Notes," (abbreviated as "A/N" and appearing in parentheses and italics.)*

Think of these added comments as a kind of "author over-voice," as if you and I were confidants or friends sitting together and having a casual conversation about the material being presented. My intention with these added notes is to bridge the emotional gap that invariably arises between reader and author because of the limiting venue of the written word. I also feel it's important that we develop a working bond between us because of the challenging material we'll be exploring and engaging in together. I and my Book Team, who you met in the *Forward* have also created a *Reader's Question and Answer* section at the end of each chapter. The idea is to address some of the common questions that might arise for you so you are more able to integrate the concepts and principles being presented.

Before we take our first steps into the extraordinary terrain of the human psyche, I want to say that there really is no "map" that can do justice to the majesty and mystery of our inner terrain, but the *AwarenesSphere* is still very useful for the inner traveler. And for this reason, I'm enthused and honored to share it with you now.

The DNA Blueprint For Our Spiritual Evolution

The *"Awareness"* part of the *AwarenesSphere's* title refers to the development of our higher faculty of Self-Awareness as we navigate our way through its *Four Stages* and *Twelve Phases.* The *"Sphere"* portion of the title pertains to two key characteristics of the model. The first is that the terrain of the human psyche is "volumetric" rather than linear in nature. Volume equates to dynamic capacity as opposed to linear storage or sequencing. What this means in simple terms is that while the process of traveling to our inner higher ground may appear to be a sequential and linear process, (from one Stage and Phase to the next, to the next) in actuality it's not the case. Just as unexpected leaps in genetic advancement exist in *Darwin's Evolution of the Species,* similar nonlinear leaps of consciousness can and do occur as we travel through the terrain of the psyche as it is charted by the *AwarenesSphere Model.*

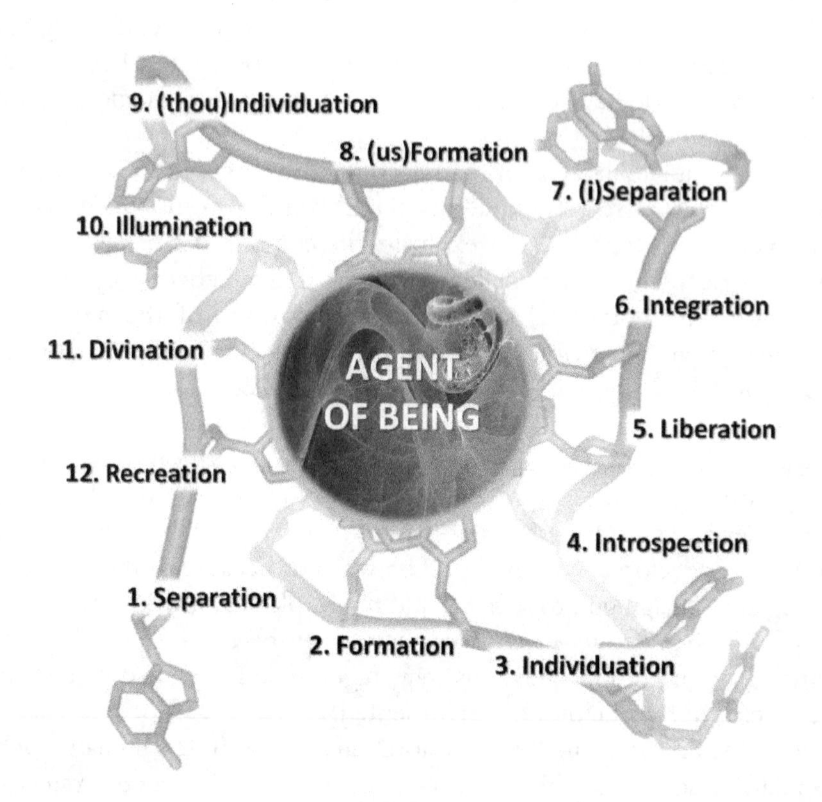

The second characteristic is that the model's suffix title of *"Sphere"* refers to a kind of "contextual container" with the traits of an infinite upward spiral. In other words, its terrain is ever-evolving and has no discernable beginning, middle or ending. Rather than being a circular process in which the map's terrain starts over again once we've come full circle around to the *Twelfth Phase of ReCreation,* reentry into the *First Phase of Separation*, (where we initially began our journey as newborns) occurs at ever-higher levels with each subsequent rotation we engage in.

In other words, there's no returning to already-taken terrain, each rotation around the Four Stages and Twelve Phases leads us to ever higher ground. I do want to point out that this doesn't mean we will never revisit challenging terrain again once we've explored and traveled it. In fact, the dynamic nature of the psyche is such that we can find ourselves in multiple locations, (and predicaments) at the same time. The other important characteristic of the psyche is that much like the stellar properties of a star, its core energy source emanates from its self-generative center. This is a crucial point to understand in that our inner Agent of Being is an omnipotent phenomenon that draws upon its own power source rather than relying on external sources. The closest body of work to the *AwarenesSphere Model* I've found is that of Carl Jung's writings on the "Collective Unconscious," a mysterious inner subconscious landscape comprised of *Archetypal*[11] forces acting upon us without our conscious awareness. While Jung's life's work is far more extensive than what I'm putting forth, I believe I've made a useful contribution to the field of psychology and personal growth by publishing the *AwarenesSphere Model.*

So what importance does having a detailed map of the psyche hold for us? The answer is that depending on where within our inner terrain we choose to travel, (and more importantly where we tend to loiter) our moods, attitudes, and behaviors are influenced accordingly. As I've pointed out previously, the terrain of the inner world is much like that of the outer world. Just as the exterior landscape is composed of a myriad of interconnected geographical locations such as mountains, plains, valleys, and oceans, the inner world also has its own intertwined geography including Stages and Phases of consciousness, emotions, beliefs and historical life experiences. And just like navigating to different locations in the outer world influences our feelings, outlooks, and attitudes, so too does navigating to different locations within our psyche.

By identifying where we're positioned within our inner terrain at any given time with a roadmap, we're able to accomplish two important things – first, we recognize the self-development ground we've already taken, and second, we identify specific practices and behaviors for navigating our way into higher ground, elevations of insight that lead to our greatest human attribute, our Agent of Being. The *AwarenesSphere* provides us with important navigational markers as we encounter and engage with the Archetypal forces moving deep within us. Much like Genetic Biologists who explore the architecture of the Human Genome, inner travelers can use the *AwarenesSphere Model* to navigate their way through their myriad of inner terrain and come into accord with their Agent of Being.

Technically speaking, the structure of the *AwarenesSphere* is based on a unique characteristic of DNA's Double Helix called the *Quadruplex Telomere*, (the faint cellular-looking background image). These special chromosome "end caps" serve two main purposes; they regenerate damaged sequences of individual DNA strands or "members," and they safeguard the integrity of strand clusters or "communities." The corollaries between these members and communities and the evolution of our human consciousness serve as powerful navigational pointers for expanding into higher ground. One way of understanding my genetic-based model is that it is the *"DNA blueprint for our spiritual evolution."*

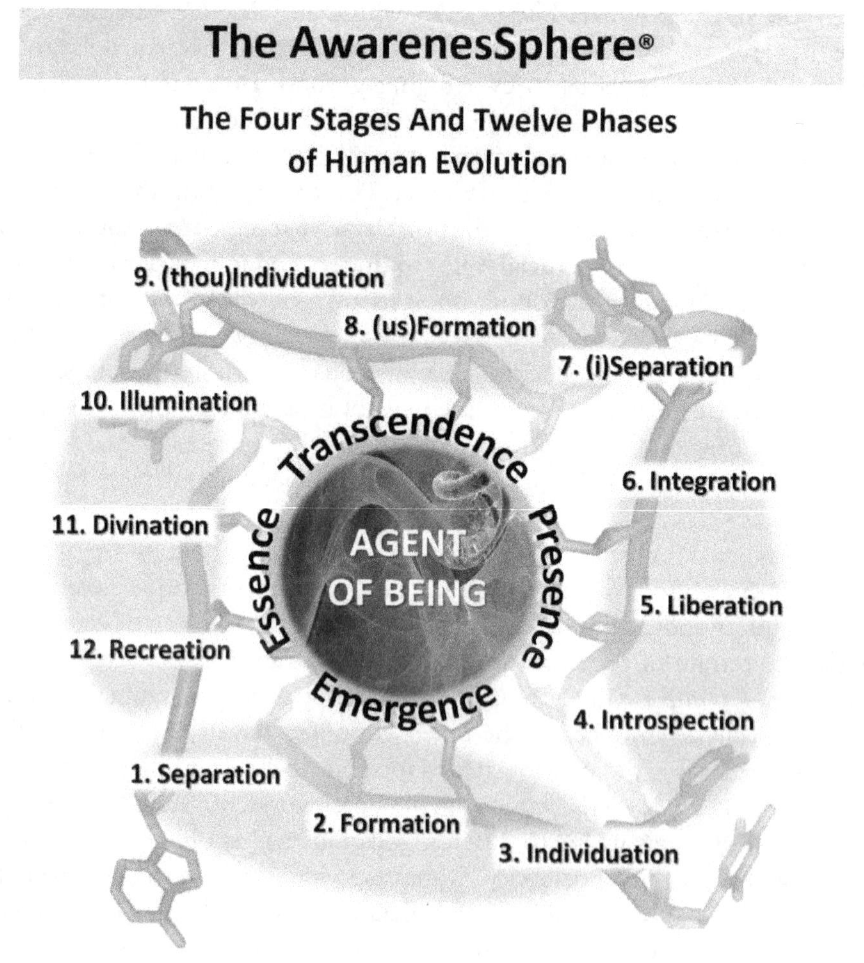

The *AwarenesSphere* is composed of a Central Core, or our Agent of Being and Four Stages of Human Consciousness that surround it, (designated by the four highlighted areas, *Emergence, Presence, Transcendence, and Essence*). Additionally, each Stage contains three Phases of development which are similar to DNA-specific species categorizations. For example, bird families are uniquely different in appearance, yet they share common genetic traits such as beaks, talons, and feathers. The same goes for Stages and Phases of human consciousness in terms of being grouped together. And while there are no physical traits to compare for the groupings, the degree of emotional maturity, personal responsibility and how we perceive ourselves in the world as a whole is the main organizing principle for how the Twelve Phases are grouped within each of the Four Stages.

The difference between the *AwarenesSphere* and other mainstream personality models is that its scope extends far beyond conventional wisdom's notions about identity and personality development. For example, my model's *"Beyond"* notions such as *"Divination," "ReCreation"* and *"Transmigration"* transcend even Maslow's controversial assertion of Self-Actualization in his well-known work on the *Hierarchy of Needs.* Venturing beyond what conventional wisdom deems as credible can be both challenging and rewarding. One perspective, which I personally hold, is that only those who are willing to explore beyond the bounds of the ordinary will make contact with the extraordinary.

Exploring the architecture of the *AwarenesSphere* in greater detail, it's important to understand that while displayed on a flat plane, the model is three-dimensional, much like an actual DNA strand. Just as the two sides of a DNA strand run in opposite directions causing its ladder formation to twist as life develops into more complex expressions, there is a similar way in which the Four Stages and Twelve Phases spiral as we attain higher ground and evolve into ever-higher human faculties.

The other striking similarity is that within both the biological structure of DNA and the philosophical structure of the *AwarenesSphere,* there exists a mysterious and invisible central core from which our life-force energy, as well as our spiritual energy arises from and is infused into our being. This extraordinary correlation has huge implications in terms of the innate importance and relevance of the *AwarenesSphere Model* when it comes to providing sound guidance for those who are willing to use it as a development roadmap. Let's take our first pass at getting to know the *AwarenesSphere Model* by exploring a summary overview of its Stages and Phases.

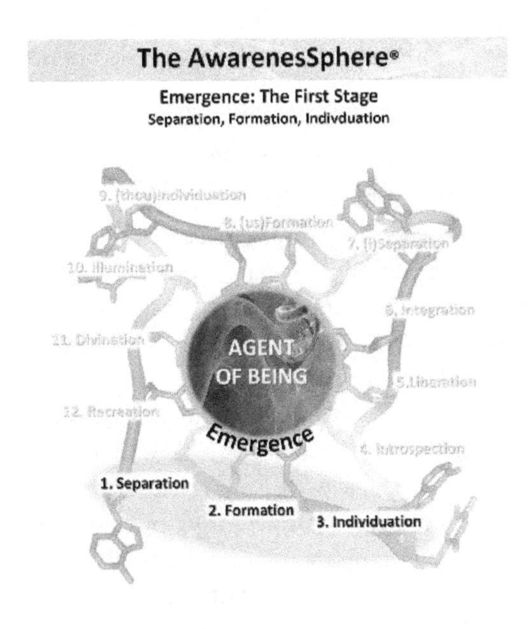

First Stage of Emergence

The *Emergence Stage,* (shown in the highlighted area of the diagram) contains the three initial *Phases of Separation, Formation,* and *Individuation. Emergence* spans the first five years or so of life, starting with inception and gestation and advancing to the trauma of birth and separation from the mother's womb. Filled with turbulent survival-based emotions, this First Stage is when our basic identity and personality fully forms. During *Emergence,* infants possess the faculty of basic awareness but lack the ability to self-reflect or observe their own behavior, and they are completely unaware of the impact their actions have on others. This is an important distinction to understand as it is the primary reason why those who are caught in Emergence later on in life have so many recurring survival issues and often display persistent narcissistic tendencies.

Separation - The First Phase of Awareness

Separation is rooted in basic survival instincts, insecurity, and fear. While still in the condition known as "Symbiosis," separating from the mother's womb as well as from the womb of the Divine is a traumatic event for newborns. This sets the stage for infants to form emotionally charged conclusions and primary decisions that influence their newly forming identities as well as their future adult behaviors. Genetic inheritance of behavioral traits by our family of origin also plays a role in our core identity development.

Formation - The Second Phase of Awareness

Formation is the active process in which our core identity develops, our ego-protection mechanisms come into being and our basic survival needs are formed into specific behavior patterns within our psyche. In this Phase, infants are aware of their existence but have no ability to self-reflect, empathize with others, or grasp the consequences of their actions. As an infant's identity develops an independent sense of "self," what we know as the "the terrible twos" comes into existence.

Individuation - The Third Phase of Awareness

Individuation is when the young identity fully forms and solidifies into a specific set of personality traits. An infatuation with one's self is prevalent with infants along with ego-based behaviors such as self-worth, self-esteem, and indulgences in self-judgment, blame, shame, guilt, and credit. Adults who display excessive self-importance and seek excessive recognition and acceptance invariably failed to mature out of these infantile infatuations. A key contributing factor to dysfunctional adult behavior is the creation of our "Primary Decision," a very specific and detrimental emotional structuring we all form during our development within the *Emergence Stage.*

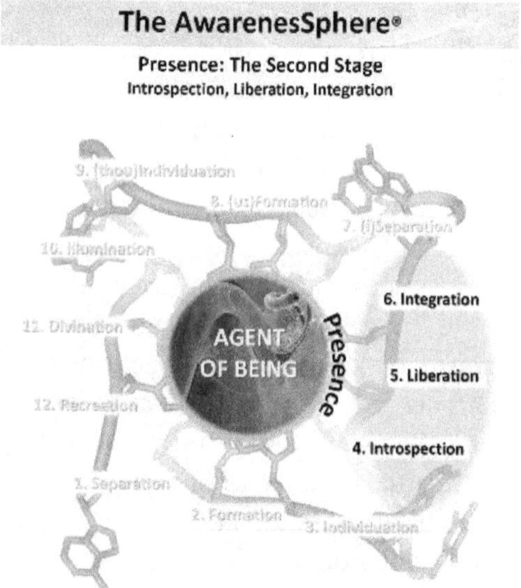

The AwarenesSphere®
Presence: The Second Stage
Introspection, Liberation, Integration
AGENT OF BEING
Presence
6. Integration
5. Liberation
4. Introspection

Second Stage of Presence

The *Presence Stage* contains the next three *Phases of Introspection, Liberation,* and *Integration.* Once we transition out of *Emergence,* if we are precocious and curious, we begin to become present to why we do the things we do and how we can best grow ourselves. Often through the self-discovery process we become "self-aware," a higher faculty that leads us to our Agent of Being. *Presence* is the ability to perceive and be conscious of our experiences, sensory inputs and most importantly, our higher faculty of Self-Awareness. In other words, we become aware of our awareness, which provides us with the capability of observing and modifying our behaviors in the moment as we are acting on them.

Introspection - The Fourth Phase of Self-Awareness

Introspection is about the dawning of our higher faculty of Self-Awareness, an inner awakening in which our capacity to not just be aware, but to be aware of being aware. This higher faculty gives rise to us beginning the process of releasing our *Emergence*-based survival issues and taking responsibility for the outcomes we produce within ourselves, with others and in our daily lives. *Introspection* is expressed as curiosity, inquisitiveness and a desire to open, take risks and grow. By "looking within" we begin to realize and understand that we possess predictable behavior patterns and set emotional reactions that may or may not serve us.

Liberation - The Fifth Phase of Self-Awareness

Liberation is about freeing ourselves from the "Box" of our infantile emotional assumptions and decisions and awakening to being at choice in our lives. In this Phase we open to embracing the deeper flow of emotions and feelings moving within us, we realize how they affect us and how they influence others, and we free ourselves from their detrimental behavior patterns. *Liberation* is also about letting go of being at the effect of our life's circumstances, at the mercy of others, or victims of the world at large. The liberating process requires the deep inner work of "Uncasting" the survival-based "Primary Decisions" we form as infants when we encountered either real or perceived threats to our well-being.

Integration - The Sixth Phase of Self-Awareness

Integration is about embracing our shadow and light sides, a paradoxical coming together of the unconscious oppositional forces dwelling deep within us. In this Phase, our higher faculty of Self-Awareness undergoes a transformation in which we begin to integrate the paradoxical aspects of our finite presence with our infinite nature. Said another way, we dare to embrace both the darkness of our primal urges and the light of our spiritual nature. This movement towards *Integration* is the beginning of releasing ourselves from the limitations of our ego-self and migrating into our Higher Self.

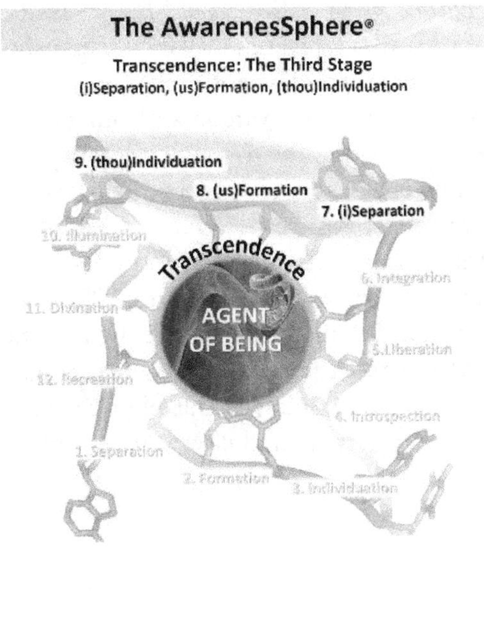

The AwarenesSphere®
Transcendence: The Third Stage
(i)Separation, (us)Formation, (thou)Individuation
9. (thou)Individuation
8. (us)Formation
7. (i)Separation
Transcendence
AGENT OF BEING

Third Stage of Transcendence

The *Transcendence Stage* contains the three *Phases of (i)Separation, (us)Formation and (thou)Individuation.* In *Transcendence,* we expand beyond the limitations of our ego-self and come into accord with our Higher Self and Agent of Being. Unlike the previous Phases, each of the Phases in this Stage is linked to the three Phases of the *Emergence Stage.* Each of the titles matches up except for the prefixes "(i)," "(us)" and "(thou)." These additions signify a cumulative expansion of our consciousness out of the survival mode of *Emergence* and into the higher awareness of our "Shared-Identity." Through the work of Uncasting our conclusions and decisions in each of the three *Phases of Emergence* we come into accord with our Higher Self.

(i)Separation - The Seventh Phase of Shared-Awareness

(i)Separation is about a profound reunification with the Divine that we've longed for our entire lives. The "(i)" represents having surrendered our ego identity up to an elevated presence of self. By taking "additional life passes" at healing our initial separation from Spirit and letting go of the survival-based reactions and Primary Decisions associated with the trauma of birth, we reunite with our spiritual origins and expand into the higher faculty of "Shared-Awareness," the sense of interconnectedness with everyone and everything.

(us)Formation - The Eighth Phase of Shared-Awareness

(us)Formation is about our further expansion into collective interconnectedness and the realization that we are not separate entities engaging in a solitary life, but are part of a vaster wholeness that includes everyone and everything. Rather than grappling with our identity development as we did when we were infants, this time around we re-engage with the *Phase of Formation* and do the work of redefining our core identity around a greater sense of self, one that includes the awareness of "(us)," an expansion of our core identity in which we become more inclusive of the experience of others and of the awareness levels they possess.

(thou)Individuation - The Ninth Phase of Shared-Awareness

(thou)Individuation is about our identity merging with the omnipotent presence of "thou," our sacred connection with the Divine. This merging occurs as we complete our history around our identity development and the remaining survival energies within the *Phase of Individuation.* Once we have embraced the expansion of "i" into "us" and "us" into "thou," our Agent of Being becomes available to us. As we take this final *(thou)Individuation* pass at the issues lodged within our psyche, our evolution as an interconnected human/spiritual being becomes fully realized.

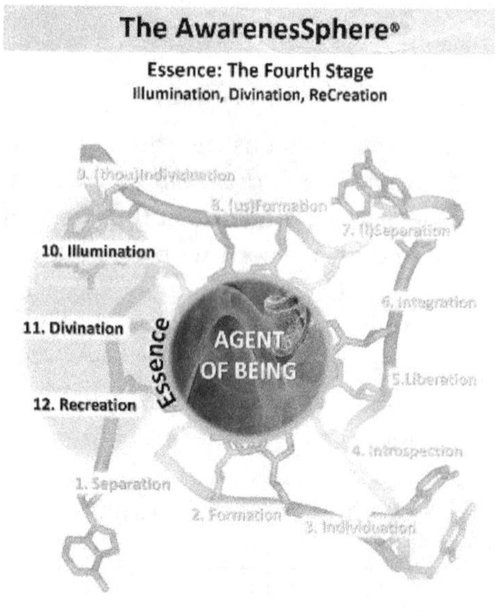

The AwarenesSphere®

Essence: The Fourth Stage

Illumination, Divination, ReCreation

9. (thou)Individuation

8. (us)Formation

7. (i)Separation

10. Illumination

6. Integration

11. Divination

Essence

AGENT OF BEING

5. Liberation

12. Recreation

4. Introspection

1. Separation

2. Formation

3. Individuation

Fourth Stage of Essence

The *Essence Stage* contains the three *Phases of Illumination, Divination,* and *ReCreation. Essence* is the awakening of our "Meta-Awareness." This expansive spiritual attunement includes not only being self-aware and experiencing the awareness of others, but it also enables us to contribute to the development of higher Self-Awareness within others. This Meta-engagement process produces deep and meaningful relationships and empowers us to support those who are on the path to their own higher selves. While our spiritual nature is illuminated brilliantly within the three *Phases of Essence,* our human presence is also enhanced through a deepening of our higher virtues of compassion, humility, and ability to love and be loved.

Illumination - The Tenth Phase of Meta-Awareness

Illumination is about becoming a "candescent presence" in which we know ourselves to be the luminous space in which life moves, rather than being a "thing" caught inside its movement. *Illumination* is hot. Like a torch, it burns away all that is fixed and rigid within us. Any remaining artifacts of our ego-self are placed upon the altar of Spirit and cremated by its stellar flames of *Illumination.* Within this high ground, we come to know that the depth of our darkness delivers us to the heights of our enlightenment and that in order to be lights in the world we must be willing to endure the burning.

Divination - The Eleventh Phase of Meta-Awareness

Divination is about embracing the dynamically changing presence of Spirit, especially in terms of what it means to authentically live into both our Humanity and our Divinity. *Divination* embodies a reunification of both our finite presence and our infinite nature. In this Phase, we come to terms with the challenge of being both temporal and eternal. *Divination* is the union of the omnipotent presence of grace and the human practice of servitude. In this place of high ground, we are devoted to traveling with others and offering them light, love, and care as they navigate their way into their own higher ground and Agent of Being.

ReCreation - The Twelfth Phase of Meta-Awareness

ReCreation is about fully moving in accord with our Agent of Being and with the grace of Spirit. Such selfless movement requires surrendering life itself back unto itself so it may be recreated and renewed over and over again. This Phase also embodies "sacred rebirth," the essence of our humanity undergoing a regenerative migration from life into death and arising again into life anew. This cyclical movement is not necessarily likened to reincarnation, but rather is the completion and rebirth process of migrating into ever-higher sacred ground.

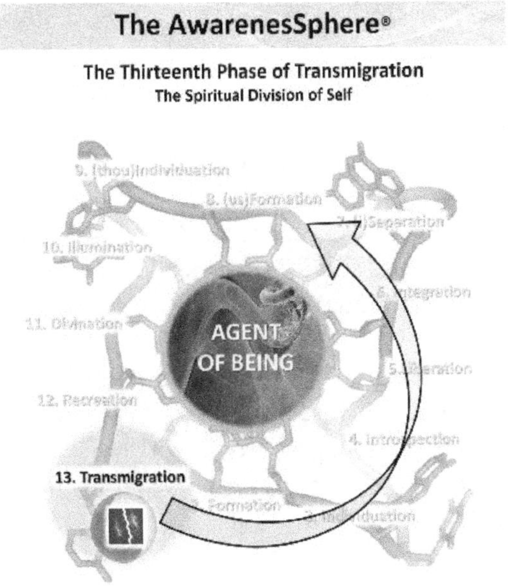

The AwarenesSphere®
The Thirteenth Phase of Transmigration
The Spiritual Division of Self
AGENT OF BEING
13. Transmigration

Transmigration - The Thirteenth Phase & Beyond

It is here, within the *Thirteenth Phase* that we come full circle around the Four Stages and Twelve Phases of the *AwarenesSphere* and re-enter *Emergence* for a second time. This evolving "Transmigration" of self into higher expressions of who we are ensures the sustainability and continuity of life and the evolution of humanity. This forever-bound migration is also less about arriving at a destination of permanence and more about realizing that the ongoing journey of "becoming" is our true place of residence and authentic home. Our travels through the *AwarenesSphere's* Four Stages and Twelve Phases and Beyond is about elevating our consciousness and coming into accord with our Higher Self and Agent of Being. This evolution means knowing ourselves beyond our self-imposed limitations, social upbringing, and even personal history. Initially, our migration through the terrain of the *AwarenesSphere* is about relinquishing our need for self-importance, (ego afflictions such as pride, control, arrogance, blame, judgment, protection, and self-doubt). The greater ongoing journey, however, is about relinquishing our fundamental assumption of being a separate object that moves through life and instead, realizing that life actually moves through us. Said another way, who we truly are is the space in which life actually moves and evolves. Ultimately, the expansive terrain we travel into and through is the embodiment of our paradoxical nature, one that is Human in every sense of the word and Divine in every vibration of the word's utterance. ~

I want to congratulate you on staying with it and arriving on "this side" of the *AwarenesSphere Model.* If you think it was challenging to digest this material, imagine what it was like to create it and organize all its distinctions. It has taken me over thirty years to understand and actually *live into* these many principles and distinctions. And while I was somehow able to articulate all the Stages and Phases, it by no means implies that I've mastered them all. Like you, I have much traveling still to do and much experience to gain in order to truly live up to, and into, what it means to be fully human.

The *AwarenesSphere* is a formidable undertaking and as a way to help you gain the most from exploring its upward spiraling terrain, I've dedicated *Volume 1* to bringing the first two Stages of Emergence and Presence to life. I will not only explain in great detail each of these Stages along with their six associated Phases, but I will also include relevant case studies from my public programs, as well as share personal life stories that illuminate and "warm" the materials for you. Hopefully, this combination of education and inspiration will provide you with enough experiential engagement to not only follow along on the journey but actually integrate the first half of the *AwarenesSphere's* principles and practices into your daily life. (In *Volume 2,* we will move on to exploring the second half of the *AwarenesSphere*, including its *Stages of Transcendence* and *Essence*, and onto the extraordinary terrain of the *Beyond*.)

Before we explore each of the *AwarenesSphere's* Four Stages and Twelve Phases I'm going to introduce the *Reader's Questions and Answers Section* I mentioned to you earlier. The questions and answers presented at the end of each chapter are designed to address some of the unresolved concerns or wonderings you may have as a reader. Because my Book Team's profiles and questions represent a wide diversity in terms of careers, religious and spiritual beliefs and interests, there should be something of use for just about everyone. The team has also included their personal experience of each chapter in a summary statement which I believe will enhance your own summary process. ~

In the next chapter, we'll travel together into the inner terrain of *Separation,* the *First Stage of Emergence.* Once you've reviewed the question and answers section, prepare yourself to venture into the deep inner terrain I call, *"As A Human Thinketh."* It is both mysterious and inspiring so prepare yourself for your first *Travelers Within* expedition!

♦♦♦

Reader's Question & Answer Section (Introduction)

Allison - Q: What if I feel I have aspects of each stage operating inside? Can I feel Oneness, connected to the Divine, and even have had moments where all suffering feels to be gone while also still having survival issues? And if so, will this work help me to finally resolve those survival issues once and for all?

Val Jon - A: Just as the physical structuring of the brain is replete with billions of interconnected neurons, the terrain of the psyche too is just as interconnected and dynamic. What this means is that we can experience multiple Stages and Phases of our inner terrain simultaneously. Your example of the absence of suffering while feeling survival is an indicator that you are occupying both a "low" and a "high" inner ground at the same time, which is normal and healthy. What this work will empower you to do is expand your capacity to hold many diverse experiences simultaneously without getting overwhelmed or becoming scattered. Some may wonder why to expand such a capacity, and the answer is that the more of life's diversity we can take in and experience, the more fulfilled and nurtured we become. In terms of a "final resolve" for your survival issues, that won't happen. As long as you and I exist in the mortal form we'll always be affected by survival. What can happen, however, is that we can resolve how we will relate to our fears, threats, and devastations. The higher we rise within the spiral of the AwarenesSphere, the greater is our capacity and ability to embrace all of life's experiences in a way that deepens and nurtures us rather than devastates and depresses us.

Allison - Q: As someone with physical health issues, I am wondering about the connection between taking this inner journey and the relationship with the physical body. Can this work of the psyche help me heal the physical body? I'm not asking if it can cure me but asking about your thoughts on this interconnection and how this journey might support a physical healing exploration.

Val Jon - A: I'm a firm believer in the healing power of *Clear Intention, Conscious Prayer* and *Unconditional Gratitude.* All three of these vital well-being resources are available to those who travel within. Clear Intention is the practice of raising our awareness, focusing our attention and energy and directing our conviction towards making positive mental, emotional and physical changes. Conscious Prayer is the act of calling upon a higher power and surrendering over our fears, concerns, and afflictions so we do not need to hold them and allow them to burden and tax us. Unconditional Gratitude is taking the lead with appreciating life even when it's rough. It's also about being our own best friend, loving ourselves and maintaining healthy optimism about our physical wellness. Having been diagnosed with Prostate Cancer last year myself, I just completed 12 months of putting these three resources into daily practice and I'm happy to report that I am now in complete remission, (and without any radiation or chemotherapy). So is there a connection between the work of the psyche and the physical body? I'd bet my life on it . . . because honestly, I already have.

Allison - Chapter Statement: As challenging as traversing the inner terrain can be, I cannot imagine not embarking on this journey. I feel called to experience the depths of what it means to be human, knowing that I have a deep spiritual inclination that has always been a part of my consciousness, even in some of my earliest memories. To embark on the traveling your books will engage me in, I am opening my heart to allow all that is ready to come forward to heal and to be in the community of support this work provides.

Anna - Q: What would be the motivation to conquer the fear of self-determination?
Val Jon - A: This is a challenging question that makes me have to really think about how I answer it. The first thing that I must consider is the conundrum between "motivation" and "self-determination." Are these two not intimately linked together? Without self-determination, it would be very difficult to become motivated. And yet, without motivation, strengthening our self-determination would also be challenging. Given this dilemma, I would say that the motivation might be that a person is aware of their deficiency and for purposes of becoming more self-determined, they would place themselves in some kind of coaching or mentoring process in which they could incrementally strengthen it.

Anna - Q: Will this journey of self-discovery help me find resolutions?
Val Jon - A: Resolutions, (re-solutions) are essential to facilitating our personal growth, so yes, traveling within provides us with an abundance of new insight and inspiration we can directly apply to find new and empowering solutions to those long-standing issues and challenges we tend to carry with us and burden us over time.

Anna - Chapter Statement: It takes a lot of courage to take the first step, especially when you have to be willing to revisit old traumas with a new perspective and be willing to accept reality instead of the status quo.

Antonio - Q: What is it about self-inquiry and traveling inward, to embark on the path of self-discovery that has so many worried and fearful to the point that they would rather not embark at all?
Val Jon - A: It's human nature to fear what we do not understand. But it's also our nature to be curious and inquisitive. While "curiosity may have killed the cat," it actually brings new life to those who trust themselves enough to explore the unknown. For each of us, there is a different process and timeline for the development of curiosity. People are only ready to engage in this work when they are ready. I've been practicing and facilitating for over three decades, and I still haven't figured out what sparks people's curiosity to begin looking within. I do however believe each of us can take more of an active role and encourage people to become more curious. It's unfortunate, but the motivation for many to begin the self-development path is painful situations they get themselves into by not being more curious and inner focused earlier.

Antonio - Q: Is fear not separate from all that is, in this experience of life, is it just another aspect of the Source or Oneness? It seems as though we begin from a space of Oneness, then separation which we perceive as duality, where we find fears among other emotional qualities and opposites. Then through our inner work of traveling within, moving into a higher space of being and non-duality.

Val Jon - A: Fear is an essential aspect of life. With life comes survival, and with survival comes fear. My personal opinion is that "Oneness" is so vast that it includes everything in existence, including fear. Also, I believe that we are always in Oneness, but that we simply forget and get distracted by thinking we are separate entities living our individual lives.

Antonio - Chapter Statement: Unpack your thoughts and allow yourself to be guided into The Great Beyond.

Cyn - Q: I am a *Traveler Within,* I'm super busy, a professional trying to collect my paycheck each week whilst forging my future path of success. I think I'd rather be out at "Happy Hour" vs taking this journey. Will you please tell me why I should be here?
Val Jon - A: There's nothing wrong with occasionally opting for a "Happy Hour." There is, however, a huge difference between getting *relief* and assuring one's *endurance.* In order to sustain your strong ambitions, and to succeed in forging your future path, it would be wise to engage in activities that strengthen your endurance. Traveling within is the way to go about doing just that. I might also add that if you do not already have a sense of why you are here, there really isn't any answer I can give that would convince you to stay.

Cyn - Q: Should I be afraid that this journey will rock my world and uproot my successful career which makes everyone else I "report to" happy? What might be my biggest fear?
Val Jon - A: If you weren't afraid it would be a bigger concern. Also, I would think that "rocking your world" would be a welcome thing, as long as it does not endanger your career. Just what your career might transform into as a result of taking this journey within is what you may want to reflect on. What if "reporting to yourself" and being fulfilled as a result of doing so becomes more important to you than making others happy? And what if facing into your greatest fear, (whatever that might be) resulted in you discovering that not only are you capable of rocking your world, you are also capable of positively rocking the world of others as well.

Cyn - Chapter Statement: I think upon reflection we can all see how we change over our lifetime, some of us evolve, some of us seem to, remarkably, remain the same, or do we? I am excited to be traveling the AwarenesSphere to "till the soil" in evolving to my best and most giving "me" and to draw closer to understanding God's purpose for me within this lifetime by unpacking those trigger points and moments that forced change and redirection.

Elise - Q: How do I accept the never-ending journey?
Val Jon - A: The "journey" will continue whether we like it or not, or whether want it to or not. The benefit of accepting its never-ending nature is that we save ourselves the misery of resisting it along the way. And on a practical level, how to accept it is just how you'd go about accepting anything that's hard to accept . . . first, reject it, then get upset about rejecting it, then consider accepting it, then reject it again and even get depressed about it, and do this process over and over again until you finally reach acceptance. There is no shortcut, and if anybody tries to tell you there is, I'd reject it, (keeping in mind, of course, the process I just shared with you).

Elise - Q: Is how I perceive myself as important as how I am perceived by others?

Val Jon - A: Both of these activities come from the same place . . . the ego's preoccupation with itself. It's important to pay attention to perceptions, but to also realize that they are just that, *what is perceived* and not *what actually is.* A more useful process would be to notice what is for you, and then take into account the perceptions others have about you with a grain of salt.

Elise - Chapter Statement: It is so very helpful to have the Stages and Phases put in an ordered spiral, so in circling around my thoughts I can come to a place where I can see what I think in a new way. Having the ability to clarify what is at the source of my thinking and steps to see if it is true is a lifetime's journey.

Mindy - Q: Do I/we always move forward or do we sometimes have to move back if we find we cannot go to the next Phase or Stage? In other words, could we think we are ready to progress and then find we are not?

Val Jon - A: I can't begin to tell you how many times I've said to myself, *"I thought I handled this already . . . why is it coming up again?"* Navigating the human psyche is not that different than finding one's way through a maze or labyrinth. We move forward and almost make it out of the maze only to learn that we need to backtrack almost the entire way and try another route. There is an important distinction between being "smart" and being "wise" that once understood helps us progress forward. Having smarts is about *what we know*, but wisdom is about *how many ways* we can know what we know. Acquiring additional ways of knowing requires revisiting our life lessons many times over and under many diverse circumstances. Some lessons can be transferred and applied to our new challenges, but emotional lessons and matters of the heart are especially challenging. Think of the forward and backward movement like dancing and it will help with minimizing self-judgment. After all, a great cha-cha-cha involves both stepping forward and stepping backward many times over, does it not?

Mindy - Q: If one is in a serious, committed relationship (partnership or marriage), would you recommend both parties take the journey in order to fully develop understanding and how it applies to relationships?

Val Jon - A: Unless you choose a partner who is already familiar with the inner journey and is willing to look within *before* you get seriously involved with them, the odds are slim that they'll be willing to venture across the bridge from Individuation to Introspection. It's not impossible, but if you find you are investing far more energy into having your partner accompany you than they're contributing, you're probably better off *traveling within* without them.

Mindy - Chapter Statement: This is entirely and completely out of my usual comfort zone, but I am fascinated by the subject(s), I am a voracious reader, and I trust the author and other members of the Team, so off I go!

Susie - Q: What might now be possible in my life, with the exploration and learnings of all of these previously unconsidered and unknown Stages and Phases?

Val Jon - A: *Traveling Within* opens new vistas of self-discovery for sure. The deeper we are willing to go within, the more possibilities become available to us. I love the Ralph Waldo Emerson quote, *"What lies behind us and what lies before us are tiny matters compared to what lies within us. And when we bring what is within us out into the world, miracles happen."* For those of us who are courageous enough to travel within, these "miracles" he speaks of are possibilities that become realities in our daily lives.

Susie - Q: Who / Where / What is this Agent of Being?

Val Jon - A: Our Agent of Being is our better conscience, inner guide, and even our "best friend." But it is also more than these things in that it has a Divine nature about it, spiritual energy that provides us insight and inspiration. I like to think of my inner Agent as my personal wise life mentor, a close confidant I can call on in times of need and during times of transition.

Susie - Chapter Statement: This introduction to an inner world I've never experienced, has woken me up to "Hmm, maybe I haven't gotten this life all figured out. There seems to be much more to be discovered and experienced and to be lived!"

Victoria - Q: What is the greatest benefit of traveling inward?

Val Jon - A: To come to know ourselves *beyond ourselves.* For just beneath the surface of who we've always known ourselves to be is a Being who is far more beautiful, wonderful and capable than we ever imagined. This has a secondary benefit to others in our lives as well. The deeper we are willing to travel into our own hidden nature, the more it draws others into the journey with us. To be with others in this extraordinary way transforms life from the mere act of living into the fulfillment of being fully alive. It is also a huge blessing to be in "sacred motion" throughout the course of our lives . . . as we travel within, we move in accord with life's grace and Spirit's intent. Communing with life, Spirit and our Higher Self is a blessing and a benefit that no one should miss out on.

Victoria - Q: Is this process going to bring up painful memories I would really like to not resurface or memories I did not consciously know about?

Val Jon - A: Yes, it certainly will. Consider the challenge to be Spirit's way of encouraging you to trust yourself and show you that who you are is greater than your fears will ever be. I do want to reassure you however that thousands of people have engaged in this work and the outcome has always been positive for those who've participated. That's not to say people don't have challenges to face both during and after engaging in this work, because they do. But with enduring devotion and by maintaining trust in the process, I believe there is nothing we cannot rise above.

Victoria - Chapter Statement: The idea that it isn't failure we fear but rather sustained success as we become more in touch with our Higher Self capabilities is worth deeper consideration and exploration and I look forward to excavating what that means for me.

♦♦♦

CHAPTER 1: SEPARATION

As A (Hu)man Thinketh

The AwarenesSphere®

Emergence: The First Stage
And First Phase of Separation

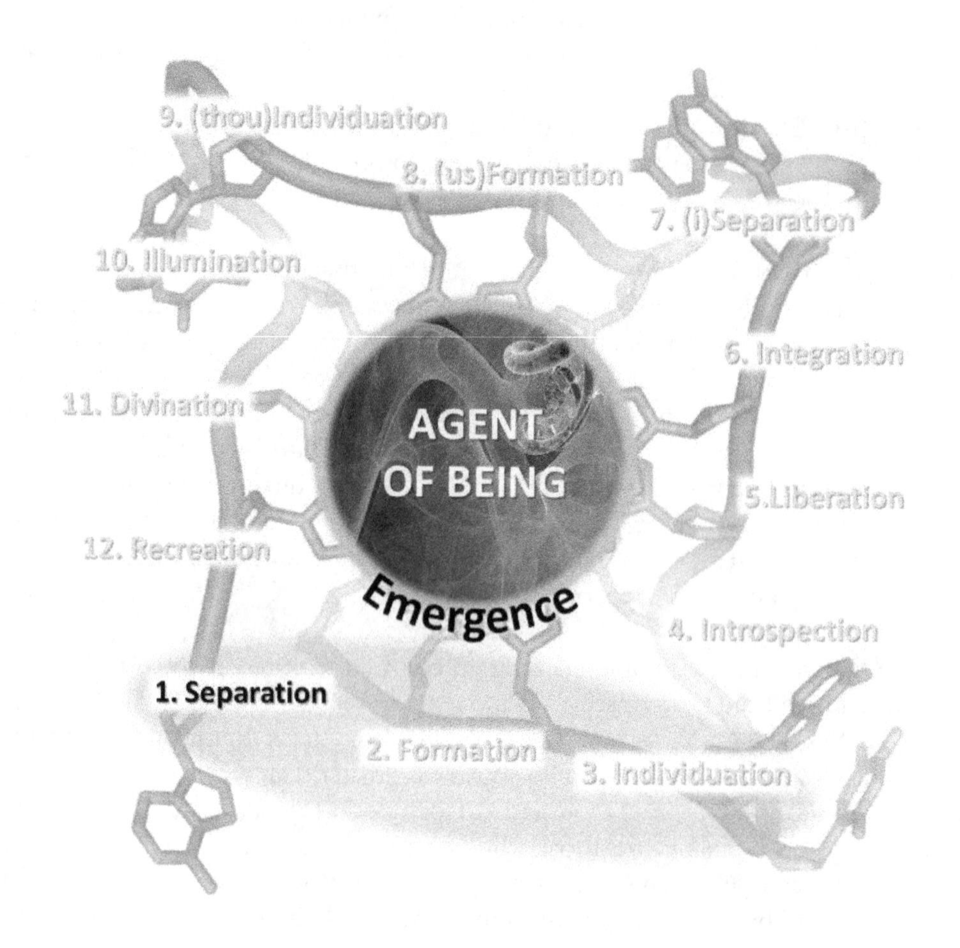

Note: This marks the beginning of the *First Stage of Emergence* within the *AwarenesSphere Model.*

"And ever has it been known that love knows not its own depth until the hour of separation." — Khalil Gibran

Emergence, the First Stage of the *AwarenesSphere* and its three primal Phases of Awareness are *Separation, Formation, and Individuation.* This first Stage is where we all begin the journey of life. Human beings, like all sentient creatures, emerge into the stream of life through a condition of extreme vulnerability, a new-born fragility freshly charged with the primal forces of survival, fear, and dependence. *Emergence* spans the first five years of life, starting with inception and gestation. It then extends to the trauma of birth and separation from our mother's womb, then on to identity formation and ending around the age of five with a fairly complete set of personality and character traits.

While infants are fully sentient and aware, they start out in life without the ability to observe or reflect on their responses to stimuli. Essentially they are relegated to "knee-jerk" reactions rather than possessing the capacity to make objectively responsible choices. An example is a newborn infant uncontrollably crying when left alone in the crib. At this primal stage in their development, they have no choice but to react with the raw emotions of anxiety and fear.

While *Emergence* is a tenuous and rudimentary stage of development, it's a necessary precursor for us to mature into fully evolved adults. In this Stage's title *"Phase of Awareness,"* Awareness refers to our level of consciousness. *"Awareness,"* (without the prefix "Self") means that in these first three Phases, infants lack the ability to self-reflect, observe their own behavior, or grasp the impact their actions have on others. This lack of self-reflection is a crucial distinction to understand as it is an indicator of two very different evolutionary behavior sets. Allow me to explain.

Students of human behavior often learn about these differing behavior sets by observing the diverse awareness levels within the animal kingdom. One such non-harmful lab experiment involves placing a dog in front of a mirror and observing its behaviors. Almost immediately the dog will start barking, but the important question to ask is, *"What is the dog barking at?"* And the right answer is, *"The other dog."* The reason it isn't barking at "itself" is that while dogs, (and cats as well) possess the basic faculties of sentience and awareness, they lack the higher faculty of Self-Awareness I introduced in the previous chapter.

(A/N: This does not mean our pets lack feelings or don't possess human-like characteristics because they certainly do. It simply means that they are not evolved enough to recognize themselves as self-aware creatures. My next segment of the experiment will make this point clear.)

Now let's compare this canine behavior with that of placing a chimpanzee in front of a mirror. Not that you would ever do it, but what you'd observe if you did is that a chimp will start entertaining themselves by making faces and preening because they know there is a "self" they are seeing. Dogs and cats are aware, chimps are self-aware. This is a clear difference in capability and behavior between these two species. The reality is that much of the adult human population behave like dogs and cats, and only those who've evolved out of *Emergence* possess the beginnings of chimp-hood. While it's a humorous assertion, it's also a sad reality because the inability to see ourselves and reflect on our behaviors is one of the primary reasons why we humans create so much strife and suffering in our world.

(A/N: I'm reminded of my preceptorship into the field of Psychology and Behavioral Science many years ago when my colleagues and I endured grueling videotaping analysis sessions. Every single gesture, word, and action we made during clinical counseling sessions was caught on tape and scrutinized by our instructors. Seeing myself as others saw me was a true eye-opener. And while it was a terribly painful ordeal, I made huge leaps in my skills as a counselor and facilitator as a result of the elevated Self-Awareness I attained. It also elevated my relationship skills and my ability to observe the impact my behaviors had on others.)

The detriment of lacking Self-Awareness doesn't only pertain to infants, dogs, and cats. Adults who haven't developed beyond the survival of *Emergence* act out many of the same immature traits, including but not limited to narcissism, self-centeredness, entitlement, bouts of pouting and withdrawal, acts of manipulation, and aggression. *(A/N: I know what you're thinking, some of your family members, spouses or ex-spouses fit this profile perfectly. Believe me, I can empathize with you. As for how to deal with them? Stay with me my fellow traveler as I promise to address it.)*

Separation: The First Phase of Awareness

The *First Phase of Separation* is rooted in basic survival instincts and is charged with the primal forces of insecurity, fear, and dependency. Within this Phase, we're aware of others and our surroundings, but we experience being separate and apart from them. As a result, we fail to understand that we are an interdependent being and that while we have individual lives, we are innately interconnected with others and with the world as a whole. In lacking Self-Awareness, we're also compelled to engage in immature "fight or flight" behaviors. The result is that we are driven to deny or destroy what we don't understand, or side with and worship what we do understand, or happen to agree with.

The detrimental effects of lacking Self-Awareness is a disregard for the sacredness of life and a lack of care for the well-being of anything or anyone, often including ourselves. In this compromised state, when we fail to get what we believe we are entitled to, we react with ploys of defiance, intimidation, withdrawal, and control. The detrimental effects of *Separation,* however, are far more profound than a mere disconnection with our surroundings or others. At its core, the deeper severance is between the wholeness of our newly forming identity and the omnipresence of the *Divine*[12]. *(A/N: Within the context of my work, the "Divine" is not necessarily a religious term or implying the personification of some entity, but rather represents a larger philosophical idea that there is an omnipotent presence that can influence us and open us to the sacredness of life.)*

This existential separation from the Divine casts us into the illusion of abandonment, and we experience a loss of connection with it and from its loving embrace. This perceived loss closely mirrors the trauma of birth and the physical separation from our mother's womb. The cutting of the umbilical cord is the ultimate mortal symbol of *Separation.* Once caught in the illusion of disconnection a deluge of primal forces overtake us and we spiral into the abyss of fear and reaction. As a result, we're compelled to either become completely dependent upon, slip into apathy about, or totally isolate from those around us. While the evolutionary path out of *Separation* is organic and natural for all infants, it isn't uncommon that as we develop, we dramatize our condition and cast ourselves deeper into the unbearable suffering of *Separation* until it becomes too unbearable for us to *not* evolve.

While this is a dismal picture of our first five years of life, it's actually a sacred process that speaks highly of our resilience. We *can* evolve out of basic survival instincts and into higher virtues, it just takes time and a good deal of wise life traveling. *(A/N: For those of you who think you've escaped the detriments of Separation because you had a gentle birth or a well-adjusted childhood, I suggest to you that just because you don't experience the detrimental effects of Emergence doesn't mean they're not there. In other words, we don't miss what we fail to realize is missing . . . until that is, we do realize it. It's like misplacing our keys until we need them. Suddenly the impact of having misplaced them hits us and all the behaviors of self-flagellation and blame begin to emerge.)*

As A (Hu)man Thinketh

For the more experienced life traveler, there's little doubt that what we entertain in our thinking and the feelings we covet in our hearts has an impact on our outward behaviors and actions. What is less clear, however, is that our thoughts and feelings can be *either* empowering *or* detrimental, but not much in between. What about a third option of neutral thinking you might ask? Perhaps, but life isn't all that different from the act of breathing in my experience. In other words, there isn't much hovering between inhaling and exhaling and the same holds true for our thought processes. And just like in the outer world, when we wander into negative terrain within ourselves, even momentarily, it can quickly escalate into a situation we really didn't want to put ourselves in. Take for example an argument with a loved one. You know if you say *that one more thing* it will result in a meltdown, but you think to yourself, *"I don't care if it hurts . . . in fact I want it to hurt!"* and you blurt it out anyway. You just allowed yourself to engage in detrimental thinking and as a result, sent yourself right over the edge of a cliff into a self-righteous abyss of spousal misery.

Basic Assumptions And Primary Decisions

To be clear about the impact of our thinking process, I'm not referring to our casual thoughts or the myriad of mental detours in which our mind has a mind of its own, but rather the more survival-laden *Basic Assumptions*[13] and *Primary Decisions*[14] as I call them that reside just beneath the surface of our obvious awareness. Much like the difference between pliable topsoil and the solid layers of bedrock buried deep within the Earth, these rigid structures of thought and feeling reside deep within our psyches and are permeated with paradoxical emotions and polarizing dynamics. On one hand, these granite-like structures serve as cornerstones of certainty and continuity for our identity. But on the other hand, they are impenetrable rigid conclusions that magnify the detrimental effects of *Separation* and disconnect us from our better judgment and from making wise choices. The way the psyche and our identity is formed is similar to the layers of an onion. The innermost core contains both the memory of our unity and the trauma of our separation. The next layer is composed of a protective veneer designed to reduce threats. The third layer is the pretense we project to others, the way in which we want to be seen, or not seen. Subsequent layers contain adaptive behaviors designed to assimilate new experiences, define our basic preferences, values, morals and so forth.

Exploring Basic Assumptions

Basic Assumptions and their more influential counterpart, Primary Decisions play a substantial role in shaping our behaviors as well as in casting our destiny. Basic Assumptions are the unconscious notions and beliefs we've accepted and integrated as "truth," and thus get added to our internal repository called "my experience." Because they are, for the most part, unexamined and virtually unquestioned assumptions, they have full reign to automatically act upon our decision-making processes without our conscious consent or awareness. *(A/N: Let me give you an example. If you've ever experienced a power outage and found yourself using the light switches over and over again even knowing the power is out, this is the Basic Assumption in operation called, "lights are controlled by the wall switches". . . which however is only true if electricity is available.)*

Basic Assumptions come into existence as a result of experiencing both real and perceived threats, and in some cases, they can be inherited beliefs endorsed by the family and community in which we were raised. An example of this is our political and religious preferences. It takes many years for an individual to begin questioning what they and their family of origin have always held as absolute truth. While after completing a full inquiry of our assumptions, our beliefs and values may change, or they may remain as they were, but what is different is that we understand *why* they are important to us, and as a result, we take sovereign ownership of them. This internal questioning process only begins once we've crossed over from *Emergence* into the higher terrain of *Presence* and its initial *Phase of Introspection.* Without the higher faculty of Self-Awareness which is present in these elevated grounds within us, there is little internal reflection or insight possible. This is so both for infants and for adults who have not developed the faculty of being aware of themselves and their behaviors.

The important distinction to understand is that such assumed "truths" are individual and not universal. What is true for me is not necessarily true for you or for others. For example, one person's truth might be that the world is a beautiful and loving place, and another's might assume just the opposite, that the world is dangerous and highly toxic. Debating over who is right and who is wrong is an energy-draining exercise in that attempting to do so merely creates emotional disconnects. Many of the world's religions fall into this trap by assuming their holy doctrines are *the only way . . . for everyone.* Couples also fall into the "truth trap" by negating each other's experience and trying to shame and control each other into believing what the other believes. The irony of this dynamic, however, is that if successful, we end up with a partner who is just like us, and we eventually lose interest in them. Most domestic arguments are fueled by conflicting Basic Assumptions and an unwillingness to validate their partner's truth as being true for them.

(A/N: To "validate" another's truth or experience doesn't mean we need to agree with it or condone it. It simply means we honor it as their valid reality and that it is important to them for some reason . . . a reason we ought to be interested in understanding if we are to sustain a loving relationship with them. BTW, I know all too well about how we justify our version of the truth as in "I'm not going to validate them because they're just wrong!" If you're stuck on this point please just let it go for now and we'll discuss relationship challenges in greater detail later on in the Presence Stage.)

Basic Assumptions have a profound influence over how we view ourselves, others and the world as a whole. Gone unchecked, they serve as fertile ground for the creation of more powerfully detrimental Primary Decisions that restrict the development of our Self-Awareness and access to our Agent of Being. Let me give you an example. Let's examine the seemingly innocent notion that *"we are born into the world."* There is a potent assumption hiding within the syntax of this phrase. And while it may seem to be an exercise in semantics, the fact is that language is not only a medium of communication, it's also a programming syntax, a kind of self-hypnosis that unconsciously shapes and molds our perceptions, beliefs, and behaviors. What is insidious about this particular assumption is that being *"born into the world"* suggests alienation, estrangement, and disconnection from the very world we are born into. Whereas being *"born out of the world"* is an expression of belonging, connection, and familiarity in which we are a part of, and a natural extension of the world. While this alternative phrase may sound cumbersome, it's more authentic to our true relationship with our planet and with one another.

This subtle disconnect between us and our world creates a rift within our psyche that sets the stage for future disconnections to be automatically made, (e.g., If I'm separate from the world, then it follows that I'm also separate from others and from the human race as a whole.) This separation from others then paves the way for believing I have no part in the detriments being committed by others. And extending my denial even further with, I don't share any responsibility for atrocities like war, the extinction of animal species and the destruction of the natural world. Without even knowing it we've separated ourselves from the world and from the human race by unconsciously condoning that we were born "into it" rather than "out of it." *(A/N: My diatribe isn't intended to invalidate anyone or cast a negative shroud over humanity, but rather to emphasize how insidious Basic Assumptions can be and how they lead to greater degrees of separation. I can, however, be a bit extreme at times, so please forgive me. Plus, I must admit that I'd never go to a party and declare that I was "born out of the world.")*

Nonetheless, just for a moment imagine actually being born *"out of the world,"* fully connected and embraced with the loving care of those who honor you as a part of themselves and them as a part of you. I'm not simply talking about loving parents and family members who happen to be present at our birth, but having an entire race of loving and supportive benefactors who share with us and travel along with us in life as we engage in the extraordinary privilege it is to be alive. Obviously, this is not our current arrangement with the human race. As a whole, we act more like dogs and cats than as loving benefactors, or even as friendly self-aware chimpanzees for that matter.

Exploring Primary Decisions

Primary Decisions are more ingrained and more detrimental than Basic Assumptions. They are composed of intense emotional conclusions and rigid structures of thought that are typically formed between the ages of zero and six. They come into being as the result of an infant being exposed to real or perceived trauma or threats. When I say "trauma" there's a scale of proportion to be considered. It's important to understand that what might be traumatic for an infant is far different than what might be traumatic for an adult. The physical size difference alone between an infant and an adult should make the huge disparity clear. What this means is that what might be considered to be a minor threat to an adult may well be perceived as a massive threat to an infant.

For example, something as seemingly small as ignoring a baby crying in their crib for an extended period of time can set the stage for a Primary Decision to be cast by the infant. *Casting*[15] doesn't mean infants verbalize, or even conceptualize emotional conclusions, but rather feel it in their core as a raw emotional trauma that overwhelms their fragile psyche and leaves a deep traumatic impression within it. This intense survival reaction can rupture the tender fabric of an infant's inner terrain. What this type of rupture means is that depending on the intensity of the trauma, the result might be anything from a minor rip to a gaping rift in the integrity of the infant's newly developing psyche.

Another important factor to consider is that all young children are susceptible to what I call *Infantile Introjection*[16], the act of concluding that *they* are the cause of any and all upsets or problems occurring within the family of their upbringing. In other words, they take in whatever negativity is occurring and blame themselves for it by concluding they are "bad and wrong." Introjection is as painful to infants as food or water going down the wrong pipe is for us adults. *(A/N: In my public workshops this information deeply alarms parents and often sends them careening into the terrain of their own Primary Decisions. I always counsel them that a child will, no matter what, create a Primary Decision even if the parents are consistently loving and attentive. Under even perfectly loving conditions, because of the nature of Separation, an infant will conclude that they are being "smothered" and "not given the chance to live their own lives." So parents, relax and don't you start introjecting because I need you present and attentive with me on this journey.)*

Examples of Primary Decisions

Okay, take a deep breath because we're now going to venture deeper into the core of our inner terrain and shed light on the more detrimental assumptions we cast called Primary Decisions. I've gathered up a brief selection of such decisions that I've come across over the years in my public workshops and counseling sessions. (There is a larger, more complete list in the next chapter's *Exploration And Integration Guide.*) As you read them, stay aware of what feelings or memories get triggered inside of you. Notice if any of them "hook" you or hold your attention longer than others do. If none of them ring a bell go back over each one, read them out loud, close your eyes to travel within and feel around inside your emotions for a stir or sign of familiarity. Even a numbness about any one of them might be an indicator that it may be a fit for you. Ok, here's the list . . . *I'm worthless," (or its antithesis) "I'm super important," "I'll show you," "I'll never trust again," "Love is too painful," "I need to be in control," "No one cares about me," "It's not safe to be me," "Please don't leave me," "It's unfair and I'll prove it," "I don't deserve this," "You won't dominate me," "I don't need you," "I can't trust anyone"* and one of the more popular Primary Decisions when it comes to relationships, *"I love you . . . but f#ck you!"*

Obviously, these are mere words and phrases, but the emotional conviction behind them to be right, to prove they are true, to act them out in order to show how wronged we were is very real. These phrases represent our "investment" in suffering at the expense of our own self-inflicted decisions. In other words, by holding onto such a decision and allowing it to dominate our behaviors, we get the "pay-off" of making others wrong and making ourselves right . . . albeit along with also making ourselves miserable. By the way, we can also make ourselves right about how wrong we are.

(A/N: There is always someone who says, "I don't relate to any of them, am I missing something here?" And the answer is "Yes, you are, and it's alright, you'll get it when you are ready to get it. People with control issues will dismiss the notion altogether and will either conclude that my assertion about such a phenomenon is incorrect, or that they simply don't share in the afflictions so many other people seem to suffer from. Then there are those who doubt themselves to the point of thinking they have a little of all the decisions in the list. And finally, those who entertain that there must be something wrong with them that they don't relate to any of the phrases. Every one of these reactions to this exercise holds vital clues about what your particular Primary Decision is. I recommend paying more attention to your reactions and less attention to your conclusions. And again, please relax into this process and trust that your Primary Decision will come to you naturally as we move forward with this journey.)

To keep this developmental process in perspective, as young children we have no control over our environment, and we certainly don't manufacture such decisions on purpose or from a self-inflictive or vindictive place. We are completely innocent in our conclusions and what we decide actually helps us to survive and get through the traumas and threats we all inevitably encounter as infants. The only problem is that these Primary Decisions dictate our adult behaviors and casts us into a victim role in which we abandon our power of choice, the ability to create our own experience rather than it being dictated by our circumstances. How do they dictate our experiences? If we have an investment in something such as us being wrong, or having made some indelible mistakes, how likely are we to easily give up our investment in being wrong about it? Or conversely, if we have a huge amount of evidence for how badly someone has treated us, and we are wedded to that evidence more than we are willing to let it go, how likely are we to ever be free of the negative judgments we harbor? If we were to "liberate" ourselves from the detriment of our Primary Decisions who would have been wrong all these years? The reality is, if we aren't willing to surrender our investment in being right, we lose the right to be happy. Why? Because it isn't possible to covet negative thoughts and feelings and expect to feel peace and joy. The opposing sentiments simply don't work well together.

As individuals as well as a collective race, our Primary Decisions are symptoms and expressions of *Separation* and its *First Stage of Emergence.* Because it's the first in the series of the *AwarenesSphere's Twelve Phases, Separation* is the most primal in that it evokes the survival reactions of disconnection, abandonment, and fear in newborns. Regardless of whether we have loving parents or not, or whether or not humanity ever evolves into a more conscious and compassionate race, the simple fact of being rejected from our mother's womb and having our umbilical cord severed is reason enough to tumble headfirst into life and into *Separation.*

I want to point out that while the experiences of belonging, sharing and love may come to us during or after our birth, if our Primary Decision preceded our actual birth or the love we received, it will still become integrated into our identity and shape how we later on in life relate to the world and others. This is why identical newborn twins often display completely different behaviors. The Primary Decision of one twin might be, *"I need your love"* and the other twin's, *"I don't need anyone."* These two emotional conclusions produce markedly different behaviors in the two infants, character traits that magnify and solidify as they mature. I also want to clarify that the timing of when we cast our Primary Decision does not necessarily happen only at birth, but rather can occur any time between the ages of zero and six as the entire *Stage of Emergence* is fertile ground for the casting of these detrimental assumptions and decisions.

Fear Versus Love Resides At Our Core

Regardless of what our Primary Decision might be and when we cast it, fear rather than love invariably gets forged into our core and within the formation of our young psyche. And while it may seem unfortunate, this lodging of fear within us is actually an essential rite of passage for the healthy development of our identity, especially in a world that is far from loving. Being exposed early on to survival-based energies prepares us to deal with the inevitable future threats and occurrences of betrayal, violation, and abuse we will surely encounter as adults.

On the other hand, a detrimental Primary Decision dwelling in our psyche for years on end without ever dealing with it or transcending its rigid patterning can also have the opposite effect of contributing to abuse in our future. *(A/N: I know this notion can be easily dismissed or argued with, so allow me to make an analogy that might help with the understanding. Imagine a "bullseye" target positioned just inches away from our unresolved inner terrain. "Trespassers" into our vulnerable space, those who would dishonor and abuse us will inevitably spot the target and begin shooting at it. Essentially, we bring abuse to us by harboring unresolved betrayal issues within us that give us away as easy targets.)*

I want to share a vulnerable experience with you now that will help bring to life the concepts and principles I've been sharing with you. Concepts and principles are useful for gaining perspective and understanding, but without emotional experience to warm them and illuminate their underlying meaning, they're just sterile and lifeless notions. As unlikely as it may sound, I have vivid memories of my own birth process. I've conducted countless "expeditions" into my own inner terrain and ventured into its depths many times over, so I'm going to give you a moment-by-moment account of what I encountered in the womb and during my birth process.

The Intense Survival Energies of Birth

Rather than emerging head first like most newborns, I was born breech which means I endured a feet first delivery. Such a delivery can come with some dire complications, and in my case, the umbilical cord, the very lifeline of my fragile existence was dangerously wrapped around my neck inside the womb. The further down the birth canal I traveled, the tighter its grip became. What irony, that which gives me life also threatens to take my life away! Into the confines of my mother's womb, we now go . . . or uh, since there's not enough room for us both, perhaps you can just put your ear to my mother's tummy and listen along.

Nine pounds and upside down in her uterus I am . . . but I'm oblivious to her discomfort as I'm totally consumed by the familiar heart-thumping and the rushing of fluids surging through my curled up torso. Not that I was actually hearing these sounds, but rather viscerally sensing them as they resonated within my tiny bones, soft cranium and tender limbs.

Hot moist pressure pressing in all around me, closed eyes bathed in tints of red, swirling luminous patterns dizzying me to the core. Fierce contractions bulging my tiny eyes, rhythmically forcing my mouth open, ejecting moist warmth into my throat and filling me with waves of anxiety and confusion. In raw pre-words I cast into myself, *"I'm not welcome here!"* Terror without the ability to scream suddenly rips into my familiar comfort, safety, and contentment, severing my feelings of belonging and safety. Then the shock of invasion, cold rigid pressure wedging its way up my tiny legs, twisting my hips, forcing my left arm backward and up over my head. Steel forceps jammed between my body and my mother's birth canal probing for solid anchor points, curving their way to the top of my skull, pressing down with intense force, drawing me downward into a dark vortex of oblivion, Basic Assumptions being cast now, reinforcing my already concluded unwelcome-ness, *"What have I done to deserve this?"* The umbilical cord now tightening its grip around my neck, not blocking air as there is none to be had, but squeezing-off our blood flow, the nurturance, and assurance shared with my mother, her body and my body, one comforting presence now being torn apart.

Suddenly my feet are freezing, dangling into an unknown void . . . another casting of, *"I didn't ask for this!"* Invisible demons groping at my legs, pulling my joints apart, clinging to my tiny torso, clutching around my belly, squeezing and ejecting fluids from deep in my body out through my mouth and nose, flooding my eye-sockets in hot wet terror. Intense pressure on my skull, flattening the top of my head out wide, the contrast of my legs shivering cold and my head exploding hot is too much to bear, I go numb and all is lost, and just then . . . intense white light, terrorizing buzzing sounds, massive blurred forms all around me, immediate relief and flow inside my swollen throat and a burst of cold pressure filling my virgin lungs. I have arrived! But as I do, I cast into existence my Primary Decision of, ***"I'm all alone and on my own!"***

♦♦♦

(A/N: Take a deep breath. If you feel that experience was intense, imagine what I experienced going through it. Just writing this sequence of events brings tears to my eyes and my heart is palpitating recounting the images and sensations. This was a very vulnerable thing for me to share with you, and yet I have the feeling you are compassionate and understanding. Your acceptance comforts me and encourages me to share even more vulnerable experiences with you, which I will definitely do as we travel along the pathway of the AwarenesSphere together. I can assume this response from you because I've shared this story hundreds of times in my public workshops and participants are always deeply moved and appreciative of the risk I take in sharing so intimately with them.)

I trust that recounting my birth process has conveyed the visceral experience needed for you to move into the depths of *Emergence's First Phase of Separation,* how it comes about, and what some of its challenging dynamics are. I also hope you are moved, (if not a bit terrified) to venture into your own inner terrain of *Separation* and begin to illuminate it, own it, heal it perhaps, and most importantly, learn how to recognize it and navigate around inside its dark and unfamiliar landscape. *(A/N: I want to clarify again that not all Primary Decisions are cast in the womb. In fact, the majority of them come into existence in the first five or six years of life. Also, I wouldn't focus too much on what you may have cast or when, as we'll get to that piece of work shortly.)*

The Definition of Self And The Power of Choice

There is one more key distinction I want to make about the terrain of *Separation.* It's a more advanced concept we will explore later on, but it's important to introduce it now as many who I've worked with over the years regarding their Primary Decisions have brought up a very important point. It's clear that each of us indeed does cast these emotional decisions into our young psyches, but what is unclear is *why* we select certain assumptions and decisions over others in the first place. What invisible factors are involved that predispose us to make such powerful conclusions, and why do we conclude what we specifically conclude? For instance, why out of all the decisions I could have cast did I choose *"I'm all alone and on my own?"* After all, there were plenty of people around to greet me during my birth process and my mother certainly didn't abandon me.

Let's explore the first part of the question, "Why do we make such decisions in the first place?" The answer is a philosophical one, but very important to understand as it lays the foundation for the entire context of our Agent of Being and for the extraordinary capabilities it possesses to wisely guide our lives. Many years ago as I was designing the curriculum for my public workshops I came across a definition of *Self*[17] that profoundly changed my understanding of who we are and what we are capable of. From an old mid-sixties Collegiate Dictionary I found the following definition. ***The "Self," The agent that of itself, acts in a manner implied by the word with which it is joined.*** I needed to read it many times over before it dawned on me what it actually meant. ***"The agent . . ."*** is obviously some kind of inner representative who has our best interests in mind. It's like a symphony conductor who leads the orchestra of our available choices and responses to our daily life challenges. The segment, ***". . . that of itself"*** was confusing for me at first, but I finally realized that it refers to the Self's ability to be autonomous or "self-determined." In other words, our innermost Self is not reliant upon outside forces or sources for its inspiration or positive energy; much like how stars generate their own sources of energy, heat, and light.

These first two segments were simple compared to the final one, ***". . . acts in a manner implied by the word with which it is joined."*** What could this possibly mean? The "Self" acts like the words it joins with? The implication is that we, our Self, somehow bonds or "joins" with our language syntax. But what does this joining process involve? The answer is a very important process of bonding between what we think, believe and feel and our conclusions, behaviors, and actions. A good example is the emotion of anger. What makes controlling our anger so difficult at times is that it's not so much that we *get* angry as that we *are* angry. In other words, we actually join with the emotion of anger and become it to the point that we lose control of who we are and what we are doing. *(A/N: I know there are some who have completely suppressed their access to anger so my example isn't relevant. You can take any emotion however and the same principle applies with respect to the "joining.")*

Coming across the Proverbs passage in the Bible, *"For as he thinketh in his heart, so is he"* brought the whole definition of Self into clear focus for me. Our words, (whether spoken or coveted) are powerful influencers over our behaviors and actions. When we think and feel passionately about something it has a powerful influence on us and can literally rearrange aspects of our identity, character, and actions. So in other words, if I think and feel deeply that I am "Bad," *I become Bad.* If I think I am "Alone," then *I Am Alone.* It's not just that I *feel Alone*, it's that *I Am Alone.* Who I know myself to be literally becomes *Aloneness* to my core. Given the tendency of infants to internalize everything they take in, this dynamic makes total sense and must not be underestimated.

This brings us to the *Power of Choice*[18], our ability to choose how we respond to life's challenges. Choice is about taking personal responsibility for how we experience our circumstances, as well as for getting ourselves into the circumstances we find ourselves in. We may not always have a choice over what happens to us in our daily lives, but we always have a choice regarding how we will relate to them and deal with them. "Choosing" is an essential aspect of our Higher Self and it literally transforms our relationship with our life circumstances. Rather than empowering the Basic Assumption that we are at the effect, we live into the reality that in fact, we are at cause.

Choice is about being self-aware enough to monitor our internal reactions and the meanings we assign to things. Think of Choice like an intentional buffer we use to "catch" our incoming circumstances and assess how we want to respond to them rather than reacting to them directly. This added moment of self-assessment enables us to either "unjoin" from a negative conclusion we previously cast, or to divert the "joining" process to something more beneficial to us and others. *(A/N: When I was a boy, because of my extreme independence, my mother would often advise me to "count to ten" before opening my mouth. While this is a simple explanation of the Power of Choice, it's a good example that we all can relate to. So did I often follow her advice you might ask? Uh . . . No.)*

Fundamentally our Agent of Being, along with the higher faculty of Self-Awareness enables us to choose what emotional conclusions we join with moment-by-moment. It also gives us the power to "unchoose" detrimental conclusions we've already joined with. So why then can't we simply unchoose our Primary Decisions right after we join with them? Because as infants we don't possess the Self-Awareness needed to self-monitor and buffer the intense reactions that instantly form within our psyches. Without Self-Awareness, we literally become our reactions, and in most cases, during the *Phase of Separation,* we join with fear rather than love.

Joining with fear sends us into greater separation, but more importantly, it disables our ability to exercise Choice. This is so because joining with fear automatically bonds us with being a victim, and there is a fundamental truth we simply cannot ignore which is that in this gross physical reality, two different things cannot exist in the same place at the same time. In other words, we can't be both a Chooser and a Victim. It's either one or the other.

If we initially bonded with love rather than fear, the outcome would be different. Why? Because love carries with it total acceptance and the lack of reactionary judgment, two virtues essential for being the Chooser in our lives. There is no way to Choose from a place of victimhood because as a victim, our investment is in being at the effect of our circumstances rather than being at cause of our reactions. And the final but essential point I want to make about the Power of Choice is that rehabilitating our Power to Choose requires not only un-choosing the initial Primary Decision we cast, but also *"Choosing to be the Chooser."*

(A/N: This final point is of utmost importance as the entire developmental process of coming into accord with our Agent of Being depends on understanding and embracing this crucial distinction. We'll explore Choosing to be the Chooser in the Liberation chapter to come.)

The Genetics of Our Energetic Disposition

The final insight I want to explore before we move on has to do with the second part of the question I asked earlier in the chapter, "Why do we decide what we decide?" Given that we are "Choosers" it's clear that we become what we choose. But what causes us to make the choice we do in the first place? Given I wasn't really abandoned at birth and not really left alone, where did my conclusion come from? While I won't answer it completely now, because doing so later will make much more sense as we move further along in our travels, suffice to say that just as the nature of Self is to "join," and just as we have learned from Jung that we share in a "Collective Unconsciousness," we also possess energies within us that were pre-existing to our conception. Said another way, we possess an *Energetic Disposition*[19] that contains a predetermined array of forces and energies our family of origin and ancestors also possessed.

I want to clarify that I'm not talking about past lives per se, or that we carry karma forward from our ancestors into this life, but rather that much like a pure droplet of water falls into an already existing pond or lake, that droplet takes on the chemical and energetic composition of that which it merges with. Likewise, the Self that exists beyond the bounds of the individual and prior to our arrival as a human, has also joined with a vast pool of personhood elements and forces, some more prominent than others.

I want to step back from a metaphysical discussion about our Energetic Disposition and ground what I'm suggesting in science. It's a given fact that we all share in the same DNA gene pool as the whole of the human race, so the common physical traits everyone possesses reside within us. And just like our physical traits are shared and can be passed from one generation to the next, there is now evidence that our genes also pass emotional and histrionic traits forward. (There are at least five such genes that have been recently discovered that contain emotional-based coding.) It's not a huge leap of faith to draw the conclusion that our individual droplet of individuality carries within it traces of the larger gene pool of collective elements of personhood Carl Jung suggested. *(A/N: We will explore later on how the Energetic Disposition comes into being, how it influences our identity formation and behaviors.)*

The AwarenesSphere's Linkage To Eastern Theology

As an additional point of reference, I've added an Eastern Theology linkage to each of the *Twelve Phases of the AwarenesSphere.* By doing so I believe it honors and includes those *Travelers Within* who have an Oriental approach to the process of self-development. I believe the characteristics of each Phase will be better understood for those with an Eastern orientation, and even if you don't particularly relate to metaphysics, the linkages will provide you with an added way to understand and integrate them. Allow me to offer some background before making the linkage between *Separation* and the energy present in the first of *Twelve Chakras* called the *"Root." (A/N: We will use the lesser-known Twelve Chakra rather than Seven Chakra model for purposes of this inner work.) Chakra*[20], in Sanskrit, means "wheel" and according to Eastern Theology, the name refers to the rotation of our life force energy or "Prana" as it travels up and down our spinal cord and through each of our Twelve Chakra centers. This rotating energy starts below the base of our spine and moves up to above the top of our head, traversing each Chakra center as it travels. Each of the Twelve Chakras has a different vibrational energy and correlation to our physical, emotional and spiritual selves. Chakras are much like "gates" a traveler might encounter while venturing out in the wilderness in that when we come upon them they can be either open, closed, or in some cases, dilapidated and in need of repair.

An "open" gate indicates that the way forward is clear and our passage is unencumbered by obstacles in the form of emotional baggage, unresolved hurts, conflicts, and emotionally charged decisions. A "closed" or "dilapidated" gate contains these detriments and blocks our life-force energy from being able to pass, which in turn, inhibits the advancement of our Self-Awareness, access to our Agent of Being and our access to higher spiritual ground within. Each of the Twelve Chakras matches the *Twelve Phases of AwarenesSphere.* Let's explore the first linkage now.

Separation's Linkage With The First Chakra: Root Energy

The First Chakra or "Root Energy," just as the name suggests is the most primal of the twelve centers. It is located at the very base of the tailbone and matches the *First Phase of Separation* in that the energy of basic urges, survival, and disconnection are shared between them. The official name of this Chakra is "Muladhara," from the words "Mula," which means root and "Dhara," which means support. Our Root Chakra is grounded close to the Earth and when it's balanced and open, it provides us with stability and a sense of continuity and contentment. And much like when our *Separation* issues have been resolved, we experience a sense of peace, presence, and accomplishment, particularly with respect to money, safety, and shelter. Likewise, when our Root Chakra is closed and our issues of *Separation* are dramatized or acted out, we slip into survival, feel unstable and anxious and tend to stop paying attention to our basic needs.

Exploration And Integration Guide

As a way to integrate the material presented in this chapter, and so you can gain insight into some of the conditions surrounding your own birth process, I've crafted a few key questions and processes for you. *(A/N: I will include this section in all the coming chapters as a way to provide you with a working forum and means for integrating and implementing the concepts and principles I introduce into your daily life.)* Let's review the key questions and processes that pertain to the chapter we just completed.

1. Not many people recall their birth, so try not to struggle with it too much. If you do happen to remember, what stands out most for you about it? And what is your sense of any emotional assumptions and decisions you may have made either in the womb or during your birth process? First impressions are usually correct, especially if you find yourself second-guessing them.

2. If you don't remember your birth, if your mother is alive you may want to ask her about it as she will most likely recall the experience. If she is no longer alive, try imagining the process, close your eyes, place yourself in her womb and allow your curiosity and feelings to lead you into the experience.

3. Don't worry about "making things up" as it's all valid material and will assist in you becoming more familiar with your inner terrain. That's the point, to gain experience in navigating within your psyche, not necessarily accessing specific material relevant to this inquiry.

4. Review old photographs of you around the time of your birth. If you can locate pictures of yourself just after you were born, see if you can get close-up views of your face and your eyes. What is your emotional expression? Do you look happy, sad or distracted? What about your mother's demeanor? Is she smiling, how is she holding you and looking at you? All these details will help you piece together what your birth experience was like for you. *(A/N:*

Take your time with these questions and processes and remember to relax and trust that you will gain the insights and experiences needed to succeed in this work. I have faith in you, so I ask that you too have a similar faith in yourself. Oh, and one more thing, don't delay doing this work or it will slow your forward progress.)

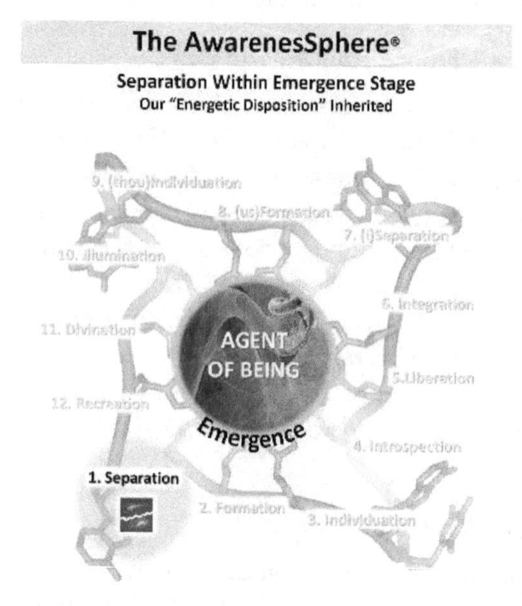

Let's move on by recapping *Separation, Emergence's First Phase of Awareness. Separation* occurs during our birth when we are expelled from our mother's womb. This abrupt severance from our mother and from the Divine infuses fear and insecurity into the core of our being. As infants, and throughout most of the *Emergence Stage* we possess only a rudimentary level of awareness that lacks Self-Awareness, the ability to self-reflect and observe our own behaviors. Without Self-Awareness, we have no ability to reflect upon or understand the processes that are impacting us, and no capacity to do anything about it or make any positive changes.

Separation occurs sometime between conception and birth and its fear-based energies pave the way for us to make emotional conclusions called Basic Assumptions and the more insidious Primary Decisions. Much like the structure of a "Box," these emotionally-charged conclusions play a prominent role in shaping our newly forming identity and evolve into rigid behavior patterns in our adult lives. As with my own Primary Decision of *"I'm all alone and on my own"* I can attest to the enduring effects of having chosen such a ruggedly independent conclusion, as it took years to liberate myself from it. While such a fate seems unfortunate, the reality is that having a Primary Decision is a natural and normal part of our development process. It becomes a detriment only if we fail to do the work of freeing ourselves from its rigid patterning at some point as we mature into adulthood.

Our Higher Self and its Power of Choice empowers us with the ability to choose how we respond to life's challenges. Choice is about taking personal responsibility for how we experience our circumstances, as well as for getting ourselves into (and out of) the circumstances we find ourselves in. We may not always have a choice over what happens to us in our daily lives, but we always have a choice regarding how we will relate to them and deal with them. This vital principle of personal responsibility stems from Webster's definition of Self which is, *"The agent that of itself, acts in a manner implied by the word with which it is joined."* Essentially, this means that whatever we empower in our thinking and feeling becomes realized in our behaviors and actions. The "joining" is the coupling of what exists within our inner terrain and what gets projected into our outer world. We can only "un-join" from our Primary Decision when we take the ground of being the Chooser, which includes the process of identifying, re-experiencing and "un-doing" or *Uncasting*[21] our initial childhood traumas. Once we fully complete this process, we are free to declare to ourselves that we are no longer a victim of our circumstances.

Other than the *Eastern Theology Linkages* and *Exploration And Integration Guide,* the final section in this first chapter was devoted to introducing the notion of Energetic Disposition, a genetic passing of emotional material between generations. Just as we inherit physical traits from our family of origin, we also inherit behavioral traits from them. This material is infused into our core being during the moment of our conception and plays a powerful role in predisposing us to choose a specific Primary Decision that fits with the behavioral patterning of our ancestors. ~

In the next chapter, we'll venture together into *Formation,* the *Second Phase of Emergence.* This aspect of human evolution is where our identity begins to develop, where our survival-based conclusions continue to get cast into existence, and where we lose touch altogether with our Agent of Being. Put on your hip-waders because, after the question and answers section, we're going to enter the mysterious collective genetic pool called, *"From Everyone To Only One."*

♦♦♦

Reader's Question & Answer Section (Chapter 1: Separation)

Allison - Q: I am one of the people who, when reading the different Primary Decisions you listed, felt to have some of each statement as a truth inside of me. As I say this, I also see this aspect of myself that wants to connect to everything and everyone I encounter. (I experience myself as so deeply empathic that it can become hard to create boundaries, which can lead to overwhelm.) How do I support myself to create more clarity of vision to know what is truly me and what is not?

Val Jon - A: Wanting to connect with "everything and everyone" is, for the most part, a healthy desire, and yet exploring the underlying motivation for it is important. As you hinted at, having insufficient boundaries tends to have one scatter their awareness. This is so because the material in the psyche tends to flow out of the inner terrain and merge with the terrain of others, (as well as with Nature and the natural world). And what is "truly you" cannot be validated through referencing the outer world, but rather only by traveling into the entire expanse of your psyche, and as you do, placing "identity-markers" much like you would personalize your living space. A few family pictures here, a favorite flower vase there, and a colorful painting above the couch. Only by "getting to know and marking" all the diverse and hidden facets of yourself will you gain the clarity of vision you seek. Focus on the practices and exercises I outline in the *Exploration And Integration Guide* sections and work them with dedication and resolve, as doing so will help clarify your vision and the unique nature of who you truly are will shine like a bright light in the darkness.

Allison - Q: Even though I have already accepted personal responsibility and am being the Chooser in my life, I still grapple with moments of "victimhood." Will this dance between the two fall away more effortlessly as I become clearer about my Primary Decision?

Val Jon - A: Absolutely. The aspects of victimhood that sneak into our awareness and behaviors stem from repeated attempts on our Primary Decision's part to regain control over us so it can carry on with its selfish agenda of proving how right (or wrong) it is. I suggest reviewing the Q&A sections in the next few chapters and integrating what some of your teammates have to say (and how I respond to their questions) regarding the challenge of identifying their Box.

Allison - Chapter Statement: The experience of Separation isn't something to run away from but rather, something to embrace. The clarity and courage that results in becoming empowered in the experience of Self-Awareness and Choice is the gift of being fully alive and fully realized on the path of the human journey. In my own embracing of this and in the recognition that comes with choosing this path of Self-Awareness, I am humbled at the work that comes forward and how opting into this experience of life brings the most beautiful gifts, even if they are sometimes hard to take.

Anna - Q: How do we overcome the need to be right and be in control to allow ourselves to accept being "incorrect?"

Val Jon - A: Needing to be right is an automatic behavior set arising from our Primary Decision, and held in place by an ego-investment. There are two genres of righteousness to consider - public and private. The public version is all about not losing face and maintaining a pretense of perfection. The private version is about denial, self-invalidation and the deeper fear of not being enough in life. The public investment is usually tied to earlier similar incidents in which we were humiliated, made fun of, chastised, or otherwise embarrassed in front of others. By Uncasting these previous events, we free ourselves to place more importance on being authentic than on protecting our self-image. The private investment is deeper and usually tied to an underlying fear of being inadequate or "damaged goods." This core Basic Assumption can only be undone by doing the Box Uncasting work outlined in this chapter. There is, however, a shortcut practice I often use, but you may not like it. Any time I catch myself needing to be right while in conversation with others, I immediately stop and "bust" myself by acknowledging my defensiveness and insistence on being right, and I do so right while in mid-sentence! It devastates the ego, but it empowers the Self. I find that if I commit to this ego-busting strategy, my ego prefers to give up being right *before* it starts being right, rather than facing the humiliation that comes through my intentional ego-busting exposure tactic.

Anna - Q: How does one become willing to accept the emotions that go along with those realizations that bring that flood of awareness and insight to us?

Val Jon - A: It's all in making the choice to live as a Chooser rather than as a victim of our own limitations and circumstances. If growing and deepening my life is more important to me than being comfortable is, I will be much more willing to face into and experience the emotions and situations I most want to avoid. We have a saying in our retreats and programs, *"Go where you don't want to go, step where you don't want to step and feel what you don't want to feel."* The key is to realize that facing our inner demons and limitations will never be something we want to do, *and* by doing so anyway, we become stronger and ever-more true to our Higher Self.

Anna - Chapter Statement: When I took that step off the edge of the cliff like the FOOL in the Tarot it was with blind faith that what I would find could be no worse than the hell I was living. I've known Val Jon for many years and have had a multitude of deep conversations with him. It was knowing that he would be guiding me through this process of awakening that I trusted enough to take that leap of faith. It was the best conscious choice I've ever made. And boy did it make my life make sense, however, it also showed me where my poor blind faith choices created the hell I was living. So I decided to do a very FOOL-ish thing and continued to embark on this journey with nothing but my wits about me and my trusted friend to guide me.

Antonio - Q: What are the signs that we are becoming aware of our Agent of Being?

Val Jon - A: The signs of coming into accord with our Agent of Being usually come in the form of intense curiosity and in asking ourselves questions we've never asked before, and specifically those pertaining to our personal growth and spiritual nature. Another sign is when our conscience kicks in and informs us that we're doing something detrimental and ought to reconsider our choice . . . and we actually consider taking the inner advice. These are all signs that our inner Agent is reaching out to us and wanting to make itself available to us in our daily lives.

Antonio - Q: How can we trust that we are connecting with our Agent of Being and not an ego voice?

Val Jon - A: The ego has a very distinct "feel" about it. It's reactive, opinionated, exclusive and self-serving. Our Agent of Being, on the other hand, is spacious, inclusive and is always looking out not only for us but for others as well. If caring for everyone involved and being honest and forthright is part of the message, then you can trust it's your Higher Self and your Agent of Being connecting with you.

Antonio - Chapter Statement: The first step in healing the wounded child from our Primary Decision is recognizing that we were/are not victims.

Cyn - Q: Is the Separation Phase always rife with fear and negative experiences?

Val Jon - A: Having facilitated thousands of workshop participants through the terrain of Separation I can say with certainty that almost all of them experienced some degree of fear and uncertainty, and enough doubt about the strange newness of life to cause substantial anxiety within their tiny core. The "negativity" factor varies greatly, however, as in your case, where you may have been greeted and attended to with consistent love and reassurance the negativity you experienced may have been minimal.

Cyn - Q: In this crazy high-speed world are there tips to quickly get beyond our brain clutter to focus on discovering our internal workings? To clear away distractions and find our root?

Val Jon - A: Our mind, or brain clutter, as you call it, is deeply interwoven with our crazy high-speed world. The two are inseparable, locked in an obligatory symbiosis that can only be transcended through sustained practice and attention. There are no quick tips or fixes, and if there were, I would have used them myself instead of spending many years traveling through the terrain of my psyche and working hard to declutter my being-ness.

Cyn - Chapter Statement: Although I think I need to take many passes at continuing to define my Primary Decision with trips within the Box, there is so much profound love, happiness, and joy I feel around remembering my birth and meeting my mother, (all nine pounds of me)! And, there is no doubt in my mind that, not the separation, but the welcome I received grounded the positive energy that has been pervasive throughout my life – "Choosing" light.

Elise - Q: How does one form the Agent of Being with an initial experience of non-validation?
Val Jon - A: An initial experience of invalidation is certainly a challenging personal experience to endure. Fortunately, the forming of our Agent of Being isn't a personal action and doesn't come about through our individual will. It is rather an omnipotent phenomenon that arises through the intent of the Divine, or a force that is greater than ourselves which is capable of manifesting in and through us.

Elise - Q: "Rebirth" is used in so many contexts, are they all valid?
Val Jon - A: The validity of a context is a subjective thing. Rather than debating the validity of all the contexts out there regarding rebirth, it might be more useful to engage in an inquiry process and come to your own truth about it. I certainly believe in rebirth in a few specific contexts. Nature rebirths constantly with its perennial magic. Life as a whole and humanity rebirths itself through the wonder of reproductivity. And the cosmos rebirths its stars and celestial bodies through its quantum alchemy. Beyond these specific contexts, I personally have less faith in the claims that are made about rebirth. For example, reincarnation is a context I remain neutral about. Not because I don't believe it's possible, but rather because, while I've explored "other lives" I just don't resonate with having been any single individual in the distant past . . . perhaps *all* individuals to some degree, but not any one personage.

Elise - Chapter Statement: This chapter was a remembrance of the deep process of uncovering my Box and the ideas that had driven my life until age 35 in one of Val Jon's workshops. Those discoveries in his programs changed my life and reality completely. To become the conscious Chooser of my actions, freed of the reactive mind, was the start of a blossoming self that continues today.

Mindy - Q: I am a Christian. Will I be conflicted by the references to Eastern Theology as we progress through the AwarenesSphere?
Val Jon - A: As you read on, you will find that I reference a wide variety of theologies and religions. (Traveling within is a secular journey that is not tied to any one faith.) I chose to add the "Chakra Center" materials at the end of each chapter because I have a personal affinity and respect for Eastern philosophy. I have also devoted a substantial portion of my manuscripts to

Christian beliefs, such as *The Three Temptations of Christ*, which I introduce later on, as well as a variety of other Biblical lessons, quotes, and references. There are bound to be conflicts for some readers because of my all-inclusive approach to religion, spirituality and empirical philosophy. What I recommend is simply skipping over the sections you are not interested in and trusting that because your faith runs deep, a small exposure to conflicting materials will not in any way sway your devout convictions.

Mindy - Q: My experience of birth was "sMOTHERing." My brother was 9 years old and my mother had several miscarriages before I was born. She was so relieved to have me, I don't think she ever put me down. Is this, then, the difficulty I still have wanting to please my mother? She thinks I'm the perfect child, and yet I constantly feel I must live up to her expectations of that perfection. My father, on the other hand, allows me to be me. Is this why I'm drawn to him, yet bristle if my mother simply asks me a question?

Val Jon - A: I call this dynamic "womb worry." There is clear behavioral evidence for the transference of emotional distress from the mother to the fetus. Research by prominent obstetricians show that if a pregnant mother is going through high levels of fear or anxiety, she creates a "metabolic cascade," powerful hormonal reactions that affect both mother and fetus. Chronic anxiety in the mother can also set the stage for a whole array of challenges such as prematurity, birth complications, and post-birth behavioral and emotional deviations. Where I would focus however is in the time shortly after your birth regarding incidents in which your mother held you too closely and perhaps inhibited your breathing accidentally. Skin to skin contact or wrapped too tightly in a blanket. As you review potential incidents use your breathing ease or difficulty level in order to zero-in on the primary incident in which you made a decision about you and your mother.

Mindy - Chapter Statement: As a Christian, the concepts of separation and fear can be pronounced, and yet I have often been one who has to have the last word. I almost doubled over crying when I read, *"It isn't safe to be me."* Yes! That's it. That is what I was feeling and experiencing so much of my life! I have learned – painfully so – the art of "zipping it" or saving that last word for another time has a profound impact on relationships. I *intentionally choose* to save it, and then I find I don't need to use it. I want to be the one showing grace rather than the one seeking it. This creates a choice to *be safe – as me.*

Susie - Q: Can I be courageous, and identify with my Primary Decision, even if I didn't know I had one before I opened this book? It seems to me that identifying with one makes me look bad.

Val Jon - A: "Looking bad" is a fear that is directly generated from our Box or Primary Decision. What "looks bad" and what "is bad" are two very different things. We need to commit to endorsing one or the other. We can't grow ourselves if we're worried about looking bad, because the ego always wants to look good. We must come out from behind the mask of "good and bad" and have our original face be seen by the world. And what face is that? The face of the Divine, who is beautiful beyond all looking, be it good or bad.

Susie - Q: Is it really possible to re-experience our birth?

Val Jon - A: In my thirty years as a facilitator of the human psyche, I've learned that most people can indeed re-experience their birth, once they've worked their way through all the distractions and diversions first that is. There are a few who were so unconscious in the womb, or so bent on not wanting to be here that they missed the entire event, but these cases are rare. Could you be one of them? Sure, but it would be more useful to set that fear aside, trust the inner traveling process and work with all the practices and exercises I'm outlining in this work. In doing so I believe you will indeed be able to recall your birth.

Susie - Chapter Statement: I realized that identifying with my Primary Decision, "seemed" to make me not the self-aware person I know myself to be. Yet, it is at the root (pun intended) of my separation from my divine nature and Agent of Being, and it is the first step on the path of reunification.

Victoria - Q: A few months before reading this first book, I had a pre-birth memory of feeling, *"I don't belong here."* I now see that this is what you refer to as the Basic Assumption. How does this assumption relate to my Primary Decision, and how does it play out throughout my life? I know the answer for myself, but I think it may help other readers who might have a similar Basic Assumption.

Val Jon - A: Let's explore your assumption, *"I don't belong here."* This is a powerful conclusion that in addition to being a Basic Assumption, could also very well be your initial Primary Decision. The slight difference is that the assumption of "not belonging" is usually an afterthought that comes about as the result of a more primary incident of fear and separation. Only those who feel separated or cut off become susceptible to such an assumption. How this Basic Assumption plays out later in life is in one of four ways. Needing approval, always feeling less than, constantly being violated by others, and in repeatedly failing to honor one's own inner wisdom.

Victoria - Q: In looking at the list of Primary Decisions it seems like one or another stands out more in different phases of my life, rather than just one being a thread that runs through my life. For me, I've discovered a Primary Decision I created at 14 months of, *"I can't trust anyone."* Is that a variation of one that you have listed, and are the others just layers on top of this primary one?

Val Jon - A: All the Primary Decisions run together and are aspects of one another to some degree. This is so because while the psyche has clearly defined inner terrains, those terrains merge together on their "edges." This is not unlike physical geography in the sense that one cannot really find any defining line between say, a flat meadow and a high mountain range. "Not trusting" is a common issue for many people, but much like the feeling of "not belonging," it must be understood that it's also usually, but not always an afterthought, a secondary conclusion that does not come into existence immediately, but sometime shortly after an infant encounters a primary incident. The good news is that realizing the depth of one's lack of trust can lead to the initial Primary Decision. Also, why you may have trouble locating your specific Box is that the list in this chapter is just an introduction. There is a more complete summary of Primary Decisions in chapter 3 that will help you clarify what yours is. I suspect it has to do with neglect, but do check out the "Ten Box Categories" I've posted in chapter 3's *Exploration And Integration Guide.*

Victoria - Chapter Statement: I've always had a fascination with Psychology, Spirituality, and Science and see them as inseparable. I appreciate how Val Jon uses all three as complementary to each other and how they work in symbiosis, rather than as separation as it seems has been a common thread through many systems of belief.

♦♦♦

CHAPTER 2: FORMATION

From Everyone To Only One

The AwarenesSphere®

Emergence: The First Stage
And Second Phase of Formation

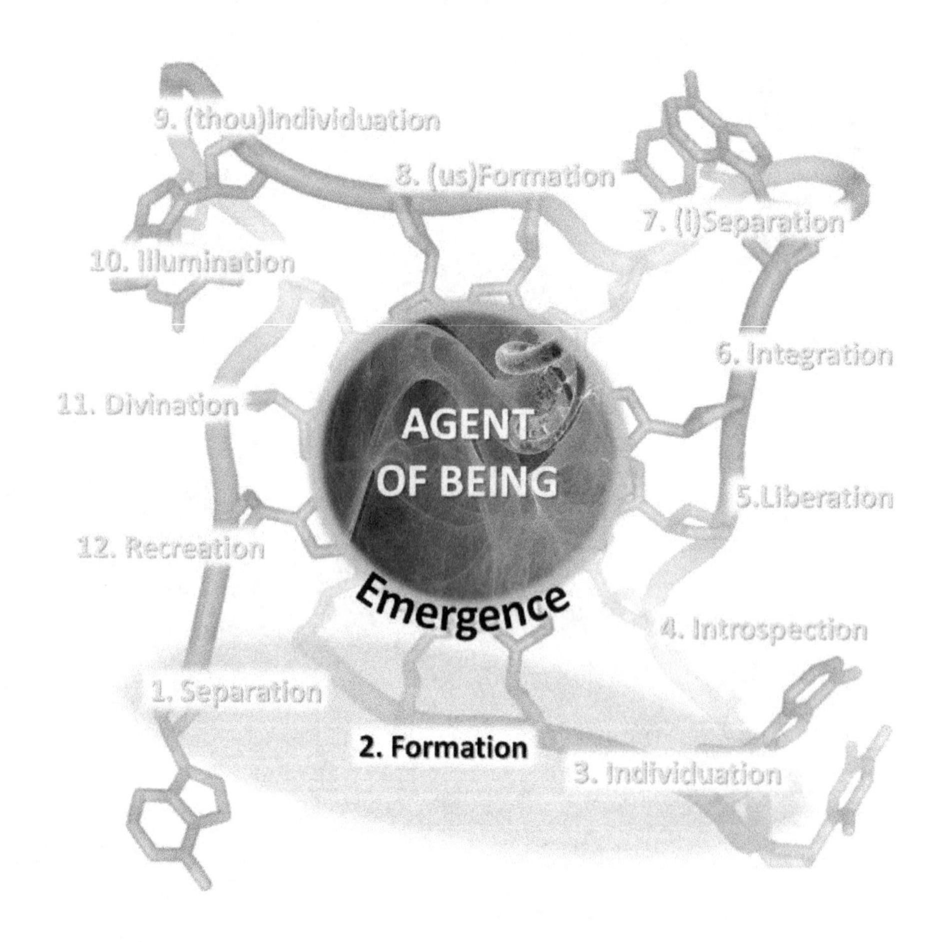

"What lies behind us and what lies before us are small matters compared to what lies within us. And when we bring what is within us out into the world, miracles happen."
— Ralph Waldo Emerson

Formation, the Second Phase of Awareness is the early childhood development time when our core identity forms and comes into being. Within this Phase, infants are aware of their surroundings, but just as in *Separation*, they have not yet developed the ability to be self-aware. As we've learned, Self-Awareness is a higher faculty that includes self-reflection and observation, and the ability to monitor and adjust our behaviors as we are acting them out. It also involves understanding the consequences of our actions and the impact our attitudes, moods, and actions have on others. *Formation* is a wonderful miracle of life in that our core identity undergoes full-on development, but at the same time, its downside is expressed in tantrums, pouting, and a litany of innocent, yet mischievous behaviors. Parents know this condition well as "the terrible twos." In *Formation*, just as in *Separation*, without the higher faculty of Self-Awareness, the only development path available to us is to endure the consequences of our actions until we learn about the ways of the world and how cause and effect actually work.

Our Collective Pool of Humanity

The Psychologist Carl Jung had much to say about identity development and what goes into making us humans "Human." Unlike most of his contemporaries, in addition to Freud, who narrowly based identity development on the dynamics of sexuality, Jung pioneered a revolutionary approach with implications not yet fully embraced by many astute personality experts of our day. Jung believed that rather than our identity forming in an iterative fashion as a result of being exposed to a series of external stimuli, all the elements of our individual nature reside within us from birth in a kind of "blueprint" or "collective pool of humanity." From this joint pool, specific elements of personhood are called forward into our individual identity depending on our environmental conditions and the choices we make with respect to them. The way I like to put this lofty notion is that *"who we are is everyone, narrowed down to only one."* In other words, we share *all* of the possible human traits that exist within the entire human race within the core of our collective being. *(A/N: This puts a new spin on the reasons for our marital problems and the unfortunate end of many marriages. Given our collective sharing of human traits, perhaps our dissolution papers should read, "Irreconcilable Similarities?")*

Jung believed that these collective blueprints residing within the human psyche are influenced and shaped by Archetypal forces, powerful unconscious energetic influencers of our identity development such as our parents and relatives, major events like births and deaths, as well as other meta-forces existing in Nature like the Sun, Moon, Planets, and the elements of water, fire, earth and air. According to Jung, all of these forces and elements combined have a hand in shaping our newly forming identity. *(A/N: For those interested in learning more about Archetypes, I suggest reading Jung's theory of the "Collective Unconscious" as it's a fascinating exploration into the nature of our shared humanity.)*

The idea that who we become as individuals is the result of narrowing down humanity's plethora of shared "personhood elements" is, on one hand, comforting, but on the other a bit unnerving. I always knew I shared genetic material with the entire human race, but the idea that I also share every last intimate element of personhood with them as well is somewhat disconcerting. While it's an unpleasant thought, it's kind of like the experience of wearing other people's underwear . . . both before and after they've worn them. Seriously though, this notion of the human psyche possessing a collective blueprint turns child development on its head in that it points to a very interesting process infants must engage in during the *Phase of Formation.* The reality is, as infants, each of us unconsciously makes specific selections from this vast pool of personhood elements, and the emotional decisions we make in the face of both real and perceived threats narrows them down to a very specific set of identity traits and characteristics.

The Unconscious Nature of Primary Decisions

While infants are obviously incapable of making conscious choices about which elements of personhood they integrate into their newly forming identities, it doesn't mean such a selection process isn't unconsciously going on. In our last chapter, we discussed Basic Assumptions and their more insidious counterpart, Primary Decisions and learned that they are powerful emotional conclusions we cast without any conscious awareness on our part. Likewise, the re-triggering of them in our adult lives is just as unconscious, yet with very real consequences. Because these decisions were cast into the core of our identity as it was forming, we must realize that they will remain with us for the rest of our lives as part of who we are. The good news is that just because they are a part of us does not mean we need to dramatize them.

Formation is the process of forming anew. Our identity, along with our Primary Decision forms into a cohesive whole between the ages of zero and five, and our personality is fully developed by the time we reach six years of age, except for more refined distinctions having to do with our preferences, values and adaptive behaviors. Once surviving the trauma of separation from our mother at birth, as well as a disconnection from the Divine, we enter into the *Second Phase of Formation* in which our identity develops into the familiar "I," we are all accustomed to.

Symbiosis, Assimilation, And Adaptation

The early development process known as *Symbiosis*[22] is one in which there is no distinction between the mother and the infant, and it typically lasts until around the age of one or two. During this crucial identity-forming period, the main processes going on within *Formation* are *Assimilation*[23] and *Adaptation*[24]. Infants Assimilate through touching, feeling and "mouthing" everything they can get their little hands on. Everything goes into our mouth as a way to take in life's myriad of mysterious facets, and it's at this stage in our identity development that there are little or no barriers between the inner terrain of our tender psyche and the outer landscape of the hardened external world.

The other developmental process, Adaptation is the act of learning through cause and effect, with pain rather than pleasure being our primary means of education. Somewhere around the age of two, we evolve out of Symbiosis and begin to develop the concept of "I" as distinct from "You," and particularly in the unnerving form of "I am not You!" The terrible twos we discussed earlier are the result of the newly forming psyche coming into its own as a separate entity. In *Formation,* infants begin to develop a "self-concept," the attributes, abilities, attitudes, and values that define who they are from others. By the age of three, we've developed a concrete way of viewing our independent selves through specific labels. For example, infants entering into selfhood typically label themselves as "children or adults," "boys or girls," "short or tall" and "good or bad," self-distinguishing concepts they were previously incapable of making.

The Dawning of Self-Consciousness

Toddlers also naturally demonstrate their developing awareness through their ability to use and understand self-referential language such as "I," "me," "you," "my" and "mine." The appearance of self-conscious emotions, (different from the higher faculty of Self-Awareness) such as embarrassment, pride, guilt, and shame also come into existence as the identity forms. As "I" emerges within an infant's psyche, as a parent you can sit them down across from you, show them your right and left hands and ask them which is *their* right and left hand. They will be able to transpose them and give you the correct reverse-answer, their *left* hand is directly across from your *right* hand. Prior to this elevated capability of self-consciousness, however, toddlers will invariably make the mistake of misidentifying their left and right hand because they have no ability to place themselves in your experience or see from your perspective. Adults who display narcissism, the lack of ability to empathize or see things from anyone else's point of view other than their own is an indication that their capacity for Self-Awareness was inhibited by the casting of a detrimental Primary Decision somewhere around two to three years of age. *(A/N: Isn't it reassuring to finally understand why some people are so darned inconsiderate?)*

The influential power of Primary Decisions during this *Second Phase of Formation* must not be underestimated. Even though the young psyche is not yet fully formed, the fact that emotional material and behavioral programming is present from the moment of our conception means that we are susceptible to unconsciously forming powerful emotional conclusions. As a way to make clear Jung's assertion that we formulate our identity based on pre-existing internal forces, and to emphasize the Power of Choice, I want to share a case study with you from one of my *"LifeChoice Intensive"* workshops which I have been delivering to the general public for over thirty years. While the specifics of the process are accurate, the names of the participants have been changed to maintain confidentiality. This particular case study is extremely useful in clarifying the Power of Choice each of us has, even all the way back to the time when we were infants.

A Classic Case Study About "Choice"

"James" and "John" were identical twins in their mid-to-late thirties, and both attended the same *LifeChoice Intensive.* The pre-work they submitted prior to attending indicated what they each wanted to get out of the workshop; goals that were quite different from one another and with completely unique challenges. John was going through a painful divorce at the time and was dealing with depression, anxiety, emotional numbness and issues of "projection," (the tendency to blame his ex-partner for all the problems and breakdowns they had). For John, relationships were, as he put it, "a pain in the ass" and that loving someone "just wasn't worth the effort or cost."

James, on the other hand, was single and experiencing frequent bouts of loneliness and unhappiness. As a result, he was distracting himself with drugs, alcohol, spending large sums of money and blowing through a series of unfulfilling one night stands. For him, it seemed that just when he met a woman he liked, something would go wrong and she would end up walking out of his life. The way James characterized it was that he desperately wanted love, but he just couldn't seem to keep it.

"The work" as I call it in this particular workshop comes down to revisiting early childhood traumas that have a long-standing impact on our adult behaviors. Most of the incidents are relegated to dysfunctional family dynamics such as physical and sexual abuse, alcoholic parents, issues of abandonment, neglect and general mistreatment. There is the occasional "totally loved child," but even they show up discontent with issues of entitlement, a lack of fulfillment and are often overworked, exhausted and at the effect of mounting obligations. *(A/N: For purposes of clarification, and to represent all those who attend my retreats and workshops, these people are not "sick" or "disturbed," but rather are well-adjusted adults who are successful and happy with most areas of their lives. There is actually something extremely healthy about investing in venues of personal growth that deepen our sense of self and adds to the enrichment and happiness we already possess.)*

Through the introduction of principles and processes, interactive group sharing and guided closed-eye processes, participants travel deep into their psyche and re-experience specific events, places and times in their pasts, times when they first cast their Primary Decisions, powerful emotional conclusions in reaction to threatening moments of trauma, abuse, violation or neglect. The "re-experiencing" of these events includes recalling very specific threatening incidents and revisiting the trauma locked within them moment-by-moment as if one were replaying a movie scene frame by frame.

Recalling primary incidents from our early childhood can be challenging in that we tend to block out unpleasant memories and bury them deep within our psyche. Uncovering them requires opening our vulnerability and "feeling our way" into very small fragments of scenes until we gain access to the entire film strip of the incident. Often the key to recovering these traumatic memories is by tuning into what our body feels. The body stores painful memories in very specific pockets of sensation such as sick feelings, heat or cold, tension, numbness, and an intuitive sense of violation, especially in and around our genitals, stomach and chest areas. *(A/N: I will provide more guidance on how to access and "uncast" these primary incidents in the Exploration And Integration Guide section of this and the next few chapters.*

As I stated previously, such decisions are a survival reaction to either real or perceived threats to our newly forming identity, and while they help mitigate the emotional intensity that arises at the moment, their long-term effects manifest as pervasively detrimental adult behaviors, much like the ones being reported by our workshop participants, James and John.

Normally in my programs participants go through the childhood regression process individually, but because these two brothers were identical twins, I decided to have them do the work together, taking turns recalling the same incidents from two different points of view. The regression processes can last up to four hours or more per participant, and the expanse of terrain covered is vast, spanning from adulthood, to adolescence, to childhood, infanthood and as far back as birth and even before. The array of emotions re-experienced by participants range from love to terror, joy to anger, deep sadness and grief, betrayal, numbness and utter shock regarding what they can actually recall when they focus on it. And as intense as the process always is, I have never had anyone emerge from any of my programs or counseling sessions feeling disabled or worse for the wear. Everyone gains a huge amount of clarity about their Primary Decision as well as experiences the enlivening outcome of *Liberation,* which we'll cover later on in the *Presence Stage.*

Both brothers had their eyes closed, sitting in an upright position in their chairs and in a semi-circle along with their other fellow participants. James suddenly covered his face with his hands and was markedly shaken by what he was recalling. John could sense his brother's elevated anxiety and reached out to comfort him. "I can't do this!" James blurted out. "I don't want to relive it, please, it's too painful!" "Alright James, breath and relax, John, what about you?" I continued my gentle inquiry with, "What is James referring to?" "He's talking about the train accident in which our mother, father, and sister were killed." "Ok, can you take us to what happened James?" He nodded and proceeded to recount the devastating sequence of events they both survived so many years ago.

The boys were three-years-old and their sister Julie was eleven. The entire family was riding in the car on their way to Julie's school piano recital. The boys were in the back seat, and Julie and their parents were in the front. All of a sudden the car in front of them stalled, leaving their car dangerously straddling a railroad crossing. In a blur of terror, they helplessly watched as the huge yellow and red striped safety arm came crashing down on the hood of their car, pinning it to the tracks. Recalling this horror, both brothers burst out crying, their faces tinted red and their bodies shaking uncontrollably. "Breathe guys, breathe and take it slowly. It will be alright, you survived it then, you can survive it now. Tell us exactly what you are seeing and feeling and go very, very slowly as if you were watching a movie frame-by-frame."

Gaining courage from his brother's lead, James speaks up. "Johnny and I are in the back seat and I hear mommy screaming" . . . "The train! Oh my God, get the kids out, get them out!" "Then I hear a loud horn blast and the smashing of glass and metal . . . tearing the car in half in slow-motion, twisted shards of steel cutting us . . . blood everywhere . . . blood everywhere!" "Ok James, stay with it now . . . what did you say to yourself in that moment? What did you decide?" Silence, more silence . . . and then he blurts out his Primary Decision with the force of a train-wreck, *"Mommy, Daddy,* ***I can't live without you! I need your love!"*** "Oh my God," John immediately blurts out his devastating decision, *"Mommy, Daddy,* ***I've lost you! It's too painful to ever love again!"*** Suddenly it becomes clear to everyone in the workshop, *the exact same incident produces two completely opposing Primary Decisions!* Two brothers unconsciously casting two completely different conclusions, which in turn produced two completely different sets of adult problems.

(A/N: No matter how many traumatic events I facilitate in this work I'm always deeply humbled by what we humans endure in our lives. I'm sure by reading this recount you feel the devastating impact of what happened

with these two boys, their sister, and parents. And while you may not have encountered such a traumatic experience as theirs, I promise you that deep inside you there is a devastation that was as impactful to you as the train wreck was for them. I want to also say to you that the more we understand the traumas, abuses and abandonments people endure in their early childhoods, the more compassion we can have for them, and the more we can reach out and offer them loving and well-grounded assistance in beginning their own inner journeys.)

Affirming The Power of Choice

This example of how Primary Decisions get cast into our young psyche is a profound revelation and a fundamental precursor to understanding the Power of Choice. Identical twins experiencing the very same devastating circumstances, and each casting their own unique fate by the emotional decisions they individually concluded. This vivid example sheds light on the undeniable reality that it's not our life circumstances, or what happens to us that shapes our identity or determines our destiny, but rather how we choose to interpret what happens to us. This is the essence of the Power of Choice. And once this reality becomes clear to us, we can never go back to the *Stage of Emergence* and its context of being at the effect of our circumstances.

I hope my sharing of this extraordinary case study has conveyed just how powerful Primary Decisions are, and how deeply they impact our newly forming identity as children. I also hope you are moved, (if not also a bit hesitant) to venture into your own inner terrain of *Formation* and begin to illuminate it, heal it perhaps, and most importantly, learn how to identify your own Primary Decision and begin Uncasting it.

Reactive Formation And Recurring Patterns

The Primary Decisions individually cast by these twin brothers sent them in totally different directions with their adult behaviors. For one brother, love was too painful to ever open too again, and for the other, love was too important to ever lose again. Once these opposing decisions were in place within their young psyches, their inner terrain began forming around their individual decisions. As our developing identity wraps itself around our Primary Decision, it becomes firmly lodged in place, setting the stage for future recurring patterns to occur that reinforce our initial emotional conclusion. In the case of what these two brothers concluded, the truth is, love is neither "too painful" nor "too important." Love is simply "love." We are the ones who color it with additional dramatic meanings and embellishments that then shape our future behaviors.

In John's case, once love was *"too painful to open to,"* his forming identity generated subsequent similar layers of protective patterning in the form of caution, suspicion, paranoia and eventually, closed-heartedness. In James' case, once love was *"too important to lose,"* his forming identity generated more impulsive layers of insecurity patterning in the form of dependency, need, attention and eventually, the insecurity of excessive neediness. It's not difficult to recognize that with these detrimental behavior patterns, each brother attracted partners with the very characteristics that triggered their individual Primary Decisions, especially if they were resisting such outcomes. Why is this? Because the more our psyche focuses on what it doesn't want and what it is unwilling to experience, the more it attracts those very same traits.

This isn't "woo-woo" magic, but rather is the result of a very real psychological phenomenon known as *Reactive Formation*[25]. The reaction is driven by the two developmental dynamics we covered earlier, Assimilation and Adaptation. In other words, the more we refuse to be like someone, the more like them we actually become. This is so because we are holding their negative traits in our consciousness and embellishing them with highly charged reactive emotions and judgments. The more we focus on resisting these negative traits, the more we assimilate them into our developing psyche. *(A/N: I can't begin to tell you how many of my clients have spent their lives trying to not be like one of their parents, and sure enough to their dismay, they invariably act out the very same characteristics and behaviors with their own children.)*

These recurring patterns that stem from our initial Primary Decisions will continue in our lives and even escalate in severity until we come to terms with them through the work we will be engaging in as we explore the *AwarenesSphere*. Subsequent incidents we encounter in our lives that have any resemblance to our childhood traumas compound our initial decisions through what are called *False Validations*[26]. Allow me to clarify this important psychological patterning by sharing my own encounter with such a repeat incident in my own childhood.

My "Smoky" False Validation

In the last chapter, I shared the traumatic experience of my breech birth and the danger of the umbilical cord being wrapped around my neck as I came down the birth canal. The Primary Decision I cast during this entry drama was that *"life isn't safe and I need to do it alone."* As I stated previously, that emotionally-charged decision lodged in the core of my psyche, along with a few other survival-based incidents in the first year or two of my life. Somewhere around the age of three, I had my first False Validation and recurring pattern of my initial Primary Decision. Through taking what I call "additional life passes" into my affected inner terrain I was able to recall in vivid detail a traumatizing False Validation incident involving my father.

Through discussing my early childhood with my mother, I learned that she and my father separated for a brief time between my second and third year of life. Apparently, my being born was an unwanted development for my father. As my mother described it, he wasn't very well suited to care for a family. I vaguely recall an incident in which he came into the room during a middle-of-the-night fit I was having. The image that came to me was of him leaning over my playpen bed rail making faces at me.

At that point in time, he wasn't a familiar face to me, and I recall feeling frightened as his huge presence towered over me. I also smelled something awful that made me gasp for air as he got closer. I didn't know it at the time, but it was cigarette smoke permeating his clothing and the overwhelming smell sent me into a panic. I wanted the comfort of my mother . . . and I wanted *him* to go away. I remember him yelling at me to "shut up and go to sleep!" My body jolted and shook, causing me to cry out even louder. My mother came into the room and my father told her to get out. In the next moment, he had a cigarette in his mouth and was blowing smoke into my face to make me stop crying, causing me to choke uncontrollably. My eyes burned and the smell was so terrible I couldn't breathe . . . I couldn't breathe, just like when the umbilical cord was wrapped around my neck during my birth. In a moment of suffocating terror my Primary Decision of *"It's not safe and I need to do it alone"* was falsely verified!

This kind of abuse is totally unacceptable for any child to endure. The most detrimental outcome of the incident, however, was the False Validation of my Primary Decision which compounded its recurring patterning, imprinting it as a "danger zone" within my still-developing identity. So now I had two survival-based incidents lodged in the core of my young psyche, with a third clincher on the way soon to follow. I want to emphasize that while these kinds of experiences are terribly troubling and can produce long-standing negative effects, the most detrimental aspect of them is what we ourselves decide as they are happening. Keep in mind the two totally different outcomes with James and John. The train wreck was a tragedy to be sure, but the deeper devastation had to do with what each of them decided about the tragedy. If there is any good news at all here it is that since we were the ones who initially cast our Primary Decision into existence, we can also be the ones who "uncast" it. When that is, we have sufficient Self-Awareness to do the needed work. *(A/N: As a way to assist you in discovering your own Primary Decision I've outlined some questions and processes below in the "Exploration And Integration Guide" you can use to begin your own inner work.)*

Formation's Linkage With The Second Chakra: Sacral Energy

The Second Chakra is that of "Sacral Energy" or "Svadhishthana," which means "the place of the self." This Chakra, located just behind the belly button is much like that of *Formation* in that it's all about our identity as humans, how we define ourselves and how we go about navigating the experiences of being alive. As our identity forms, we have a permanent place from which to engage with life. There is sufficient "I" at this point in our development to begin to appreciate pleasure, nurturance, joy, and happiness.

In terms of the linkage between *Formation* and the Sacral Chakra, the "place of self" is the common connection. Both share in the essential aspect of our core identity. The energy of sexuality arises both within our newly forming identity as well as within the core of the Sacral Chakra, and when open, this energy is nurturing and positive. When closed, however, just as with "the terrible twos," we become frustrated, irritated and generally unhappy. This is when addiction and excess becomes a concern. The more unhappiness we feel, the more pleasurable experiences we crave. But more is not necessarily better as it usually leads to less fulfillment, because the reality is we can never get enough of what we really don't want.

Exploration And Integration Guide

As a way to integrate the material presented in this chapter, and so you can gain insight into your own Primary Decision, as I mentioned earlier, I've outlined some "Key Uncasting Questions and Processes" for you. The list below was taken from the support materials provided in one of my public workshops and counseling sessions. While it's unrealistic to expect to access the deep terrain of your psyche through simply reading my books or following the guidelines I outline, it isn't unreasonable to expect that you'll take a solid first pass at it. Here are the questions and processes to help you get started.

1. Do I have any sense of what my Primary Decision might be? Ask yourself, "When I was a young infant what might I have decided?" Rather than efforting at it, simply allow yourself to feel your way. Trying to "figure it out" or "do it right" will just get in your way. Relax and let your natural emotive processes lead you into the terrain.

2. What recurring behavioral patterns have I had to deal with over and over again in my life? Review your history for recurring issues. Recall childhood feelings you had about your family and friends, people you felt close to, role modeled after or avoided. Also, like James and John in our case study, what patterns have played out in your intimate relationships? Notice any recurring themes, challenges, and outcomes. It is these common themes that will point to your Primary Decision.

3. What, if any, hurt feelings am I holding onto with my past or current relationships? Notice any hints of avoidance, withdrawal, or negative reactions with certain people, or certain types of people. Open to any sadness, fear, anger, resentment, love, pain or loss you may feel or have glimpses of.

4. Recall towns or cities you lived in, and school friends, relatives, neighbors, special toys or friends and animals you cared about. What images, memories, and feelings are associated with them?

5. Locate an early incident where you felt loss or pain, embarrassment, anger, sadness or hurt. Get as specific as you can. Where were you? Get it down to the exact location, where you were, your age, who was there, what was said or done. Pay attention to your body sensations. Notice any sick feelings, numbness, tension, and heat or cold. They will lead you to flashes of images and incidents.

6. Once you locate an incident stay with the feelings. Images may appear as "fragments" or like shards of glass until you open to them fully. Move into the fragment that is most clear to you or contains the most emotional charge. No matter what arises, engage with it fully, even if it seems unreal, doesn't make sense, or is too uncomfortable to recall. It's all-important material to engage in.

7. Every Box has its "corners," or the predictable ways it acts when triggered.

While your Box is invisible, you can certainly feel its effects. Much like a goldfish occasionally bumps its nose on the aquarium glass, we bump into the predictable behaviors generated by our Box. You may recognize some of them – easily overwhelmed, lacking trust, blaming others (or self), making bad decisions, self-sabotage, being in control, avoiding conflict, being self-critical or short-tempered, unable to say "no," shy and unassertive, demanding or reactive, over-sensitive, impulsive or obsessive, non-committal, manipulative, arrogant or quick to judge. It's the behaviors that you repeat often and tend to arise during upsets, stressors or when you are in fear that are the rigid corners of your Box.

To clarify, these behaviors arise out of your Primary Decision and are not to be taken as possible Boxes. Think of them as the effects of your Box causes. By identifying the effects or "corners" of your Box you'll come one step closer to identifying it. *(A/N: I want to encourage you to take this process slowly and with trust and faith as your guiding light. If you relax into the process without efforting at it you'll have a much better chance of accessing your Primary Decision. I always counsel people to take their time and "trust the process.")*

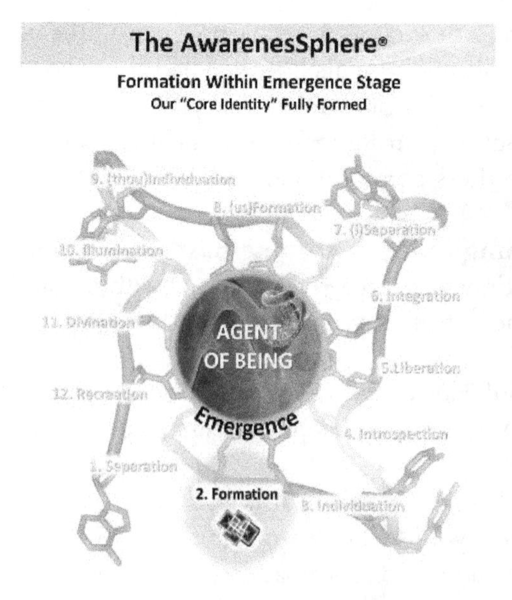

Let's move on by recapping *Formation, Emergence's Second Phase of Awareness*. This Second Phase is when our newborn identity undergoes its basic development. All of the elements needed to complete our individual personhood reside within us from birth in a kind of "blueprint" or "collective pool of humanity." Carl Jung believed these blueprints are shaped by Archetypes, powerful influencers of our identity development such as our parents and relatives, major events like births and deaths, as well as other natural meta-forces.

Formation and the familiar "I" we all know so well include the three identity-forming activities of Symbiosis, Assimilation, and Adaptation. It is at this stage of development that we possess little or no boundaries, no barriers between our tender psyche and the tough exterior world. As our identity forms, "I" and "You" become distinct from one another. "I am not you" is the outcome that gets expressed as "the terrible twos." The concept of "self" (with a small "s") comes into being and we begin to define ourselves as separate from others. In terms of awareness level, infants undergoing *Formation* still do not possess any Self-Awareness, but they do begin to show preliminary signs of self-consciousness. Embarrassment, pride, guilt, and shame begin to form within the young psyche which sets the stage for the higher faculty of Self-Awareness to develop.

The intense workshop case study of James and John I shared with you highlighted the influential power of Primary Decisions. It also revealed the undeniable reality that it isn't our circumstances that cause our long-term challenges, but rather how we interpret our circumstances, what we say to ourselves and the decisions we make about them and ourselves. Once we cast these powerful emotional conclusions into our psyche, our core behaviors begin forming around them. They then mature into recurring behavioral patterns that have long-term effects on us as adults.

Finally, I introduced the notion of False Validations, recurring incidents throughout our early childhood and adulthood that reinforce our initial Primary Decision. I gave the example of my father blowing cigarette smoke in my face, which reinforced my Basic Assumption that *"It's not safe here"* which reinforced my Primary Decision of not being able to count on anyone and needing to take care of myself. With each repetitive False Validation, our Box strengthens its grip on us. The good news, however, is that because we were the ones who initially cast our Primary Decision into existence, we are also the ones who can "uncast" it. ~

In the next chapter, we'll venture together into the *Third Phase of Emergence,* called *Individuation.* This next Phase of our human evolution is when we finally arrive in life as a unique person unto ourselves. It is also a major transitional time in which we possess the ability to traverse the development gap between the Second Phase of *Formation* and the Third Phase of *Individuation.* After reviewing the Q&A section, let's pack up our gear, hook up to our safety lines and prepare to engage in an extremely challenging inner navigation I call, *"Traversing The Valley of Ignorance."*

♦♦♦

Reader's Question & Answer Section (Chapter 2: Formation)

Allison - Q: Can you elaborate on and explain a bit more about projections in relationships, and is there any connection between projections and what one might be resisting or unconscious about in one's Primary Decision?

Val Jon - A: As you know, projection is when we externalize our own unresolved issues and assign them to others as if they were harming us or violating us in some way. I'll give you an example of how it's connected to our Primary Decision. As I've shared, my Box is basically *"I need to do it alone."* The way I project when I get triggered is to look for evidence about *how badly* I'm being treated by my mate. Once I find the evidence, it justifies my withdrawal and feelings of not being appreciated . . . blah, blah, blah. The other version of projection is "introjection," in which rather than blaming others for our troubles, we blame ourselves. *"I must have done something to deserve this,"* is an introjection in that it presupposes being wrong, bad or guilty in some way. What you might be unconsciously resisting if you find yourself projecting onto your mate, or introjecting into yourself, for example, is an unresolved issue with one of your parents. It's a well-known dynamic in the field of psychology that men tend to marry their mother, and women invariably marry the father the first time around. (Second marriages tend to be just the opposite, which creates a whole different set of projections and challenges.)

Allison - Q: Have you done this work with younger people? I'm thinking specifically about teens? As someone who works with teens and also has a young teenager, I'm wondering about supporting their process with this early on so they can begin Uncasting way earlier in life, and I'm curious if you've had any experience with this work and younger people.

Val Jon - A: Yes, I've facilitated many young person's programs and found that a good deal of deep work can be done with them in the area of Uncasting. Early on in my career I supervised a "youth at risk program" for Children's Hospital in Los Angeles, California and worked with homeless teens between the ages of 12 and 16, as well as with their counselors who were facilitating their therapy sessions. (The counselors required more support than the teens did!) The only downside of working with teens is that the clearer they become about being Choosers in their young lives, the more challenging it becomes dealing with adults who have authority over them. (Over 80% of all the teens who were rehabilitated in the programs I supervised and who were sent back home, were repeatedly abused or molested by the very parents or family members who violated them the first time around. The 20% that were not violated were in special programs in which the teens and all their family members participated in counseling.)

Allison - Chapter Statement: Knowing that the Primary Decision is part of life's journey to get to the Uncasting of it and to stand in re-choosing who we really are is a path of liberation.

Even with all the work I have done and the work I put forth into the world, the desire to have not had certain experiences happen to me in the past still resides in my consciousness. Doing this work moves me one step closer to true forgiveness and hopefully, freedom, from the depths of my psyche that still asks: *"What did I ever do that was so wrong to deserve this?"*

Anna - Q: Do you think that Hypnosis would facilitate with unlocking one's Primary Decision?

Val Jon - A: While Hypnosis might help in locating childhood incidents that were traumatic or fearful for us, there's an element of being consciously "awake and aware" of the details of the experience as they play out during our Uncasting that is essential. It's by bringing Self-Awareness into the recalled incident and consciously engaging with it, consciously feeling its effects, specifically identifying what we decided, and then consciously re-choosing who and how we are going to show up in life that liberates us from our Primary Decision.

Anna - Q: How do you keep yourself from slipping back into denial if the memories seem to be too painful to relive, especially if you are engaging in the journey alone?

Val Jon - A: It's always wise to have traveling companions, friends and supporters who can empathize with your journey and your challenges. Doing it alone is terribly difficult, and for this reason, we've established what we call the *Travelers Within Society And Member Resources* which you will find at the back of this book. Upon completion of their work with me, I give all my clients and program participants the following advice. *"Your Box will be waiting for you in your morning slippers the moment you're unwilling to embrace being the Chooser in your daily life."* I want to clarify that it's perfectly alright to slip back into your Box once in a while. In fact, I recommend it. One never ever wants to forget what it's like to be stuck in their inner "danger zones." While many fear that if they slip back in, they'll never be able to get back out, it's actually an unfounded fear. This is so because if you were able to liberate yourself from it just once, you will always be able to do so in the future. It's much like learning how to ride a bicycle in that once you grasp "balance" you will never forget it, even if you haven't ridden a bike in years. The sustained ability to extract one's self from their Box is just another kind of balance.

Anna - Chapter Statement: Over the years I have read many self-help books, different spiritual philosophies and dabbled in Astrology. I searched for clues to unlock the pain my psyche was in. I had come to accept that I was in control, but what was standing in my way was holding me back. I could not find the answers. I went through a ten-session Rolfing experience and many of the micro spasms that were holding deep-rooted emotional reactions were released. But then what? Not one of them helped me define the root. I knew it was buried in there somewhere, but how to find it? I could not get past the sentry guards of my programming. Not good enough, not smart enough, not, not, not . . . I was well aware of the circumstances of my birth and my infancy. Most of my generation was raised by Dr. Spock. But before that, I was also a breech birth and had the cord wrapped around my neck as well as being extremely jaundiced. I was whisked away immediately and placed in an incubator and left in the hospital for six weeks. When I was brought home I was placed in a crib in a room at the end of the hall and allowed to cry it out. It became quite easy to identify my Primary Decision of abandonment and inability to bond to others in a relationship, *"I don't need anyone, I can handle this on my own."*

Antonio - Q: If we are no longer empathetic to our fellow beings, how can we cultivate other virtues to remind ourselves that when one is suffering, we all are suffering to a degree, *"from everyone to only one?"*

Val Jon - A: Allow me to use an analogy. Seeds that land on solid rock do not grow, nor can they be cultivated. If someone is acting as rigid as a stone by displaying a lack of empathy towards others, I don't believe any "reminding" will reach them. There is however the high probability that life will get their attention by delivering a painful enough blow to them that drops them to their knees and opens their heart. This does not mean we should avoid trying to reach such individuals but to simply know that it is actually life's job to do the kind of reminding that brings about permanent change for the better.

Antonio - Q: How does it feel to forgive yourself?

Val Jon - A: Forgiveness literally means "to give as before." To give to ourselves as before through the act of forgiving returns us (and others) to the equanimity of our original sacred Self. It's like the blessing of coming upon an oasis after having been lost in the desert. One of the greatest tragedies we can endure I believe is to live out our entire lives without forgiving ourselves for the mistakes we've made, or for the pain we may have caused others. I suggest watching an old classic movie called "The Mission" as it has a forgiveness scene that will touch you deeply and will convey the experience quite vividly.

Antonio - Chapter Statement: I too felt the rejection of my father from the earliest recollection of my journey into this world. This chapter is a reminder that our parents simply took on all of the false beliefs dumped upon them by their parents and ancestors. There is no blame, only acceptance, and love.

Cyn - Q: Is it possible that we can have the capability to "foresee" the future in some way, even as infants, so that the Primary Decision we select and hold fast is selected almost as a shield or teddy bear, as it were, to hold onto tightly and keep us safe?

Val Jon - A: I've never come across a clairvoyant infant, but I've definitely observed a behavior set of vigilance that scans for potential trouble to avoid. Such hypervigilance is the result of those Primary Decisions that were cast around uncertainty and unpredictable family dynamics, (such as alcoholism, violence or neglect), or as the result of the parental manipulation tactic called, *"I'll withhold love from you if you don't do as I say."* The other thing to keep in mind is that while "keeping safe" seems to be the healthiest option, the truth is we need to come into contact with at least a minimal level of threat and detriment as infants in order to learn how to cope with an unpredictable world. Those who were protected from every possible threat as children are usually stifled in terms of adult spontaneity and are in my experience, the least likely to become interested in their own self-development.

Cyn - Q: Can we select the incorrect Primary Decision as our own?

Val Jon - A: If you are referring to the literary selection process we are engaged in within this chapter, without actually participating in the deep facilitator-led processing work, identifying one's Primary Decision can be challenging. The accuracy of your selection as it were, is contingent upon which faculty you employ as you do your selecting. The mind struggles to understand what the heart has always known, and because of this, you must *feel* rather than *think* your way to the correct selection. You can't really go wrong with this process however, as any selection is better than none. And the selection you make, if you feel and let your body sensations and memories lead you into deeper terrain, you will eventually come to the primary incident in which you first cast your Box into being. A useful "test" is that once you locate and re-experience the incident, and work through its associated fear or trauma, check to see if you return to a state of "innocence and peace." If you do not, you can bet there is an earlier similar incident you have not yet accessed. The other test is to notice if the incident is more negative evidence for you about whoever was involved or was it an initial shock that changed your relationship with them. And finally, our Primary Decision repeats many times over in our lives, so it will be fairly evident in the patterning. While the circumstances and players will change, the "theme" of our Box always remains the same.

Cyn - Chapter Statement: *"I need to be in control."* Although my childhood was bathed in love and positive energy, with my mother instilling in me I could do anything and when people teased me, it was only because they liked me. I realize now the same Primary Decision played out again and again as I lived a life of "the new kid at school" 22 times. I'm excited to learn how much our external environment plays a part in our internal spiritual development, which controls which, when it is that I added *"I'm leaving soon, so I better not get invested,"* and when it is that I finally learned being in control all the time is exhausting and not a lot of fun.

Elise - Q: In projecting blame on others for any experience is there "final" ownership we can take, or is it circular and undefinable?

Val Jon - A: "Who started it?" is always a dead-end inquiry in my experience. It's like which came first, the chicken or the egg? If there is a final ownership for blame, I think it has to do with realizing that when we blame someone, (or blame ourselves) our focus is not on growth and betterment, it's on making someone wrong and gathering evidence for how we were mistreated, or for how "stupid" we were. The true "finality" to the pattern of blaming arises when we shift our focus from negation and make wrong to betterment and learning.

Elise - Q: The experience of "I" always felt empty for me. Is that a normal condition being raised in an abusive family, or is it tied to a certain kind of Primary Decision?

Val Jon - A: It depends on the kind of "empty" you mean. If you experienced yourself as being empty in the sense of lacking something, then your experience of yourself has most likely been influenced by past neglect or abandonment and the specific Primary Decisions associated with these kinds of abuses. But, if by empty you mean spacious, then it is a sign of inner wholeness, and while it may not be "normal," it is certainly healthy.

Elise - Chapter Statement: In revisiting my birth, I have had many aspects of myself made clear. My assumption that I should not be here and subsequent emotional/ego enmeshment and empathetic dance with my mother's malignant narcissistic disorder was truly set and contributed to my disabling self-conclusions.

Mindy - Q: Can Primary Decisions developed in childhood be discarded as part of the AwarenesSphere journey, or will we learn to redevelop them, or will the development of new Primary Decisions work to diminish and possibly delete previous ones?

Val Jon - A: Just as each of us has a very specific eye color and retina pattern that remains with us for our entire lives, each of us also has a specific Primary Decision that does not change. There is no "discarding" our Primary Decision as that would imply elimination. Once deep emotional patterns are cast into our psyche they remain there for our entire lives. What we can do however as you suggest is, "redevelop" them, (or in my terminology "uncast" them). To uncast past wounds means consciously, and with positive intention, re-experiencing our threatening childhood incidents until the emotional charge they hold releases and then surrendering our "investment" in being a victim of our circumstance. These two key actions are what frees us from our detrimental conclusions and decisions.

Mindy - Q: Do we work with our Basic Assumptions as they are, or should we attempt to filter, edit or change them? Or is this knowledge part of our journey?

Val Jon - A: Basic Assumptions are deeply held beliefs that act as the foundational underpinnings for our faith, morals, character, and values, which in turn, drive our moment-by-moment behaviors and actions. If your underpinnings are sound and work well for you and for others, there's little reason to change them. But if you are unhappy or experiencing repetitive issues that are detrimental to you or others, then change is recommended. Think of your Basic Assumptions like the roots of a tree, and your behaviors and actions like its limbs and leaves. Just as it's possible to change the shape and form of a tree's limbs, and even improve its overall health by "pruning" and "trimming," if the tree suffers from a deeper systemic condition, attempting such changes will be ineffective. (You can even "cut a limb off" in the form of leaving an unfulfilling relationship, but you'll discover later on that some form of the underlying issue will reappear in your next relationship.)

The best approach to changing unwanted behavior patterns is to identify where the issue is arising from and get to the root of the problem by doing the Uncasting work I outline in this section of the book. Just as Basic Assumptions are like the roots of a tree, our Primary Decision is the "soil" or ground of being those roots are planted in and sustained by. By identifying our Primary Decision and doing the deep emotional release work, we free ourselves from the detrimental soil that is buried within our inner terrain. (Think of it like transplanting a sad little tree that is struggling in low nutrient soil into higher fertile ground and watching it flourish and you'll have the picture.)

Mindy - Chapter Statement: I had a nervous laugh at the description of "totally loved child." I was that child, and living up to the expectations therein did make me frequently feel inadequate. I know I manage life best when I believe I have my mother's approval. This is a Primary Decision, and I look forward to learning what to do with it.

Susie - Q: Is it so that you and I come from a family with "similar" Primary Decisions, blueprints from our collective pool of humanity, going back for centuries? If so, one could blame all previous generations for these traits, that are seemingly annoying, embarrassing or degrading, or we could thank them, because in some wonderful, magical, mystical way, all those previous serendipitous events, generation after generation, got us here today, and if it would've happened differently, we wouldn't be here.

Val Jon - A: Yes indeed, we share the same blueprints, gene pool and behavioral tendencies with our ancestors. And in terms of blaming our family of origin for our shortcomings? Absolutely, we do it all the time, (e.g., *"If my parents would have only blah, blah, blah, I would have had a better life.")* It's one of the main reasons why there is so little personal responsibility in our world. And finally, getting to the place of "thanking" our ancestors for our inheritances, it's a wonderful notion, but that kind of gratitude may very well take lifetimes for humanity as a whole to embrace and act on . . . but then again, as Bucky so wisely mentored me, I'll remain open to the great possibility you brought up!

Susie - Q: I wonder, is it possible to raise a child to avoid all of these Primary Decisions and Boxes that they will find themselves living in?

Val Jon - A: While the Box can seem like an unpleasant addition to the human psyche, it's also an essential survival mechanism that protects infants from abuse and emotional trauma, much like how shock protects us from the effects resulting from severe accidents. What people don't realize is that shock is a life-saver. In the face of trauma, the body draws all its blood to its torso as a way to protect its limbs. A lack of blood to the brain also triggers unconsciousness, another vital process that buffers us from emotional trauma. Given the state of the world, and the fact that it's not a safe place to be without taking precautions, the Box is actually a service to us in that it prepares us to deal with life as we know it. The only issue is that if we never liberate ourselves from the detriments of our Box, it can actually lead to more abuse and trauma in our adult lives. For this reason, the work of Liberation is essential for us, at least until the human race evolves out of its current state of unconsciousness and patterns of detrimental behavior.

Susie - Chapter Statement: I just discovered an underlying fear of the scary world I was born into. As was common at the time, my mother was put into "twilight sleep" for the birth and wasn't really very present just before, during or after. And I was all alone, the world was a scary place and perhaps it was because I assumed that I wasn't lovable enough. I didn't realize where that came from. Whenever I am confronted with seemingly scary or mean people, I become like a deer in the headlights. Now I have a chance to do something about it, instead of it having a machine-like automatic reaction running my life.

Victoria - Q: What would you recommend is the best way of seeing how our Basic Assumptions and Primary Decision play out together throughout our lives?

Val Jon - A: Take note of the recurring patterns that arise in your life, especially in your intimate and close relationships. Also, observe the "inner-voice conversations" you have with yourself when you are at your lowest points, or circling around depression, or in a bad mood. There will be a consistent "theme" that emerges, and while your life partners may change, the underlying issues that caused just about every relationship breakdown you've ever had will remain the same. To clarify this point, your Primary Decision is the deeper structure that fuels your Basic Assumptions. So for example, a Box of say, *"Please don't leave me!"* will be reinforced with the assumption of, *"I'm unworthy and damaged goods."* The two play hand-in-hand quite insidiously.

Victoria - Q: Is there a formula or methodology you have found that works best for uncovering and processing these assumptions and conclusions or is it different for everyone?

Val Jon - A: I've developed a "standard" process that works with everyone in my programs and counseling work. Why it works, however, is because within the workings of my standard process is years of diverse experience that enables me to adjust and customize my interventions to address the unique behavioral issues my clients come to me for guidance about. It's not unlike being a seasoned surgeon who has developed the skill to implement standard operating procedures but does so in a manner that meets the actual moment-by-moment surgical needs of their patients.

Victoria - Chapter Statement: I can now see clearly how my pre-birth belief of *"I don't belong here"* became solidified by my toddler decision of, *"I can't trust anyone"* after I came to see that I could not trust my mother or anyone else to look after me. My entire life I felt as though I didn't belong anywhere and I never felt at home in any situation. This led me to constantly changing jobs, friends, homes . . . until I learned how to be at home with myself. That homelessness fed into the already existing distrust of other people, and I've been on-guard my entire life, keeping my walls up except with my children, who have taught me what love really is. The more I feel at home with myself and the more I learn to trust myself, the more I am open to being at home with others and trusting them to not harm me.

♦♦♦

CHAPTER 3: INDIVIDUATION

Traversing The Valley of Ignorance

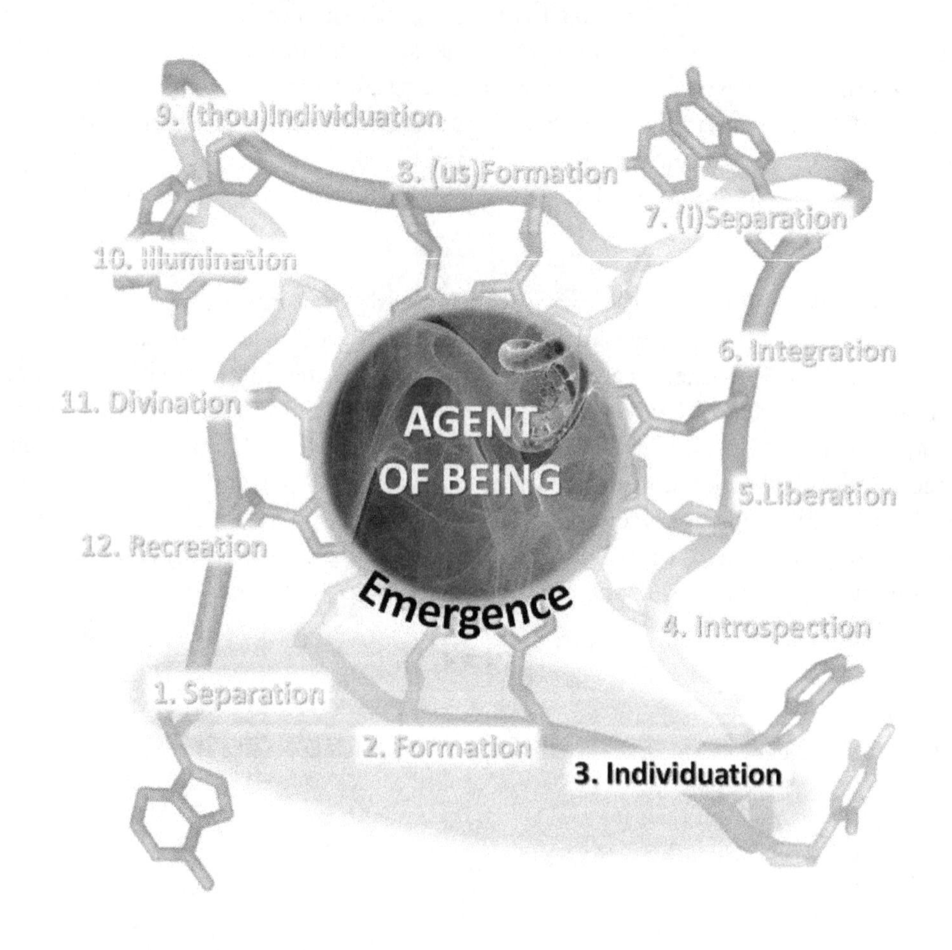

"In each individual the spirit is made flesh, in each one the whole of creation suffers, in each one a Savior is crucified." — Hermann Hesse

Individuation, the Third Phase of Awareness is an extension of the development process begun within the first two Phases of *Emergence*. It is the window of time in which the young identity evolves a complete set of character traits and behaviors. In this Phase, the developing psyche enters into the very personalized process of exploring the behavior patterning of self-worth, self-esteem, self-judgment, blame, shame, guilt, and credit. These are perfectly normal budding attributes that must come fully into maturity in order to ensure a healthy young psyche. The problem comes in if we never mature out of them, which unfortunately is a reality for a large population of adults. Within this window of *Individuation* infants still do not possess the ability to self-reflect or observe their own behaviors, other than the faint beginnings of narcissistic guilt by association.

Individuation is the height of self-importance and while it's a healthy beginning, if this ego trait remains unchecked, it can manifest as self-centeredness which is wrought with deep attachments and narcissistic tendencies. These traits mature into deep-seated ego-based agendas such as "my truth," having control over "my life," the need for "my purpose" and vying for credit, praise, belonging and attention. This "me," "my," "mine" drama plays out by resisting what is, avoiding reality and longing for something or someone outside ourselves to save us and make us happy. *Individuation* in adults also perpetuates its fixation on self-importance through over-identifying with exclusive mystical rituals, rites of passage, moralistic mandates and socially acceptable or unacceptable belief systems.

Expanding our awareness beyond the *Stage of Emergence* to include the next *Stage of Presence* can at the extremes take an entire lifetime, if not longer. The majority of our race is trapped in the karmic cycle of *Separation, Formation,* and *Individuation* and never escapes its cyclical trap. The more separate we feel, the more drama we are driven to act out, and the more drama we act out, the more isolated and separate we become. This vicious cycle repeats itself over and over again with an ever-escalating deluge of detriment until we can no longer bear the suffering, and we either implode, destroy ourselves (and others), or crack wide open into humility. It is only by dropping into a humble-hearted opening that we can truly show up in life and be present to the challenge of reaching higher ground and attaining greater Self-Awareness.

Individuals As "Humans Being"

The *Third Phase of Individuation* describes the manner in which we humans identify and distinguish ourselves from others. In essence, it's the difference between an individual and a collective presence. The *Individuation* process yields a person who believes that they exist on their own, separate and distinct from the collective personhood we all actually share in. Hesse's opening quote contains a sobering reality regarding the process of *Individuation*, one which we will investigate in great detail in this chapter.

The first part of the quote, *". . . the spirit is made flesh"* points to our separation from the Divine. It is referring to the act of departing from the realm of spirituality and entering the realm of humanity. The next part, *". . . the whole of creation suffers"* points to the loss experienced through the act of separation by the Divine itself, as well as by that which the Divine brings into mortal form. And finally, *". . . in each one a Savior is crucified"* while this is a Christian phrase, in a more secular context, it refers to the loss of our sacred connection with our spiritual nature as we transition out of the omnipotence of the immortal and into the ominously mortal *First Stage of Emergence.*

Being alive as an autonomous being is a paradoxically challenging journey. Life and death are juxtaposed upon one another just as is light and darkness, good and bad, and positive and negative. On a personal and practical level, within every "hello" there also exists a "goodbye." Likewise, for every journey, we embark upon in life we experience both gains and losses. We gain new experiences and make new friends when we arrive at a destination, and we lose them when we depart it. Indeed, we may keep a precious and detailed journal of all our friends and experiences throughout our travels, but our memories of them are much different from the vivid reality of actually having been in their presence.

One of the most extraordinary aspects of our Agent of Being is that it operates not as a memory of the Divine, but as a "navigational bridge" into the Divine's actual presence. What this means is that we never need to settle for a recollection of the sacred, but can rather, place ourselves within its actuality and experience the fullness of its grace whenever we choose. But there is a caveat . . . our ability to navigate across the terrain existing between the mortal and immortal is dependent upon our ability to navigate *through* its abysses, plateaus, and ravines. This is the reason why we must become expert *Travelers Within.* For the more familiar we become with our inner terrain and how to navigate our way through it, the more capable we are at venturing into greater vistas as fully realized "Humans Being."

Traversing The Valley of Ignorance

The journey into *Individuation* may seem like a crucifixion of sorts, but the reality is it's a necessary and even blessed rite of passage in our evolutionary process. Without becoming an individual who is separate and distinct from the collective presence of the Divine, we would have no personal experience of it. For the sake of clarification, the entire evolutionary process into Divinity is that we must lose ourselves before we can find ourselves. But then, once we are found, we must surrender our new found persona to an even greater presence, one that can never be lost or found in the first place.

The most we can honestly hope for in the *Phase of Individuation,* however, is developing a healthy identity, one that possesses enough curiosity to make the life-changing journey across the "bridge of insight" that links *Emergence* with *Presence.* Those who fail to develop sufficient curiosity about their inner nature are oblivious to this metaphorical foot-bridge and find themselves caught in the *"Valley of Ignorance,"* a miserable wasteland in which they are constantly at the effect of their circumstances, forever locked in a cursed state of emergency, and over and over again falling victim to detrimental issues of their own making.

As we discussed in the previous chapter, through the two developmental processes of Assimilation and Adaptation, our identity fully forms and our sense of "I" matures into a unique and fully fleshed-out persona. Again, there is a trade-off between what we gain and what we lose in this development process. As we gain specific personality traits and identity definitions, we lose our collective connection with the Divine and with our Agent of Being. Many wonder why this is an either-or arrangement, and the answer as best as I understand it is that as a race, we are not yet mature enough to warrant having both. The degree of polarization and unresolved forces of opposition residing within us is simply too overpowering to allow it. Perhaps when enough *Travelers Within* complete the journey around the full spiral of the *AwarenesSphere,* this limitation will be dissolved, we shall see.

As we have seen with *Emergence's* previous two *Phases of Separation* and *Formation*, the terrain of *Individuation* is also fertile ground for the casting of, and solidification of our Primary Decision. However, as we approach the age of six, and as our personality fully forms, we become less prone to casting such emotional decisions. But, the decisions we've previously cast do indeed become solidified and sink into the subterranean soil of our psyche to serve as future obstructions in our adult lives until we uncast them.

My Crystallization of "The Box"

At the age of five, just as my identity was fully forming the Primary Decision I had cast around the circumstances of my birth, *"I'm all alone and on my own"* became solidified through surviving a terrifying event with my father. When I say "fully solidified" what I mean is that while the decision I previously cast was firmly lodged in the core of my psyche, it had not yet completely formed into an entrapping "Box-like" structure. *(A/N: The Box*[27] *is a simple term I use in my programs to describe these charged emotional decisions. The name fits because it acts like a tomb-like container or rigid encasement that traps us within the confines of its emotionally charged conclusions and control.)*

What causes a Primary Decision to fully solidify into a Box is confirmation of its validity and its perceived necessity to act as a protection mechanism for us. These False Validations as I previously explained, come as a result of experiencing similar traumas and threats that we survived when we first cast our decision. Much like crystals that form in the Earth's mantle due to intense pressure and heat, our Box crystallizes into a rigid structure within the soil of our psyche as the result of being exposed to repeated emotional threats. Allow me to bring this point fully to life by sharing a very vulnerable experience with you.

(A/N: I want to prepare you to read this story. Many children go through episodes of trauma in their young lives. Some traumas are more intense than others, but honestly, to the fragile conditions within the young psyche, even the most subdued traumas can have a devastating impact. What I'm about to share with you is very intense and will require your full presence. If you find it becomes too intense, simply stop and return to where you left off later. If it helps at all, I want you to know that I obviously survived. Not only that, but I have also used the abuse I survived to deepen my capacity to embrace challenges and live with an open and loving heart. I'm a better man for it, so let's face this "trauma" together.)

It was Christmas Eve and my father was indulging in another one of his terrorizing drunken rampages. When I say "terrorizing," I mean it. He was an extremely unstable and violent man with life-threatening behaviors that could be triggered on a moment's notice. Having survived World War II as a waist gunner on a B-17, my father's psyche was as war-torn as a shattered and smoldering airplane fuselage. The "wreckage" in his psyche manifested in unpredictable and extremely volatile behaviors, which I will now illuminate for you in vivid detail.

Earlier in the day, my father had been drinking with my aunts and uncles and an argument broke out between them over a game of cards. As a result, he stormed out of the house, cursing and yelling at the top of his lungs all the way out to his pickup truck. My mother tried to ease the tension by apologizing for his behavior, but everyone in the family, (along with all the neighbors) knew he was a loose cannon. Hours passed and once all the relatives left for the day, my mother, my little brother, and sister and I were left alone to obsess in the anxiety of what was to come. Sometime around midnight, I heard the familiar sound of my father's truck pull up to the curb in front of the house. As the truck door slammed shut, my stomach tightened and I broke out into a cold sweat because I knew what was coming. I heard him enter the house and after a few moments of agonizing silence, I began hearing the sickening sound of fists striking flesh.

My mother begged him to stop, but the attack continued. The sound of her crying and screaming sent me into a blinding panic. I catapulted out of bed and raced down the wooden staircase crying out, "Don't you hurt my Mommy anymore!" He had her pinned over the kitchen counter with his hands around her throat . . . blood streaming from her face, dripping onto her limp right arm. I grabbed my father by the back of his pants and pulled with all my might. He swung around and slapped me to the floor, blurting out, "You little son-of-bitch . . . now it's your turn!" My mother slid to the floor beside me and covered my head, begging him to stop. He went to the gun cabinet in the den and came back into the kitchen . . . with a .30-06 deer hunting rifle clutched in his left hand. He reached down and pushed my mother out of the way and grabbed me by the shirt, jerking me up to my feet, and in one swift and brutal moment, slammed me up against the refrigerator. The metal handle dug into my upper back as he thrust the barrel of the rifle into my forehead, pinning me squarely to the refrigerator door.

The unmistakable metallic sound of the rifle bolt being cocked and the safety being released weakened my knees as I stared up the long bluish barrel into steely-cold vacant eyes. I was paralyzed. My breathing stopped and my chest collapsed. I couldn't breathe! Again, I couldn't breathe! The very same recurring pattern I experienced at birth as well as with my father in the playpen bed. This time, rather than smoke, the smell of gun oil and booze stifled my breathing as my father blurted out these exact words, *"I'm going to kill you, kill your brother, kill your mother, and let your sister live*!" In slow-motion, like a bullet being fired through my heart, I vividly recall my False Validation of *"Kill me if you want, but you won't hurt me!"* How hauntingly similar to my previous conclusions of a lack of safety and to resort to my own willful way of dealing with such a threat. In that terrifying moment, my father was no longer my father. He was a stranger to me. I was alone, an orphan who for the rest of my life would need to take care of myself.

I impulsively began throwing up all over my chest and onto the kitchen floor. I honestly believe this reaction saved my life, as my uncontrollable heaving caused him to lower the rifle, and as he did, the rage within him subsided just long enough for him to catch a glimpse of the monster he was being. He walked away into the living room and passed out with the gun leaning between his legs. It was a sheer moment of Divine grace, just enough of a respite to change the course of history in our family, an altered course that would exclude *that monster* from my life for many years to come.

Suffice to say I survived that violent incident plus many more, but my fully solidified Primary Decision haunted me well into my late-thirties until I finally came to terms with it. Through intense counseling, the assistance of mentors and friends, as well as much Uncasting work on my own, I was able to liberate myself from the prison of my devastating Box. While my survival conclusion of being indestructible was a protective barrier between my fragile young identity and the intense abuse I endured as an infant, the solution it provided me in the moment caused many years of behavioral challenges, a trade-off that in retrospect really wasn't worth it.

This recurring patterning reappeared as familiar False Validations in every intimate relationship from my teen years all the way into full adulthood. I could never drop my guard and be vulnerable and emotionally exposed. My Box, *"I'm alone and need to take care of myself,"* and *"no one is going to hurt me ever again"* was so prevalent that any time someone got too close to me, and too close to the wounded emotional terrain deep within my psyche, I would push them away and tell myself that I didn't need them. This pattern of behavior was so extreme that I would literally "set up" relationships so I was always in charge, always the one who held the upper hand of threatening to leave.

By protecting my vulnerability and deflecting the natural feelings of loving someone deeply, the "payoff" was that I would not be hurt if my partner ever left me. But the "cost" or price I paid was that I completely missed out on the amazing experience of having a deeply loving, intimate and fulfilling relationship with a woman all the way until my forties. I want to clarify the terms "payoff" and "cost." A payoff isn't a positive benefit to us, but rather a benefit to our Box in terms of keeping it firmly in place and in control. Essentially, we get to be right about the need for our Box's existence and we get to make others wrong for violating it. The cost is to our authentic Self in that we lose the experiences of deep love, aliveness and joy, and the experience of freedom that comes with being unencumbered by such rigid and detrimental decisions.

♦♦♦

What I experienced as a child was extreme, but I want to assure you that events with far less intensity or physical threat can evoke just as devastating a result. Keep in mind that the young psyche magnifies everything, takes everything personally, and what we as adults might consider to be a minor infraction, is a major devastation for infants. I also want to point out again that carrying a Primary Decision within us is not a liability per se, not until later in life when its unconscious structuring begins to dictate our behaviors and choices. And finally, I want to mention that we have only one Box and not a collection of them. *(A/N: I know it may seem like we have an entire collection of Primary Decisions, but all the variations can be narrowed down to roughly ten main categories, and each of us is saddled with only one decision, and that one decision exits within only one of the ten categories. I'll outline the categories in the "Exploration And Integration Guide" at the end of this chapter and will go into greater detail about them once we enter the Presence Stage and its Phase of Liberation.)*

Three Ego Layers of The Persona

Let's explore the terrain of the individual personality in a bit more detail now. Our persona is composed of three main "ego layers" or personality facets. They are, *Who we present ourselves to be. Who we are afraid we are. And Who we really are at our core.* According to Jung, the First Layer of *Who we present ourselves to be* is a kind of social mask designed to make impressions upon others and at the same time conceal and protect our more vulnerable selves. In general terms, our "ego" is the great masquerader, the one who wants credit, assigns blame, seeks to belong and seduces others into complying and serving its selfish needs. The main challenge of *Individuation* is the infatuation with the self that comes with becoming an individual.

In this Phase, as I mentioned at the start of the chapter, it's all about the self-importance of "me, my and mine." Until *Individuation* is revisited from a much clearer and higher terrain, selfishness reigns as the operative behavior in this Phase. I want to emphasize that the ego is not a detriment however, nor should we ever try to "get over it." The biggest ego trip in the world in my opinion, is to not want one, or worse yet to pretend that we don't have one.

Being "selfish," while being an inconvenience to others, essentially ensures and maintains our identity's continuity. Without a sense of "self," we would disperse out into becoming everybody else, or what in psychology is called borderline personality disorder. Without a border or ego boundary between us and others, the material contained within our psyche would spill out and merge with the emotional material of others. Early molest and sexual abuse can produce "rips" in the fabric of our ego boundaries, fractures that result in this oozing of our inner material. The outcome is emotional dependency, codependent behavior, protecting the aggressor and an inability to define and maintain one's own healthy boundaries, values and needs. *(A/N: For more information about character disorders I suggest looking into the "DSM-5," or Diagnostic and Statistical Manual of Mental Disorders, a compilation of all the main afflictions of the human psyche, a truly joyous read . . . not.)*

The Second Layer of our persona, or *Who we are afraid we are,* is our terrain of self-doubt and at the extremes, self-loathing. This self-referential facet of our identity is generated, maintained and protected by our Primary Decision. Casting the emotional decision that *"I'm bad and wrong and unworthy"* sparks a litany of self-esteem issues having to do with personal invalidation. As evidence mounts for our perceived lack of worth, our fears of being found out or judged for it magnify, thus feeding our conclusions of unworthiness. After all, only an unworthy person, someone who is "damaged goods" would feel the need to hide it from others.

The Third Layer of our persona is *Who we really are at our core*, our true Self which existed prior to the Primary Decision we cast into our young psyche. In essence, our authentic Self is our Agent of Being, the Divine presence within us that brings grace, love, and wisdom into our human condition. *Who we really are* requires no credit, experiences no blame and is uninterested in controlling anything or anyone. It has no personal needs, no beliefs to defend, and it requires no faith of any kind in order to carry out its selfless mission of being of service and contribution to all it encounters. I want to emphasize that our Agent of Being is not all goodness and light however, because it possesses the entire spectrum of Jung's light and dark Archetypal forces. What keeps our inner Agent's intentions pure is its wise integration of the full spectrum of these forces as well as its intent to sustain and nurture life. Our Agent of Being manifests goodness and is intent upon nurturing us just as life itself sustains and nurtures all its living creatures.

The paradoxical nature of our inner Agent's plethora of diverse forces should not be a surprise. Take all the stars in the universe for example; get too close to a star like our Sun, and it will incinerate you, but maintain a healthy and safe orbit around it and you will be warmed and nurtured by its life-giving energy. The omnipotent power of Spirit can be both infinitely supportive and infinitely destructive depending on how we interact with it. Our free will is what determines whether we are blessed or cursed by the Divine. Also, the term *Spirit*[28] originates from *"Spiritus,"* or *breath of life* and the term refers to the "breathing" process of inhaling the grace of Divinity and exhaling the challenges of Humanity. This exchange between the infinite and the finite infuses us with new life and grounds us both on Earth and in Heaven. Living in the presence of this sacred exchange is what I believe it means to be "spiritual."

As challenging as the developmental *Phase of Individuation* is, every bit of what we endure as children, including everything that happens to us and every meaning we assign to those happenings contributes to our healthy identity development. This essential Phase of development also paves the way for our eventual expansion into higher ground and prepares us to one day come into accord with our Agent of Being.

Individuation's Linkage With The Third Chakra: Solar Plexus Energy

The Third Chakra is the "Solar Plexus" or "Manipura" which means "lustrous gem." It's located in the center of the belly button and extends up to the center of our chest. This is where our self-confidence, specific personality traits and capabilities of personal power are forged and brought into being. Just as the *Phase of Individuation* marks the maturing of our persona, this Third Chakra is all about the full presence of ourselves as individuals.

Manipura is about developing our sense of wisdom and the beginnings of Self-Awareness arising into our consciousness. And just as in the *Phase of Individuation* we begin to craft "our experience" and "our truth" within the core of this Chakra. When Manipura is closed or unbalanced, we get triggered to fight and do battle both with ourselves as well as with others. This reactive tendency plays out as having "won the battle, but lost the war." When open and balanced, Manipura energy paves the way for understanding, which leads to empathy, compassion, and love. Those who clear out the obstacles of resentment, blame, and shame from the terrain of Manipura are able to hold both anger and care simultaneously and never allow the energy of anger to supersede the energy of care.

Exploration And Integration Guide

As a way to integrate the material in this chapter, and so you can gain insight into the Three

Layers of your own ego persona, as well as pinpoint your Primary Decision, I've listed all the Primary Decisions in the "Ten Box Categories" below as well as outlined just how insidious they can be in terms of influencing our moment-by-moment behaviors. Feel free to browse the individual Primary Decisions or Boxes within the ten categories and "try them on." When it feels like you've found a "fit," reflect on your life and the patterns that have played out in your relationships as a way to confirm your selection. Please be aware that there's a tendency to obsess over which is the "right" Box. You can be sure that whatever your Box is, it will be activated as you browse the categories. Be advised, however, as there's no way your Box wants you to discover it, because the moment you do, it loses its edge of control over your life. Take your time and feel into the Box options and try not to over think the process too much as it will get in your way and inhibit your clarity.

Defiant and Control Boxes: "Go Away! / I Need You!" "Damn You! / I'll Show You!" "You Won't Get To Me / I'll Ignore You" "I'll Never Be Like You _____!" "You're Wrong! / And I'll Prove It" "You Hurt Me / I'll Hurt You Back" "I'll Take Care of Myself! / F#ck You!" "I'll Be Strong / I Won't Let You Love Me"	**Dependent "Needy" Boxes:** "Please Don't Leave Me / I Need You" "I Can't Live Without You / Please Love Me" "Why Don't You Want Me?" "Don't Leave Me / I'll Do Anything" "I Don't Know How / Please Show Me" "What About Me? / I Need Love Too" "I'll Be Better / So Please Love Me" "I Want Someone / Anyone To Love Me"
Violation and Molest Boxes: "I'm Bad / I Deserve To Be Hurt" "I'm Unlovable / Use Me and Abuse Me" "It's All My Fault / I'm Bad and Wrong" "There's Something Wrong With Me" "I'm Nothing / Do Whatever You Want"	**Abandonment and Neglect Boxes:** "Where Are You? / I Can't Live Without You" "How Could You Leave? / I Don't Trust You" "Where Are You? / I'm Lost Without You" "You Left Me / No One Loves Me" "I'm All Alone and Nobody Cares About Me"
Withdrawal Alone Boxes: "I Don't Want To Be Here / So I Won't" "Leave Me Alone / I'll Just Go Away" "You Don't Love Me / I'm Out of Here" "I Won't Need You / You Won't Hurt Me" "I Hate You / I Don't Want To Be Here" "I Want You / Leave Me Alone"	**Injustice and Righteous Boxes:** "I Wasn't Doing Anything Wrong!" "Why Did You Hurt Me? I Didn't Deserve It" "It's Not Fair! / You Have No Right!" "You Love _____ More Than You Love Me" "It's Not Right! / And It Never Will Be!" "It's Not Fair / But I'll Keep My Mouth Shut"
Selfish and Fixation Boxes: "It's All About Me / What About Me?" "I'll Love You When and If I Want To" "Give Me What I Need … or Else!" "I Don't Care What You Want or Think" "I Won't Make A Mistake or Look Bad"	**Hopeless and Helpless Boxes:** "It's Hopeless / Please Help Me" "I'm Helpless And Just Can't Do It" "There's Just Nothing I Can Do" "It Doesn't Matter What I Try" "I Can Never Do Enough To Get Your Love"
Non-Being Boxes: "I'm Not Wanted / I Won't Be Here" "I Want To Die / I'm Gone" "I Won't Be and You Can't Make Me" "I Don't Matter / It Doesn't Matter" "I'm Nothing and I Won't Feel Anything"	**Karmic Legacy Boxes:** Legacy Boxes often have no initial incident or specific phrase or expression. Often non-verbal "womb" based utterances or preconception inheritances are the starting point and working backward from there is how to identify them.

(A/N: I want to add that these Primary Decisions are just "snapshots" of what my workshop participants have expressed during their deep Uncasting work. The actual phrases can vary, but the main categories they are positioned within remain consistent. This isn't an exact science, so allow yourself room for variation. What is most important is to feel inside your "danger zone" for the closest emotional fit.)

Now that you've done your "Box-browsing," here's what you need to know about its insidious nature. The first thing to understand is that your Box is relentless and it doesn't care about you in the slightest. It doesn't care about what you want or what your greatest aspirations or desires are. It could care less about your spiritual path, religious convictions, love of Nature, or your love of anything for that matter. Your Box is unmoved by acts of compassion, unconditional love, prayers, medicine journeys, rites of passage or even supernatural interventions. It's impervious to tragedy, loss, divorce, assault, threat, disease and even death itself. In summary, your Box is hard-wired to indulge in its "make wrong" pay-offs and you endure the cost through a loss of aliveness, love, and joy.

(A/N: While my description of the Box is quite disturbing, I suggest letting go of any importance you may be placing on this information and breathe easy. There's a natural process of Liberation that will ensue as you engage in this work. Trust the process and keep your curiosity level high. And one more thing . . . as negative as these Boxes may seem, who you are beyond the confines of any structure is a profoundly beautiful and extraordinary Being. Also, before we move on to the Presence Stage, I want to thank you for staying with it and for being willing to look more deeply into your inner terrain. This work is challenging and is only for those who have a deep resolve and dedication to bettering their lives and being of contribution to others. I honor you as a fellow traveler and I look forward to offering you whatever guidance I can as we venture in deeper and higher into the extraordinary inner world of the human psyche!)

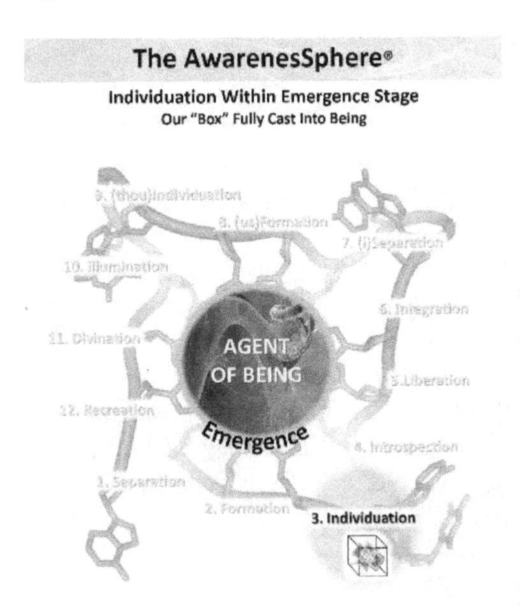

Let's move on now by recapping *Individuation, Emergence's Third Phase of Awareness.* This Phase is a further evolution of *Separation* and *Formation* that is compounded by our identity's need for self-worth, self-esteem, and meaning. Additionally, because of the emotional immaturity of infants, self-judgment, blame, shame, guilt, seeking praise and credit are prevalent. With *Individuation* comes self-importance, which gives rise to a self-centered focus that manifests as notions such as "my truth," and the "it's my life and I can do what I want with it." The higher faculty of Self-Awareness still eludes us during this primal development period.

While these behaviors may seem jaded and negative, the reality is they are a normal and healthy part of our identity and personality development. In a nutshell, *Individuation* is the process by which we come into our own as an individual, a person who exists separate from other people and distinct from the world as a whole. In this Phase, our growth into individualism is a needed separation for purposes of developing our identity boundaries. Consider it to be a healthy naiveté we must first develop into, and then grow out of in order to eventually embrace our greater Divine nature and gain access to our Agent of Being.

The terrain of *Individuation* is also fertile ground for the casting of, and solidification of our Primary Decision. However, as we approach the age of six, and as our personality fully forms, we become less prone to such castings. At the age of five, just as my own identity was firming up, the Primary Decision I cast around the circumstances of my birth, *"I'm all alone and on my own"* became fully solidified through enduring a terrifying incident with my father. Having a rifle pointed at my head was traumatic beyond belief and the emotional conclusion I drew from it not only validated my initial Primary Decision, but it also galvanized it into an ironclad Box that took me many years to liberate myself from.

My Box along with its insidious recurring patterning reappeared in every intimate relationship from my teen years all the way into full adulthood. I could never drop my guard and be vulnerable. My Box was so prevalent that any time someone got too close to me and too close to the fractured emotional terrain within my psyche, I would push them away and tell myself I didn't need them. By nullifying my vulnerability and the natural feelings of loving someone deeply I traded the possibility of falling in love for the need to be safe as well as to continue to be right about needing to do life on my own. Essentially, we get to be right about the need for our Box's existence and we get to make others wrong for violating it. The cost is to our authentic Self in that we lose the experiences of deep love, aliveness and joy, and the experience of freedom that comes with being unencumbered by such rigid and detrimental decisions.

The final piece of the *Individuation* puzzle is what I call the *Three Ego Layers.* Our identity or "persona" is composed of three main facets similar to a layered cake. They are, *Who we present ourselves to be, Who we are afraid we are, and Who we really are at our core.* The first layer of *Who we present ourselves to be* is a kind of social mask designed to make impressions upon others and at the same time protect our vulnerability. The second layer, *Who we are afraid we are* is our terrain of self-doubt and self-loathing. This includes all the things we would never want anyone else to know about us. And the third layer of our persona is *Who we really are at our core*, our true Self and our Agent of Being which existed prior to the Primary Decision we cast into our young psyche. ~

In the next chapter, we'll take an evolutionary leap out of the *First Stage of Emergence* and venture into the *Second Stage of Presence* and its three *Phases of Introspection, Liberation,* and *Integration.* This higher ground is where we free ourselves from being at the effect of our Primary Decision and begin to develop our higher faculty of Self-Awareness. Once you've reviewed the Q&A section I invite you to join me as we enter the *Fourth Phase of Introspection* and explore its life-changing terrain of *"Waking From The Slumber of Me, My, And I."*

♦♦♦

Reader's Question & Answer Section (Chapter 3: Individuation)

Allison - Q: I'm finding myself emotionally overwhelmed by the different Boxes. I, too, like others, feel a resonant energy to different ones, but I also, through reading them, feel emotionally drained - even just thinking of how some of the language in the Boxes have played out in my life. It feels that reading the statements of a couple of Boxes triggered a pattern of feeling overwhelmed, where the result is to shut down or stop "doing." Would this be a clue in finding the correct Box for me?

Val Jon - A: This process *should* produce a draining experience as it's an extremely challenging emotional activity. You are right where you need to be in the confusion and overwhelm, so don't fret dear woman. (Or maybe "relax and trust the process" would be a better descriptor in this case.) And you are absolutely correct about your sense of overwhelm being a clue. "Shutting down" and "stopping doing" is a hint as to what your Primary Decision is. If you were attending one of my programs, I would ask you these questions, *"Please close your eyes and recall an earlier time in your life when you "shut down" and "stopped doing." "Where were you and who was there?"* (My intuition is seeing you between the ages of 3 and 5 during some activity or function when you became emotionally overwhelmed and possibly felt shame or humiliation. While this may not be your initial incident, I believe it will help lead you to it.)

Allison - Q: How would you work with people in relationships that have both discovered their Box and yet now are choosing to try and be together, supporting their own journey and realizing how each other's Boxes are the biggest triggers to their own Box?

Val Jon - A: Each partner must first be clear about what their own Box is, what their "pay-off" and "cost" is, (what your ego gains and what you lose as a result) and what their Box's "corners" are. Every Box has a number of predictable mechanistic behavioral reactions such as withdrawing, getting aggressive or loud, shutting down, punishing, self-loathing, being manipulative, shaming, blaming and other negating characteristics. These corners are expressed both verbally and in our body language. Once your corners are identified, the next step is to identify how your Box and your partner's Box fit together, which is a matter of observing where your "corners" mesh together in "make-wrong" behaviors like a hand fits in a glove. For example, *"Don't talk to me that way!" "Well, don't treat me that way and maybe I won't!"* Or, *"I don't want to talk about it anymore." "That's the problem, you always avoid the tough issues!"* Or, *"Go away and leave me alone!" "I will go away because you are pushing me away!"* Couple's "Box Clearing" is the most challenging work and almost always requires a third party or counselor, (preferably someone who doesn't insert their own Box dynamics into the counseling sessions). Stay tuned as I will be offering online sessions for couples who have read my books and are interested in participating in this clearing process.

Allison - Chapter Statement: Doing this work left me overwhelmed and emotionally triggered as I felt connected to so many statements in the various boxes but also had me looking deep into my childhood where I do not have many readily available memories in my mind. But thinking about my birth and how I have been told that I came so fast that my father wasn't able to get there in time, (he was parking the car) and how my mother was very angry about that has made me think about the conclusions I might have drawn regarding my presence and arrival here.

Anna - Q: I find that I am more of a combination of two Boxes rather than have all the polarities within a particular Box. Is this common to find overflow between two or more Boxes?

Val Jon - A: It's a common struggle for people to narrow their choice down to a single Box because many of the behaviors and aspects are shared between Boxes. The key is in identifying *the very first* threatening incident in your life where you cast your Primary Decision into existence. It is there, within the sequence of events that your actual casting took place. While you are in the process of diving deeper and clearing away the layers of denial and protection that hide your primary incident, choose the Box that most fits the repeating patterns in your life. By doing so you will have the correct starting point to dive deeper and uncover the initial event and what you actually decided.

Anna - Q: Does one "teeter-totter" between the two polarities within the Box, or is one more dominant than the other?

Val Jon - A: It's common to cycle back and forth between the polarizing dynamics of one's Box. This is so because while we were initially casting it there were conflicting energies in play . . . the unpredictability associated with whatever threat we were experiencing. In one moment everything was fine and in the next, it was total chaos. Also, in many cases, the same person who threatened us was the person we loved or relied upon for our safety and nurturance.

Anna - Chapter Statement: I'm finding myself reflecting on many moments in my life as I searched for my Primary Decision. The Boxes were helpful in narrowing it down to two, one related to my birth trauma and the other to extreme forms of bullying in elementary school and abuse within my family home. I have never overcome the feelings of abandonment and believing that no one will come to help me no matter how loud or how much I ask. This was reinforced many times within my relationships. I seemed to draw to myself men who treated me how my father treated me. My father was a deeply wounded soul who suffered extreme abuse as a child from his mother. I felt I was all alone in this world. My early years were spent with an abusive father who tormented my mother, my sister and I. The emotional, physical and mental abuse solidified in me a belief that *"I can handle this" "I can survive this and anything else you try to throw at me" "The only person I can trust to help me is myself."* I remember these emotional conclusions clearly. Throughout my life, they were reinforced by the relationships I chose. I read so many self-help books, metaphysical books, I meditated, I did yoga, and I chanted Buddhist mantras, all trying to figure out what was wrong with me. What did I ever do to deserve this? I searched and searched to find that "thing" I must have done, otherwise why would people feel they had the right to abuse me, molest me, rape me, beat me, gaslight me? Was it because people as a whole were just really horrible at their core, or did I have a flashing neon sign on my back that said *"use me, abuse me, and kick me when I'm down?"* Yet when I look at who I am and the compassion, empathy, and care I show others, I know in my heart of hearts that I did nothing inherently wrong. It was my karmic knot that I need to untie, and for the first time in my adult life, I feel like it is possible to do so.

Antonio - Q: Is it possible for me to have several aspects of Formation from different Boxes?

Val Jon - A: The answer is Yes and No. The "No" is that we only have one Box and the core of our identity forms around it. The "Yes," is that there are some Boxes that have a split dynamic or fragmentation patterning to them, (*"I love you/I hate you"* or *"I need you/leave me alone"* for example). Multiple Personality Disorder is an example of this kind of split, as can be Borderline Personality. (This does not mean if you have a split Box you automatically have either of these disorders.) Explore your Box from this perspective, Antonio, and see if you can identify the opposing expressions that arise from it.

Antonio - Q: How can children grow up to be responsible, logical, ethical adults, when what we see being rewarded is narcissism, selfishness and the pursuit of material gain for happiness, not to mention childhood sexual abuse running rampant among all demographics of society?

Val Jon - A: It can be disheartening, especially for those of us who are devoted to being of service to others. The best course forward I believe is to raise parental awareness and put the tools we learn into practice in our own daily lives. Also, it is reassuring to know that whatever damage has been done to the psyche can in most cases be undone. I've personally participated in the reintegration of many terribly abused children's psyches and watched them "uncast" the devastating wounds lodged within them. Also, everyone I know who has truly taken themselves on and done the Uncasting work is a better person for having done so. And the even more encouraging news is that under the right conditions, the deeper the wounds, the greater the person is who liberates themselves from them.

Antonio - Chapter Statement: It's a wonderful reminder of how important it is to take the time to get to know who I am, at the deepest level of being. In addition, reminding myself that each of us along this journey of life has endured a similar Primary Decision. How I choose to engage or not with this underlying decision is where growth or stagnation manifests.

Cyn - Q: Is it possible we exchange Boxes at different times of life or evolve out of one into another?

Val Jon - A: Absolutely not. Like "diamonds," our Box "is forever." As we mature and evolve, however, the "exchange" that does happen has to do with maturing our understanding of how our Box operates, what its agenda is, and how we go about dealing with its controlling ways. For example, as I've shared, I have an *"I'll do it alone"* Box. As I've gained a deeper understanding of this isolating structure, I'm now more able to protect my autonomy without the need to disconnect from people who try to impose their truths on me. Since mine is a control Box like yours I suspect, you might want to take some larger risks, with the awareness that you may well get hurt as a result of doing so. By authorizing manageable degrees of risk and potential painful outcomes, you may well enjoy life more. To clarify what I'm suggesting, recall when you were first learning how to ride a bike . . . while falling was painful, you also knew that scraping your knee was part of the process of riding. What I'm encouraging you to do is much the same regarding your inner travels.

Cyn - Q: Once identified, does our entrapment fall away? Or at least allow us to find an easily definable path back to our Agent of Being?

Val Jon - A: The good news is that every time we catch ourselves acting out the agenda of our Box, we gain greater traction to be able to step out of its control and back into the grace of our inner Agent. The challenging news is that our Box waits for us in our slippers every morning, in that the very moment we deny being the Chooser, that is to say, the moment we entertain blame, shame, guilt, or projection, we fall right back into our Box again.

Cyn - Chapter Statement: It is so interesting when we take time to think about our Primary Decision and go over our lives, consider the Box elements and which resonates with us . . . as I landed on the "one," I could see how the self-sabotage played out over my life. Enlightenment began to appear when I realized I was seeking my mother's approval, (as you may have surmised I grew up in a matriarchal environment) even allowing her to choose (among other things) the men I dated and married–great for her, wrong for me. The moment I grabbed those famous words of Cher's, "Snap out of it!" my life changed forever. I think at that moment I discovered my Box and broke free, no longer did I need to be seeking approval, (i.e., giving up control) or on the other side of the spectrum be totally in control.

Elise - Q: I find myself believing the fear that arises within me more often than not. Is this because of ingrained "training" or an aspect of personality?

Val Jon - A: I have to be honest and say that the answer is "neither," because in my estimation it's actually indulgence. When we place more validity on our fears than on our capabilities, we do ourselves a huge disservice. That's not to say that your fear isn't real, just that the greatness of who you are, Elise, is well . . . greater than your fears will ever be.

Elise - Q: Is "drama" always negative?

Val Jon - A: By definition "drama" is a state, situation, or series of events involving an interesting or intense conflict of forces. In my understanding, drama is nothing more than a magnification of "what is." What is, (or reality just as it is) can be negative, positive and anything in between. Perhaps why drama seems to be expressed through negative behaviors more often is because as a society, we've judged positive drama as ego-boosting and selfishness. The media also uses negative drama as a lure to grab people's attention and manipulate them into ever-more mindless venues of consumerism.

Elise - Chapter Statement: The seeming never-ending brutality around my Box formation truly served to keep very ethereal aspects of myself hidden from me until I was adult enough to bear the undoing. It's very humbling to see the path in its "fullness" now looking back at my life.

Mindy - Q: Do the Three Ego Layers cause us to think we know our Box or want to be in a certain Box, but then discover what it actually is at certain points in our life's journey?

Val Jon - A: When I was a young boy my mother made costumes for me of the Lone Ranger, Superman, and a Fireman. When I first discovered my Box of *"I'm all alone and need to do it on my own,"* while it was not a pleasing experience, it seemed like a respectable and even "heroic" Box to me. The reality is that my ego was basking it in a romantic light. While I had the right Box identified, my ego distorted it to meet its own selfish ideals. By consistently doing the work and becoming intimately aware of how our Box operates our understanding of its true nature finally puts our ego's ideals to rest . . . but until then, in my own mind I'm a solitary and lone superhero.

Mindy - Q: In relationships, is it possible that certain "Box" personalities are completely volatile - and therefore a very bad idea - combinations? Or, can experiencing the journey of our Agents of Being and working through the AwarenesSphere create the possibility of incompatible Beings becoming compatible?

Val Jon - A: It depends on what you mean by "incompatible." If the volatility has devolved into repeated bouts of verbal or physical abuse, or perpetual emotional withdrawal, it's much harder to reach a state of loving compatibility. This is so because the psyche is wired to store negative experiences in precise detail, and with a profound conviction to guard against future infractions, which closes the heart and places a huge barrier between the couple. If the volatility is merely what I call a "Battle of The Boxes" that erupts from time to time, then yes, reconciliation is possible, but requires a devout commitment on both peoples part to take 100% responsibility for how their Box gets triggered and what they will do to remain ever-vigilant to not allow it to do battle. I could address how to deal with this challenge for chapter-upon-chapter and may do so in the future, but in the meantime, I will be hosting a series of online *"Couple's Box Clearing"* sessions for those who truly want to come to a place of loving and authentic compatibility. Watch for the announcement on my website.

Mindy - Chapter Statement: Based on my reading and experiencing this chapter, I can see that certain periods of difficulty in my life are the direct result of trying to "be" what I was/am not. This journey is a constant lesson, and it can be very uncomfortable and even disturbing at times.

Susie - Q: How can I view my Box, as anything other than "embarrassing?"

Val Jon - A: It depends on where you view it from. If we assume a mindset of "humiliation," our Box will always be an embarrassment to us. But from a place of "humility" and acceptance, it transforms into an unwitting reminder of "who we're not," and of what behaviors and actions not to fall into or dramatize. Having compassion for our Box is essential to not getting trapped in it. This is so because the more we judge it, the more control it has over us. Why? Because our Box is the master of control and judgment, and if it can get us to play its game, it wins.

Susie - Q: How can a child put together such a convoluted and alienating identity coming from such simplicity, love, and connection to begin with?

Val Jon - A: As we enter human life we inherit all the forces that exist in the "personhood pool" as Jung calls it, and not just those virtues and positive experiences we assimilate from our immediate family of origin. Children are super sensitive and impressionable and because the identity is still forming, any and all negative experiences get integrated into the development process of our young psyches. Besides, it's human nature to focus on what's wrong rather than on what's right. Consider test-taking. We can get 96% of the answers right and what do we focus on? The 5% we got wrong. (Did you catch the wrong percent calculation I did?)

Susie - Chapter Statement: I'm so interested to learn that tho' I meant well, and only wanted to live a happy life, I see that I was under the spell of an invisible cloak of inevitability that wasn't of my design. Phew! What a relief. Turns out that I wasn't a bossy, judgmental kid because I was a brat, I was just experiencing life's natural process!

Victoria - Q: I find my life has been made of complete opposites, one of ego-based personality beliefs and apparent internal opposing truths. The *"I can't trust anyone"* decision was about not trusting anyone to take care of me and also feeling like a failure. At the same time, my inner-truth was unconsciously guiding me with the knowledge that I can take care of myself and I don't "need" anyone else. I only recently discovered this as my core thread as I continue to go deeper into my Being. My mind was running the *"I can't trust anyone to take care of me."* My inner-truth was holding, *"I can take care of myself as my own source of love and support"* and my external environment was feeding me, *"girls aren't capable of taking care of themselves and need a man to take care of them."* Yet, the men in charge of me were the ones who hurt me the most. This conflict in beliefs led to internal conflict that stunted my self-confidence most of my life and prevented me from pursuing my most heartfelt desires. Would you agree that this cognitive dissonance of opposing beliefs can be found within the context of one's Box and make it all the more difficult to navigate its terrain?

Val Jon - A: Pretty much every Box has such dissonance because not only did we experience fear and trauma, it was almost always connected to someone who we loved, relied upon, or shared some kind of bond with. So, for example, the Box, *"I need you / leave me alone"* represents both sides of the primary incident. This inner opposition does indeed complicate the terrain, but once we realize that both sides are valid and that one side does not negate the other, the work of Uncasting (and staying out of our "danger zones" altogether) becomes easier.

Victoria - Q: I'm having a difficult time locating a Box that works for me. I have perhaps one sentence in each Box. What I feel tugging at me is the Karmic Legacy Box. It seems the assumption I made in-utero that *"I don't belong here"* might also be my Primary Decision upon which the cycle of everything else throughout my life was made. I was never angry, except as a teenager, and always felt like an alien in my environment, even in my own body. I preferred to be alone and also always felt lonely. Does this sound more like a Karmic Box?

Val Jon - A: Perhaps Victoria, but my tendency is to think that you cast your Primary Decision while in the womb and in reaction perhaps to your mother's critical and self-judgmental patterning. Uncasting Karmic Boxes require crossing the line between what is retrievable in this life, and what might be uncovered in lives previously. (This requires some degree of belief in reincarnation, so it's not for everyone.) Suffice to say that one can still do the Uncasting work by either exploring the dynamics of being in the mother's womb or by identifying post-birth incidents that carry the same emotional charge. Doing the Uncasting work on any of these birth, or near-birth incidents will reach back in time and undo any previous unconscious incidents. The same goes for the "Non-Being" Boxes, which may well be a better fit for you based on the behaviors and patterns you've shared so far. Keep in mind that not all the nuances of behavior are listed in the Boxes I've outlined in the *Exploration And Integration Guide.* As long as you are aware of the detriments that repeat in your life and are clear about how to navigate around them, you'll be just fine.

Victoria - Chapter Statement: I've always been fortunate, even as a young child, to have communication with my inner Agent, although my parent's religion insisted it was the devil tempting me to think outside their teachings. That inner-voice rescued me on many occasions helped keep me safe and stopped me from committing suicide as a teenager. I can see how my Box was created to keep me safe in an unsafe environment and also prevented me from self-expansion. It's fascinating to look at life experiences from both the *"I need someone to take care of me"* and *"I can take care of myself"* dichotomy. It led to a continual struggle between wanting a life of independence and needing codependent relationships and a struggle between, *"I can do this"* and *"someone else needs to do it for me."*

♦♦♦

CHAPTER 4: INTROSPECTION

Waking From The Slumber of Me, My, And I

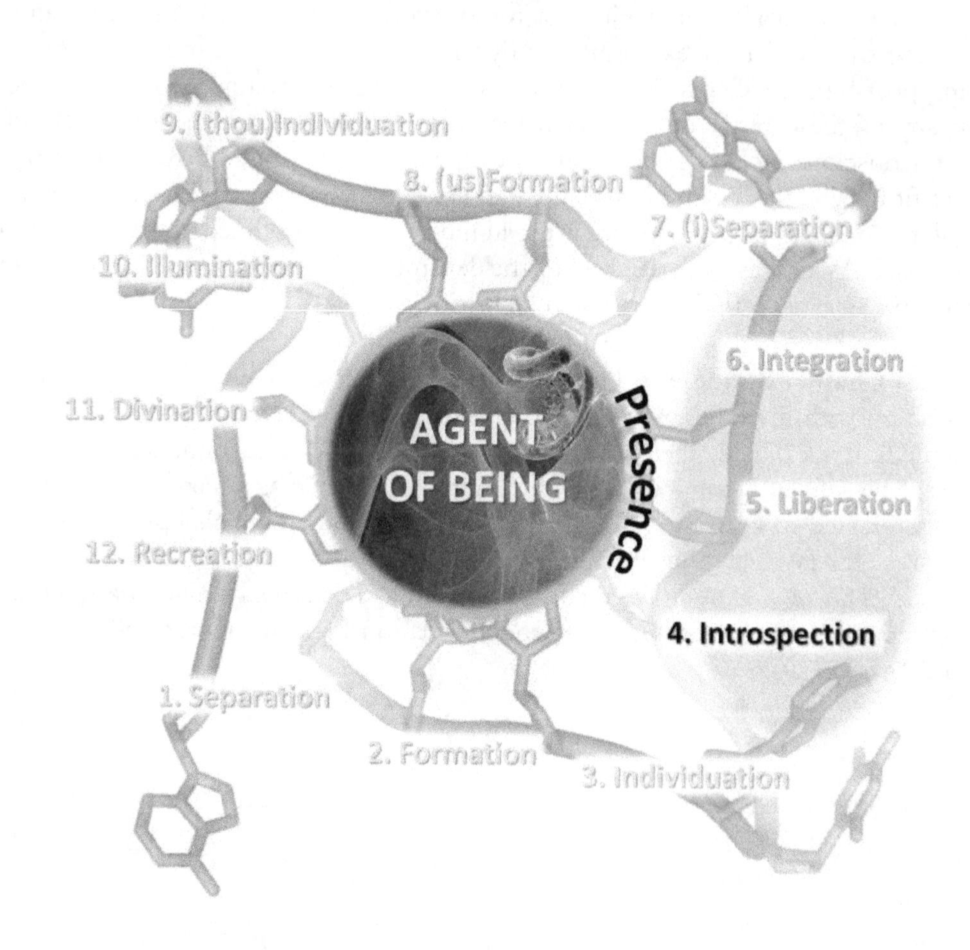

Note: This marks the beginning of the *Second Stage of Presence* within the *AwarenesSphere Model*

Your visions will become clear only when you can look into your own heart. Who looks outside, dreams; who looks inside, awakes." — C.G. Jung

The *Second Stage* of the *AwarenesSphere* is called *Presence,* and its three *Phases of Self-Awareness* are *Introspection, Liberation,* and *Integration.* Once we finally break free from the vicious cycle of *Emergence* our presence of self and level of awareness undergoes a radical transformation. The difference between our previous level of awareness in the *Emergence Stage* and our *Self-Awareness* in the *Presence Stage* is that we're not just aware and sentient, we become aware of our awareness. This higher faculty of Self-Awareness is a transformative expansion in our consciousness that matures our level of personal responsibility, thus opening the way for our ever-expanding growth. It also opens the way for us to make initial contact with our inner Agent of Being. *Presence* arises within us sometime after our basic personality is formed and begins to mature, and perhaps most notably, once curiosity and the inclination for looking within dawns on us.

Presence is the ability to perceive and be conscious of our experiences, sensory inputs and most importantly, our faculty of awareness itself. At this intermediate state of consciousness, we become aware of our ability to choose our responses rather than merely reacting to them. However, we have not yet developed enough reflective insight to possess empathy, compassion or understanding for that which exists outside our immediate sphere of awareness. An example might be an infant who accidentally strikes a sibling with a toy, causing him or her to cry out. The infant inflicts pain on the other child without reflecting on their own actions, essentially committing a hurtful act without any remorse.

Much like *Emergence,* the conditions of detriment commensurate within the *Stage of Presence* not only pertain to infants, but to adults as well, and specifically to those who have not yet elevated their level of awareness. The behaviors that often get acted out are a false sense of self-importance, entitlement and constantly needing to prove one's value or worth. On the flip side, the feelings of inadequacy, the need to belong, to be included and respected are acted out. *(A/N: Either an inflated or deflated sense of self is what I'm referring to here. Like being somewhat of a legend in one's own mind, or on the flip side, never feeling good enough, smart enough or attractive enough.)*

Introspection: The Fourth Phase of Self-Awareness

Entering *Introspection* brings about our higher faculty of Self-Awareness, an evolution that gives rise to us taking responsibility for the effects we produce within ourselves and with others. Rather than tending to blame ourselves or others for our challenging circumstances, we develop the capacity to assume an objective state of personal responsibility, un-tempted by the demeaning bindings of invalidation, shame, and guilt. *Introspection* is expressed as curiosity, inquisitiveness and a desire to open, take risks and grow. Within this Phase of development, we are self-reflective, yet our reflections are mostly limited to mental constructs rather than full-on heart openings. This developing mental reflection, however, enables us to explore and experience cause and effect, and as a result, we begin to feel our way into taking personal responsibility for our lives. While *Introspection* is freeing in many ways, we still remain somewhat attached to our fundamental *Emergence* patterning, personal agendas and the need to be in control of "our life." We also tend to fall short of being maximally empowering with others because of our need to help, rescue or save them rather than facilitating them to leverage their own inner resources so they can help themselves into their own higher inner ground.

In terms of gender issues, for women the focus of *Introspection* usually includes gaining insight into their negative self-image, never feeling good enough or pretty enough, and the incessant need to fix men, shape them into acceptable partners, and then become disenchanted with them when they fail to comply with the program. For men, the focus of *Introspection* typically includes coming to terms with their insecurities, wanting a mother as a mate, minimizing women's needs and generally being self-centered and unwilling to open to their vulnerability. *(A/N: Again, as your guide into the terrain of the human psyche, I know this material can stir up turbulent emotions. It, however, also provides useful answers as to why we act as we do. In future chapters, I'll address the practices and approaches that will enable you to deal effectively with gender issues and relationship-oriented challenges.)*

Awakening And Being Fully Present

Our opening quote, *"Look inside . . . into your own heart"* is the essence of *Introspection.* Awakening and being fully present to life is about parting the veil of our obvious reality and boldly venturing into the terrain of the unknown. It's about questioning that which we have never before called into question, risking our complacent selves by exploring unfamiliar terrain, and sailing off the edge of the world beyond the buoys and boundaries of our familiar identity. It's about opening our heart wide and traversing to the depths of our emotions while at the same time, climbing to the heights of our aspirations. It's about stretching the arms of our willingness out so wide that we actually *become* that which we want to embrace. These are the "heart-traveling" activities that awaken us to *Presence* and to being vividly alive.

On a more humorous note, regarding personal responsibility, the key principle of *Presence,* there is one question I always ask my program attendees after they've gone to great lengths to complain about their problems with spouses, friends and family members. The question I ask them is, *"Who was always there every time you ever had a problem in your life?"* And when they stare at me blankly I offer them a second question, *"So, do you think it's a coincidence that it's always been you?" (A/N: This doesn't mean you are the sole cause of all your problems or the creator of the problems arising within others. It simply means that you have a responsibility in the matter of placing yourself in certain circumstances or tolerating them to the point that they negatively impact you. It's uncomfortable to take personal responsibility for all we experience, but it's also very empowering to do so.)*

There is much more to being awake and fully present than meets the eye in that, "the porchlight may be on," but it doesn't necessarily mean anyone is home. The majority of us humans are asleep, absent rather than present, and for the most part "checked-out." We may be in our bodies, walking around and engaging in our normal daily activities, but many of us are living in a dream-state. We dream about everything we don't have, or more accurately, about what others have that we don't have. We dream about a different life, a different body, a different partner, but not about the life, body, and partner we actually have. We dream about being well and vibrant but are in denial and asleep about how we damage our bodies and our well-being. We dream about being wealthy and well-off, but the reality is that many of us are deep in debt and struggling to get by in life. We dream about an afterlife filled with joy and love and muse over going to "a better place," rather than making *this place* the best place, the only place where Heaven and Earth can truly co-exist. *(A/N: These may not be your dreams or how you approach life, but there are many who dream in exactly the ways I'm describing. Waking up to just how many of our fellow life travelers are asleep is sobering to say the least.)*

Intense Curiosity And Ego Control

Introspection requires waking up to being more curious about the world within us and less enamored with the world around us. The practice of *Intense Curiosity*[29] as I call it requires placing greater importance on self-reflection than on self-gratification. But for those caught in the survival-based grips of *Emergence,* there is no awareness of Self present to do any reflecting. It's true that infants are extremely curious about life; everything is new and mysterious to them until that is, they cast into being their Primary Decision. Once our Box is calling the shots, our curiosity goes comatose, and our ego's need to be in control goes ballistic.

In addition to the influence of our Box, as we mature into adulthood our fascination with learning new things wanes, and we become set in our ways. There's nothing wrong with settling into a fixed identity, but when it's at the expense of our inquisitive nature, we slip into apathetic disinterest, a condition in which the mystery of being alive gets replaced with the misery of merely living. But why would anyone trade curiosity for disinterest? For one simple reason, adults must contend with something infants are yet to confront, the insecurities of a mature ego. To a child, curiosity evokes an enthusiastic opportunity to learn and grow. But to the adult ego, it conjures up the risk of embarrassment and humiliation. It's important to realize that although our ego remains safe in the absence of risk, our aliveness diminishes because we've removed ourselves from being present to the astounding mysteries of life. The poet e. e. Cummings speaks of the opportunity to engage in curiosity this way. *"Once we believe in ourselves, we can risk curiosity, wonder, spontaneous delight, or any experience that reveals the human spirit."*

While an infant doesn't necessarily believe in themselves, prior to casting their Box, they have no trouble being who they are, just as they are without any second-guessing or self-judgment. This quality of innocent self-acceptance must be reintegrated into our adult persona if we are to ever truly believe in ourselves. Those who *do* believe in themselves have moved beyond the need to protect their ego and self-image. Rather than catering to their ego's fear of humiliation, they've chosen to embrace curiosity and the practice of *Introspection* with humble enthusiasm. So how do we deepen our sense of self-acceptance and belief in ourselves? By getting to know who we are *"in our own hearts,"* but in a very specific way; not in a way others expect or want, but in a way that arises within the crucible of our own discernment. Self-belief is borne of our own experimentation with cause and effect, our own insight and discovery while being fully awake and present, and more than anything, taking the initiative to engage in a life we ourselves deem worth living, whether anyone else ever validates it or supports it or not.

The Practice of Intentional Humility

Introspection not only requires Intense Curiosity, but it also demands being humble, but of a special order which I call, *Intentional Humility*[30]. From the Latin root, *"tendon,"* intention is about consciously applying pressure to two oppositional points of connection at the same time until the desired result is produced. An example is how the tendons in our arms and legs work. It's through the tension placed on our tendons and the act of contracting and expanding them through the use of our muscles that our physical movement is activated. The same applies to our emotional movement. By purposefully placing ourselves in tense situations in which we must emotionally "stretch," we strengthen our Self-Awareness muscle and thus expand into higher ground within.

It's easy to acknowledge our mistakes privately to ourselves because no one is there other than us to judge us harshly. *(A/N: While it's true that some people can't exercise an ounce of humility when it comes to judging themselves harshly, my hope is that you as a reader are capable of cutting yourself some slack. Being kind to ourselves in the form of being our own best friend is an essential part of succeeding with this rigorous self-development process. I fail at it myself quite often, so you're in good . . . and uh . . . self-critical company. The key, however, is in setting our self-judgments aside and remembering that we possess within us goodness and greatness that we really ought to give a fair chance to emerge.)*

The greatest challenge of practicing Intentional Humility is when we're in the presence of others and make mistakes in front of them. The fear of "em-barr-ass-ment" is a natural reaction for a healthy ego, but until we can "bare our ass" in front of others, (figuratively mind you), our fear of making a fool of ourselves will inhibit us from traversing into higher ground and growing ourselves into our greater virtues.

There are many reasons for our fear of looking stupid in front of others, but they all come down to not understanding the difference between *humility* and *humiliation*. Allow me to explain. *Humility* is the act of bowing down before that which we have not yet risen up to, and doing so with a clear conscience and joyful heart. In other words, we are grateful for becoming awake and fully present to what we were previously asleep to. We also realize that what we've not yet mastered isn't evidence for self-invalidation, but rather proof of our good intentions to grow and better ourselves.

Humiliation, on the other hand, is the act of cutting ourselves off at our own knees and falling onto the face of our ego indulgences, of how bad and incompetent we are, how we fail to perform like others, how stupid and gullible we are, and on and on goes our ego's self-flagellations. The reality is we can either gather evidence for how *we can't,* or we gather strength for how *we can . . . and will.* The irony is that by hiding our mistakes from others, we actually add to people being judgmental and critical of us.

While it may be true that some people are petty gossipers, there is another truth that dwells deeper within our hearts that has to do with grace, forgiveness and an inner knowingness about the greatness of the human spirit, a selfless kind of greatness that supersedes our fallibilities. What is amazing about practicing Intentional Humility is that if we are willing, we can lead others into higher ground and transform their petty judgments into magnanimous acceptance. The secret is in our ability to be publically humbled rather than humiliated. Allow me to illuminate the distinction for you.

As a leadership development consultant, I was called to India by a Fortune 100 company a number of years ago to conduct an in-depth training program for their top-tier managers and executives. Over five hundred high-tech professionals gathered in the ballroom of the Taj West End Hotel in Bangalore to participate in the kick-off event. Just prior to going on stage, the event staff hooked up my wireless microphone and tested to make sure it was working properly. Just after the test, and just prior to being introduced by the division head, I ducked into the bathroom to relieve myself. And while what I am about to describe sounds like a movie script, I assure you it actually happened just as I'm about to describe it. By mistake, I left the mic switch on and stepped up to the urinal. Within a few moments a staff member rushed into the bathroom shaking his head wildly, "Oh no, Mr. Farris, please sir . . . everyone in the ballroom can hear you!" "You must immediately switch off your microphone!"

Three minutes later I was standing on stage facing a sea of Indian faces, their eyes were slightly glazed over and the silence in the ballroom was deafening. India is a very formal country, people are eternally kind and proper and they don't want visitors to their homeland to be uncomfortable. In this moment I was v-e-r-y uncomfortable. I literally felt "bare-assed" in front of them. What was I to do? Ignore it? Pretend it didn't happen? So what I did was take my own introspective advice. In addition to my ego feeling totally humiliated, I chose to rise up above my ego reaction and instead be humbled. I told myself in that moment that I would demonstrate the kind of leadership qualities I was there to teach these fine human beings about. (My philosophy is that leaders must be as humble as they are confident if they are to expect their teams to be inspired enough to follow them.)

The moment I made the choice of humility, out of my mouth came, "Well now that we all know one another better, I suppose we can just jump right into the program, yes?" Everyone broke out into laughter and applauded, their heads rolling from side to side in utter delight. These were engineers at a global high-tech company, hardline professionals with a reputation for being cerebral, serious and on-task. But in this moment, they became benevolent and understanding beings who were fully with me and ready to participate, all because I chose to be *humbled* rather than *humiliated*.

Intense Curiosity and Intentional Humility are the two main practices to embrace when it comes to navigating successfully through the terrain of *Introspection*. The more curious we are and the more humble we can be, the more able we become to *"look into our own hearts"* and come to know ourselves in a whole new heartfelt way, a way that leads us into greater Self-Awareness and into the arms of our Agent of Being.

The Eternal Presence of Now

So regarding *Presence*, what exactly should we be looking for and become fully present too?

While I'll list a few guidelines and questions in this chapter's *Exploration And Integration Guide*, I'm going to address a few key pointers now. What there is to become present to is where we currently are now developmentally and where we want to be in the future. While it's a simple enough notion, the reality turns out not to be so easy. This is so because where we are "Now" is intrinsically tied to where we were just a moment ago, which is linked to where we've arrived from in our past. So without knowing where we've come from, we can't accurately assess where we are now. *(A/N: It's easy to get lost in what I'm about to suggest so I want to give you a solid example before launching into a bit of philosophy. Imagine waking up in a dense forest. You have some survival gear with you which is a relief, but upon investigation, you don't have a cell phone and there is no map to be found anywhere. Suddenly, by the grace of God, Spirit or the Universe, a map falls out of the sky right at your feet. You're overjoyed . . . until that is, you realize the map is useless because you don't have a clue about where you are in the forest. In other words, not knowing where we are is a detriment to getting to where we want to go.)*

This challenge of not knowing where we are developmentally is compounded by the fact that the moment we do discover where we are, our "Now" vanishes into the past and is immediately replaced with the next moment of Now entering from the future. Because the present vanishes into the past and is constantly being replaced, Now is a transitory space, much like a subway station populated by travelers moving from place to place, never staying in the "Station of Now" for an extended period of time, (other than the street musicians and homeless folks who operate outside of time anyway).

The transitional movement of Now is also a lot like the process of breathing, the past being the exhale, Now being the pause, and the future being the inhale. Try it for a moment. Exhale this moment of Now and hold the pause for a second or two to sense the transitional place, and then inhale your future as it becomes your Now . . . and again hold it for a moment and then exhale it into your past. Notice how transitory Now is? What if the whole notion of the past, present, and future is only an illusion? In other words, what if "time" doesn't really exist? And a much more intriguing question, "What if the reality existing outside of time is that the past, present, and future are really nothing more than an *Eternal Now* that we simply have not yet learned how to be present to in our consciousness? And an even deeper query . . . "What if we, as our Agent of Being, possess an infinite capacity to embrace all of eternity and infinity within one vast extended moment?"

And finally to ground this inquiry, what if we could directly experience this infinite capacity and draw upon it in order to calm our frequent overwhelm, quell our fears about running out of time and ground us in the breath of Spirit as it breathes its infinite grace into our every waking moment? Maybe it is the eternal "Now-ness" of Spirit herself, and the infinite abundance of love and grace available to us that we ought to focus on becoming fully present to.

Introspection and its overarching *Stage of Presence* are essential keys in expanding our Self-Awareness in that two results arise from doing so. First, is that we are released from the survival forces of *Emergence* and establish a sure-footing on higher ground to come. And second, is that these practices prepare us for the life-changing and timeless process of *Liberation* which, in our coming moments of Now . . . is surely on its way.

Introspection's Linkage With The Fourth Chakra: Heart Energy

The Fourth Chakra is that of "Heart Energy" or "Anahata," which translates to "pure and unhurt." This Chakra is where our love, compassion, and kindness are developed, deepened and expressed. Our mental processes need to be checked at the door with this Chakra because the mind struggles to understand what the heart has always known.

The Heart Chakra, when closed or unbalanced restricts our vulnerability, our ability to love and to be loved. Feeling "numb" is the result of closing our heart and stopping the vital flow of emotions which includes the full spectrum from love, to fear, anger, sadness, and joy. Yes, our anger must also be embraced by our heart, or else it goes up for grabs to our mind, which will "dis-figure-it-out" into resentment, regret, and loathing and even at the extreme, hatred. When our Heart Chakra is open and balanced, we are in accord with our Agent of Being, and we experience the grace of its open-hearted presence.

In terms of the linkage with *Introspection*, when our Heart Chakra is open, what we reflect on takes on positive energy, optimism, and a proactive spirit. When closed, our reflections devolve into thoughts of negation, blame, shame, judgment, and paranoia. The distinction between "humility" and "humiliation" is a perfect example of maintaining an open versus closed heart.

Exploration And Integration Guide

As a way to support you in *"looking into your own heart"* and becoming fully present to the aspects of your more engrained identity traits, I've taken the liberty of offering you a few questions and guidelines that will help illuminate your way forward. Our behaviors and actions are a clear indicator of what is moving within the deeper terrain of our psyches. Our ingrained behaviors particularly can be thought of as "ruts in the road of our minds." These "ruts" automatically steer our behaviors without us needing to have our hands on the wheel. Such deeply rutted behaviors invariably lead to the hidden terrain we need to become present to, much like a washed-out dirt road often leads to a ravine with much deeper fractures.

The only drawback of my rut analogy is that true *Introspection* requires setting our mind aside and opening to the emotions of our heart. The more we *feel*, the more present to the *reality of life* we become. The more we *think*, the more we get caught in the *concepts of life*. Concepts and reality are not at all the same things. It's like the difference between a "menu" and a "meal." Imagine setting down in a restaurant, musing over the menu, making a selection, and then eating the menu instead of the meal. Mental concepts are tasteless and empty, whereas emotional realities can be deeply fulfilling.

There are four heart-centered practices the *Introspection* process can take; 1) A consistent real-time assessment of our behaviors as they occur, 2) Retrospectively revisiting our behaviors after they've been played out, 3) A structured assessment of our behaviors based on a series of daily questions, and, 4) A comprehensive "life recapitulation assessment," or full inventory of every key event that has ever impacted us in our lifetime. You don't need to take on all four practices at once, but I do suggest at least adopting the first few in order to accelerate your introspective process. Let's explore each of the four practices in detail.

1. A consistent real-time assessment is about examining "incremental glimpses" of our hidden inner terrain by actively assessing our behaviors as they occur. This practice requires paying close attention to the effects that our behaviors have on others. To clarify this point, while interacting, rather than focusing on "what you said," instead observe "what was heard." If you want to be "right," validate what you said. If you want your relationships to "work," validate what was heard and then strive to understand why your partner heard it the way they did.

Another useful tip is to ask for immediate feedback on how you are coming across to others. Looking in the mirror requires another set of eyes because ours are focused only on "how we see things" and not on "how we are seen." It is the practice of seeing and feeling ourselves how others see and feel us that empowers us to become present to aspects of ourselves that were previously hidden from our view. You can ask a spouse or a good friend to assist with this process, but you need to be in fairly good standing with them, or they may be tempted to take advantage of your vulnerability.

2. Retrospectively revisiting our behaviors is about taking time on a daily basis, usually just after our interactions, or at the end of each day to reflect. There are two reflections, one is on how you treat yourself, and the other is on how you interact with others. Obviously, you'll want to be watching for self-invalidation behaviors, how you justify and rationalize things and any engrained "rut" patterns that occur without your "hands being on the wheel."

The other reflection is on how you interact with others. Behaviors such as agenda-based flattery, inauthentic accommodations, stepping over things, being impatient, being excessively forgiving, inflammatory, unexpressed, controlling, intolerant, arrogant and resentful. And on the flip side is to also reflect on acts of love, being in gratitude and appreciation, deep expressions of care and compassion, being humble, forgiving and open-hearted. It also includes reflecting on integrity issues of either staying true to your principles and values or compromising yourself. Keep a journal of your reflections and take note of the recurring patterns and trends that arise as they are very useful in becoming present to your deeper hidden inner terrain.

3. A structured assessment of our behaviors is based on a series of more formal questions rather than an ad-hoc inquiry. To take this practice on you first must acquire a journal to record your progress and then craft your daily questions, an inquiry process for the morning when you awake and another just before bed. The questions are crucial and need to be well thought out. Here is an example of a few morning questions. *"Who am I being today? What quality will I bring forth? How will I know I did so? What is my main intention today? How will I manifest it? What behaviors will I improve upon today? How will I know I've improved on them?"*

Then at night prior to bed review your day, what you committed to and how it actually went. A few added nocturnal questions are, *"What did I observe today? Who was I being? If not myself, who then? My mother? Father? Others? What intentions did I, or did I not manifest today? What do I see about it? Did I improve upon any behaviors today? If so, what specific behaviors? What patterns am I seeing and where are they leading me?"* The comparison between morning and evening is very important to pay attention to as it defines both the forward progress you are making as well as the "stretch" you need to place yourself in. I suggest not stretching too much or too little. Find a medium between where you are growing slowly but steadily. It's like weight-lifting, your Self-Awareness "muscles" must tear slightly, but not to the point of taxing you heavily or doing damage.

4. A comprehensive "life recapitulation assessment" is about taking a complete inventory of key life events that have impacted you over the years. This is a very intense practice and time-intensive exercise, but everyone I know who has completed it has reported extraordinary breakthroughs in their lives. The inventory is divided into 10-year cycles, (0 to 10, 11 to 20, 21 to 30, etc.) For each cycle you want to identify key events like birthdays, celebrations, holidays, births, deaths, accidents, first days of school, your first sexual encounter, falling in love, any abuse, molest, violence, abandonment, neglect, etc. For the first cycle recall special times, toys, animals, teachers, neighbors and friends and the happenings associated with them. Spend a full week if not more on each 10-year cycle. Locate old photos and pics, talk with family members and review old text chats, letters, and cards, anything that will spur your memory. F-e-e-l into your emotions, memories, and especially your False Validations.

Once you locate a "charged" event, review it like a movie film, one frame at a time until you can re-experience the whole event, stay present to it and release the emotional charge associated with it. The final instruction is to hold the event in your heart and ask yourself to "recall an earlier similar event in which . . ." (add any words or phrases that describe the specific event.) Let the process lead you back all the way to any original incidents in which you may have cast a Primary Decision or Basic Assumption. Once you arrive there, engage in the Uncasting process I have been illuminating and outlining so far in this book.

(A/N: This exercise can be extremely reactivating and bring up emotional material you were completely unaware of. While uncomfortable, please know that you survived it once, which means you will be okay this time around. In fact, the more you uncover and become present to, the more illuminated your inner terrain will become, and the more capable you will be in terms of navigating through it in the future. Please remember to be your own best friend as you engage in this work. Just as we deeply value and seldom judge our life-long friends, we can behave in the very same way with ourselves. The other thing I want to stress at this point in our journey together is that while you may uncover a good deal of less than attractive engrained behaviors, it is very important to remember that who you are is much greater than any of them. Keep in mind that only a good person, someone with deep a deep dedication to their own betterment would be willing to do this deeply challenging work.)

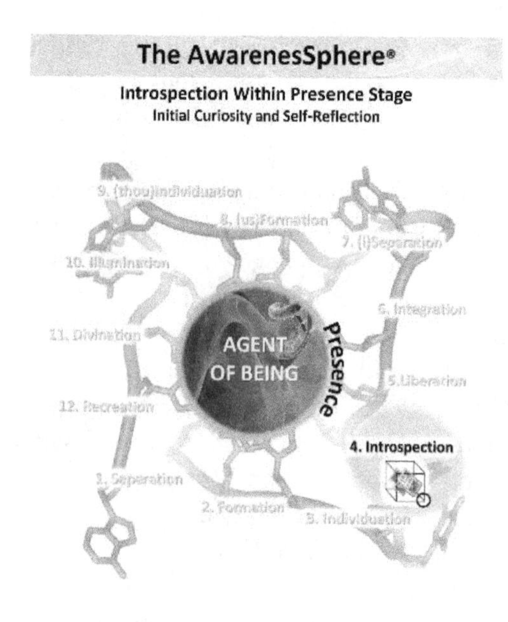

Let's move on by recapping *Introspection, Presence's Fourth Phase of Self-Awareness.* This Phase is where our higher faculty of Self-Awareness comes into being as a possibility. Prior to *Introspection,* there was far too much survival energy within our developing psyche to warrant any degree of self-reflection. With the dawning of Self-Awareness however comes freeing ourselves from the grips of *Emergence*, gaining a personal responsibility muscle and the beginnings of coming into accord with our Higher Self and Agent of Being.

The *Stage of Presence* arises after our identity is fully formed and begins to mature, and with it comes the blessing of curiosity and desire to look within. *Presence* is about being awake and conscious of our moment-by-moment experiences, sensory inputs and most importantly, our higher faculty of Self-Awareness. And while *Introspection* is freeing in many ways, we remain attached to our fundamental *Emergence* patterning, personal agendas and need to be in control. Furthermore, being of authentic service to others is trumped by our need to help, rescue or "save" others rather than facilitating them to access their own abilities to deal with the challenges they face.

Presence and *Introspection* are about being interested and constantly risking our complacencies and assumptions so we can discover the unknown. It's about opening our heart and stretching the arms of our willingness out so wide that we literally become what we are embracing. *Introspection* requires being more curious about the world within us and less enamored with the world around us. And it requires placing greater importance on self-reflection than on self-gratification. Settling into a fixed identity is healthy, but when it's at the expense of our inquisitive nature we slip into apathetic disinterest, a condition in which the mystery of being alive gets replaced with the misery of merely living.

Introspection not only requires Intense Curiosity, but also Intentional Humility, a kind of humble intent in which we purposefully place ourselves in challenging situations in which we must stretch ourselves. Holding both a firm intention and at the same time maintaining a soft humility strengthens our Self-Awareness muscle and conditions us for engaging more effectively with paradox. Humility, if you recall, is the act of bowing down before our challenges with a clear conscience and joyful heart. In other words, we are grateful for becoming present to what we were previously absent to or asleep about.

Intentional Humility also keeps us present to the reality of our better nature and inner goodness. And it helps us realize that what we have not yet mastered isn't evidence for self-invalidation, but rather is proof of our good intentions to grow and better ourselves. *Introspection* is the threshold to higher awareness and the gateway into the higher terrain where our innate wisdom and Agent of Being dwells. The more curious we are and the more humble we can be, the more able we become to *"look into our own hearts"* and come to know ourselves in a whole new heartfelt way, a way that leads us into greater Self-Awareness and into the arms of our Agent of Being. And in terms of our degree of presence, obviously, our attention must be on developing our curiosity and humility, but on a grander scale, it also includes being aware that there is a "timelessness" about our nature that we need to keep our eye on. If we are indeed connected with the vastness of the cosmos, the infinite and eternal, then we also must have access to the expansiveness of its scope and grandeur. *Presence* opens the way for us to explore beyond the bounds of our individualized experiences and venture into the mysterious and timeless terrain ahead. ~

In the next chapter, we'll continue our explorations into the *Stage of Presence* and explore its next *Phase of Liberation.* This higher ground is where our Self-Awareness and Power of Choice matures and where we liberate ourselves from the shackles of our unconscious emotional conclusions and decisions. Double-check your bootlaces, backpacks and water bottles, my fellow *Travelers*, because, after the Q&A section we're going to embark on a life-changing expedition into what I call, *"Knowing Our Self Beyond Our self."*

Reader's Question & Answer Section (Chapter 4: Introspection)

Allison - Q: In this chapter being connected to the heart, my question is based on so much evidence of women closing this in order to survive in our world today. I am experiencing more and more women friends and clients, (myself having been a part of this too) having a hardened shell protecting their hearts. Even though they all want to open their hearts, "society" and having to "make it" with work, beauty, family life, kids, etc., keep them rigidly closed. How do you work with someone who wants to experience the power of the heart-opening, to feel, receive and give love - yet has created such a hardened heart?

Val Jon - A: In one of my public programs called *"The Myths of Womanhood and Manhood,"* I've identified four major dynamics working against women (and men) with respect to opening their hearts and allowing themselves to be vulnerable. They are *Procreation, Competition, Preservation,* and *Socialization.* Gender dynamics steeped in the survival energies of Emergence plays a huge role in maintaining the "hardened shell" you speak about. The *Procreation* dynamic is composed of unconscious men who view women as sex-objects and conquests and fail to recognize the profound wisdom, power, and capability women possess. And unconscious women who buy into the superficiality of being those desirable sex-objects, and who willingly comply with the lie of being "second-class citizens," when in fact they are first-class humans.

The *Competition* dynamic is how women demean, sabotage and undermine each other in order to secure the most desirable, capable and resourceful male mate. The detrimental behaviors women wage against each other are both unconscious and conscious, ranging from matriarchal family programming in which young girls are taught to defer to men, remain invisible and hide their power, to women tearing each other down through degrading gossip and "back-biting," to women demeaning themselves through making unhealthy comparisons to other women, to outdoing one another by playing into needing to be the most alluring "prize" on a man's arm.

The *Preservation* dynamic has to do with unresolved past boundary violations and mate betrayals that women carry within their psyches, the result of which hardens their hearts. The boundary violations can include early childhood sexual, emotional and physical abuse that resulted in a loss of trust and closure of vulnerability, (the *"I'll never trust again"* Basic Assumption or Primary Decision). The mate betrayals are repeated acts of abuse from "trustworthy" mates who turned out to be as detrimental as, (or worse than) those perpetrators who committed one's initial boundary violations.

The *Socialization* dynamics have to do with peer pressure, media hype, manipulative advertising campaigns, shallow Hollywood glitz and glamour trends and degrading music and movie propaganda. It's cool to be jaded, to be a hardened woman who excels in a man's world. While Women's Liberation was an attempt at having women come into their own, how it manifested was in taking on the unhealthy behavioral patterns of men, such as becoming workaholics, dressing in masculine attire and trading the softness and caring nature of their femininity for a rigid attitude of angular male arrogance.

As far as how to counsel women, I suggest sharing this information with them and engaging them in what they can do to begin to Uncast the conclusions that have hardened their hearts. Also, let me know if I can be of assistance as I love working with women who are intent on flourishing into their true power and presence.

Allison - Q: Self-Acceptance and Belief in oneself are huge words that, for me, connect with Forgiveness. What is your experience with the intersection of these three qualities of being?

Val Jon - A: These three huge words are interconnected at a deep and profound level. To answer your question, let's explore the meaning of Forgiveness. To *forgive* means *"to give as before."* But to give what as before? To give not only Acceptance, (of self and others) but also to give back to ourselves the deep abiding Belief in the Power of Love. For those who live within Love's Acceptance, Belief and Forgiveness are Spirit's most cherished Agents of Being, true Ambassadors of Grace who have come to illuminate the darkness and help show the way forward for the human race. A big answer for just as big words.

Allison - Chapter Statement: I feel the freedom that comes with Introspection is one of the greatest gifts of being a human. We have such powerful connective links within us. To acknowledge the heart in relation to the mind, and the wisdom and transformation that the opening of the heart can bring into our consciousness is a courageous and therapeutic process.

Anna - Q: We are constantly surrounded by reinforcements through our media, religions, schools, and news that keeps us trapped within our Boxes. How does one filter all that out considering it is in their best interest to keep us trapped?

Val Jon - A: It may only be semantics, but it's important to remember that no one and nothing "keeps us trapped within our Box" other than us. I think you probably mean that all the control and consumer-driven forces we are exposed to discourage us from focusing on and maturing into our Higher Selves. It's definitely more difficult to maintain an inner focus in a society that places all the emphasis and value on being externally focused. As we become seasoned *Travelers Within* with a much more pronounced inner focus, there is a point in which we must make some major lifestyle changes in order to live true to what we are discovering. Those choices will naturally arise and when the traveler is ready the changes will appear.

Anna - Q: After discovering your Primary Decision and the incident that led up to it, how does one integrate that knowledge into their life when it changes almost every aspect of it?

Val Jon - A: There is a natural integration that happens once we have completed the Uncasting work with respect to our primary incident. Indeed, our lives change . . . for the better in the sense that the self-imposed limitations our Box placed on us are removed and we are free to be the Chooser in our daily lives. By following the steps I outline in each chapter's *Exploration And Integration Guide* you'll have no trouble moving along with the development process that ensues. Some of the "natural" integrations will be in the direction of lifestyle changes. As you gain greater navigational experience with your inner terrain you'll become more discerning about lifestyle issues like self-care, diet, exercise, devotional time and who you choose to associate with.

Anna - Chapter Statement: I've realized that the mental clutter of self-motivating and self-supporting talk fills my headspace and leaves little room for anything else. I'm so busy being my own cheerleader just to make it through the simplest things of daily life. I cheer myself with, *"You can do this." "Stop procrastinating." "Just do it."* The internal struggle just to overcome my social anxiety is draining emotionally. I found through reflection that I have spent the majority of my life trying to convince myself that I can handle it, that I can move through it, that *"it is what it is"* and keep going. Since discovering my Primary Decision, however, I realize I can now consciously choose not to fill my headspace with self-talk, but instead actually allow other positive voices in.

Antonio - Q: Why should I use discernment, regarding whom I allow into my sacred circle of beloved friends and family, even when my heart is open? Can I trust the sacred heart's wisdom that is beyond logic and reason?

Val Jon - A: Trusting Spirit, or "sacred heart's wisdom" as you say is a beautiful thing and I believe its vision is 20/20. Where the concern arises for me is whether or not we are always present to the wisdom it tries to bestow upon us. I know for myself that I'm not always paying attention to Spirit, so as a precaution I use my mortal discernment to help make choices about who I open to, trust and share life's intimate experiences with. Optimally, I believe it probably ought to be a partnership between our sacred heart's wisdom and our mortal discernment.

Antonio - Q: Do the virtues, like empathy, compassion, nobility, integrity, etc. reside in our sacred heart space?

Val Jon - A: If by "sacred heart space" you mean the "thou" that dwells within us or our Agent of Being, then yes. The reason I do not choose to position these virtues solely within the heart space is that while the heart is very wise, because some of these virtues such as nobility and integrity also require cognitive insight and the ability to discern, debate and understand, both the mind and the heart, (as well as what I call "Sacred Knowingness" which we'll explore later on) are all necessary to ensure the highest and truest reflection and alignment process.

Antonio - Chapter Statement: This chapter is a wonderful reminder to continuously check in with how I am moving through life, particularly emotionally, physically, mentally and spiritually. I recently read where a young man expressed how he felt emotions were a waste of time and energy. That saddened me deeply, as I feel our emotions are our greatest gift. To feel the heights of joy/ecstasy and yet the deepest depths of sorrow, pain and grief-everything we experience in between this spectrum is a well of information to draw life-learning experiences from. Through this process of checking in, I've realized that my heart knows best, not my mind, which is full of ideas, concepts and the tendency to over-analyze if I allow it to run wild.

Cyn - Q: They tell me I'm on the "fast-track" at work, so I'm a bit fearful noting there is a fine line in the workplace around admitting my "faults and failures" as I scale the ladder of my profession. Wanting to be humble and evolve into my best "me," how can I balance my work life with the deeply vulnerable work associated with the AwarenesSphere?

Val Jon - A: While it's unfortunate, unless your line of work happens to be in the area of self-growth, it's important to maintain a boundary between your inner travels and your outer career path. There is insufficient understanding and respect in our modern workforce for the laudable pursuit of conducting inner work. At best self-growth is viewed by society as "psychobabble" and at worst an activity for losers. The best way to be viewed in an appreciative light by your leaders is to keep your inner travels to yourself and instead demonstrate extraordinary results and do so with zero ego-attachment.

Cyn - Q: I try to connect the reality of having "high powered" privilege which causes stress for a paycheck and limited time to devote to self and how these words speak to me of not just "NOW" but requiring time in "now" and in "future," which I feel I have so little of *". . . infinite abundance of love and grace that dwells within the human spirit that we ought to focus on becoming fully present to . . ."* so I ask, although there is no shortcut, what is a practice I can embrace little by little which will lead me to the place of heartfelt Introspection without overwhelming me?

Val Jon - A: While I'm an extremist, (and my career actually encourages it) I find more value in overwhelming my heart than engaging it little by little. Like you, however, many would prefer, (and even require) a more moderately paced-process. One of the best ways to go about this is to engage in a daily "heart-share process." Each morning while brushing your teeth or combing your hair, literally ask your heart (as if it were a being) what it feels would be a kind or loving act you could initiate today with someone. (Not so loving that they think you're hitting on them, but caring enough that they are touched by your kindness.) Then each night, reflect on the heart-shifts happening within you and the effects your acts of kindness are having on others. Little by little small acts of kindness add up quickly and your heartfelt Introspection results will match or even exceed what an extremist might ever achieve.

Cyn - Chapter Statement: I can only speak for myself as a less enlightened human being, I see more clearly how I respond or react to anything in my life depends most often upon my immediate past and present–my current state of mind. This chapter is a wonderful reminder to breathe, to allow my heart to shine through, to place my overactive mind on pause, not to be too self-critical, to try and look beyond emotional upheaval and embrace experiences, acknowledge fear, failures, wins and triumphs to respect others and myself in the journey of being a human being learning how to be the best I can be.

Elise - Q: Is reaction time a marker as to the thought/feeling being a choice or a decision?
Val Jon - A: An immediate decision on our part is probably a reaction rather than a choice. Whereas if we allow ourselves a brief pause for reflection before deciding something, it's more likely to be a choice. There are certain choices that need no time to self-reflect before choosing them, but these are far and few between in my experience. Assuming that "we just know what is right" is a trap to be avoided. The hint is in the word "we," as if a group of other experts is hanging out in our psyche who also agree with our opinion.

Elise - Q: Surrendering to Intentional Humility seems to take more courage than I possess. Is there a more gentle way to process?
Val Jon - A: I think we often underestimate our capabilities. It's my belief that we possess infinite courage, but as Bucky Fuller so wisely said to me, (which I'll now say to you, Elise) . . . *"You must believe in yourself in order for your courage to be greater than your fear."* The other point I wish to make is that "gentle" is definitely a wonderful preference, however, I doubt the strength of courage we truly need in our lives can be evoked under gentle conditions.

Elise - Chapter Statement: My life inventory is depressing if looked at from a "doing" standpoint. The aloneness in the midst of being so busy makes me sad for that child/woman who had no idea of the price and reward of the journey into Wholeness.

Mindy - Q: Can we increase our level of Intentional Humility by focusing more deeply on Introspection? Is it possible to meditate to a point of purposefully doing this?
Val Jon - A: I wouldn't spend too much time meditating on Intentional Humility as the best way to gain insight into it is through experiences of in-the-moment embarrassment. Bringing about greater humility is almost always a matter of being brought to our knees, rather than sitting on a meditation mat. The value of meditation should however, not be underestimated as its deeper purpose in my opinion, is for us to set aside our constant mental chatter and open the space to drop down into our heart, as well as to rise up beyond our mind. This bi-directional meditative process, if we embrace it fully, enables us to realize that if we

travel "below" deep enough, and "above" high enough, we will eventually come full circle to the sacred ground where depth and height meet . . . and once we arrive there, Humility is everywhere.

Mindy - Q: Was your "the mic is on" moment in Bangalore and immediate reaction to the possible discomfort of your audience an intense moment of Intentional Humility for you? Did you yourself learn from this experience?

Val Jon - A: It was an intense moment of "em-bare-ass-ment" I shared in my story. I was humiliated to the point of wanting to melt into the bathroom floor and disappear. It was the walk between the bathroom, stepping onto the stage and facing the audience that I learned about my character and conviction. As I stated in my answer to you above, the place to grow one's self is in the very place one's ego does not want to be caught in. It is this massive discomfort between what the ego rejects and what we know we must embrace, that we are forged like a brilliant diamond in the intense crucible of our psyche. The pressure and heat of being completely vulnerable, honest and willing to expose our ego to devastation is what we must dedicate ourselves to if we are to fully live into Intentional Humility. Once we do this, "who we are not" gets completely annihilated, leaving only that which is indestructible . . . namely, "who we really are." So what did I learn from my "the microphone is on" experience? That who I am, (and who others are) is so much more valuable to me than who I'm not could ever be.

Mindy - Chapter Statement: I have always been introspective, but I have not always been honest with myself. In my intense desire to not be like my mother, I would choose situations where I thought I was so much more like my father. In fact, I am both of them, but I spent and wasted too much time avoiding those qualities I received from my mother. As she and I both age, I see that we are both becoming like my grandmother, great-grandmother, and great-great-grandmother. These inherited traits and behaviors are my legacy.

Susie - Q: What causes our Heart Chakra to open or close? Why wouldn't we always keep it open, given what it provides, regardless of how scary it is?

Val Jon - A: Our Heart Chakra typically opens in the presence of love and care and closes in the face of "unwitnessed" or unresolved fear. To be clear about this, fear itself does not cause our Heart Chakra to close, but rather it is unchecked fear or negative emotions that we do not act on and embrace that triggers the closure. A total embracing and honoring of our feelings, whatever they may be, is what causes our Heart Chakra to open. I want to point out that this opening and closing process is actually a necessary and healthy thing, as a perpetual opening would be much like paralysis. For example, our physical heart valves don't always remain open. Rather, they constantly open and close in order to function properly. The same goes for our Heart Chakra. The mastery is in being able to open our heart *at will.* Having the ability to choose to open, (or close) moment-by-moment is where the true power of communing with our Heart Chakra resides.

Susie - Q: When asking for another's feedback on their experience of what we said or did, aren't we just getting a response from the Box they are confined to and their Primary Decision(s)? As opposed to genuinely unbiased, helpful feedback and coaching?

Val Jon - A: Whether the sender is "unbiased" or not is not as important as is our moment-by-moment capacity to remain open to receiving feedback. Sometimes what we deem as "unhelpful" input in the moment turns out to be "invaluable" later on. If we close before what is being said to us has a chance to enter us and take its own organic course, we do ourselves a disservice. I use an analogy in my counseling sessions that clarifies this point . . . Imagine a bird flying over a meadow with a seed in its beak. It drops the seed, and as it falls to the ground, Mother Nature "trusts the process" and knows that if the seed lands in fertile soil it will grow, and if it lands on solid rock, it will die. We don't have to kill the seed of feedback before it lands in us. Trust that if what someone says has validity for you, (whether they are unbiased or not) it will grow, and if it doesn't, it will die on its own without you needing to kill it.

Susie - Chapter Statement: I realize that I've been unconsciously deeply uncomfortable and mortally afraid of asking for feedback from others. This is a new realization and a very useful one. I haven't taken any actions "yet," but I intend to, as I know that risking my comfort level is the key to accessing great breakthroughs and liberations.

Victoria - Q: Introspection appears to be where journaling can be extremely helpful. Would you recommend using a notebook with all of the practices and exercises?

Val Jon - A: Yes, creating a unique and personalized *"Travelers Within Journal"* would be my recommendation. While I keep most of my notes on my computer, there's something very cathartic about hand-writing one's insights and reflections. The personal "pen to paper" connection is very nurturing in my opinion and will go a long way towards deepening your degree of Introspection.

Victoria - Q: Do you find that there is a particular point or circumstance that occurs in a person's life that triggers Introspection?

Val Jon - A: Unfortunately the motivation for engaging in personal growth work is often pain and loss rather than curiosity and inspiration. The pain associated with losing someone or something dear to us is the wakeup call that nudges us across that gap between Individuation and Introspection. The problem with pain being our main motivator, however, is that the confrontational nature of having to embrace deep sadness, loss, and grief tends to compound depression and apathy, which triggers denial rather than greater Introspection. And when we lead ourselves into denial, we run the risk of making a "U-turn" back into Emergence or better stated perhaps, into "Emergency." Deep love and being exposed to Character Modeling as I discussed in our Introduction chapter can also be an influencer for elevating our Introspection, and hopefully, those who become seasoned *Travelers Within* will provide the kind of mentoring that members of our society need in order to access their inner goodness and greatness.

Victoria - Chapter Statement: I entered the Introspection Phase in my early twenties and it radically shifted my entire concept of the role I play in my own life. Having been raised with the belief that God had every moment of my life planned out, I had never been taught the concepts of choice and consequence or self-responsibility. Learning how to analyze my life circumstance and introspect on them and be responsible for my choices, was very liberating and empowering. The only thing I did not think to use at the time was a notebook for recording my introspections. I did not start to utilize writing until about ten years ago and wish I would have started many years earlier. I think it would have helped me not fall into some of the pitfalls I fell into over the years. I am thrilled to see you suggesting it as part of the exercises as I have found writing to be so incredibly helpful in my present phase of the journey.

CHAPTER 5: LIBERATION

Knowing Our Self Beyond Our self

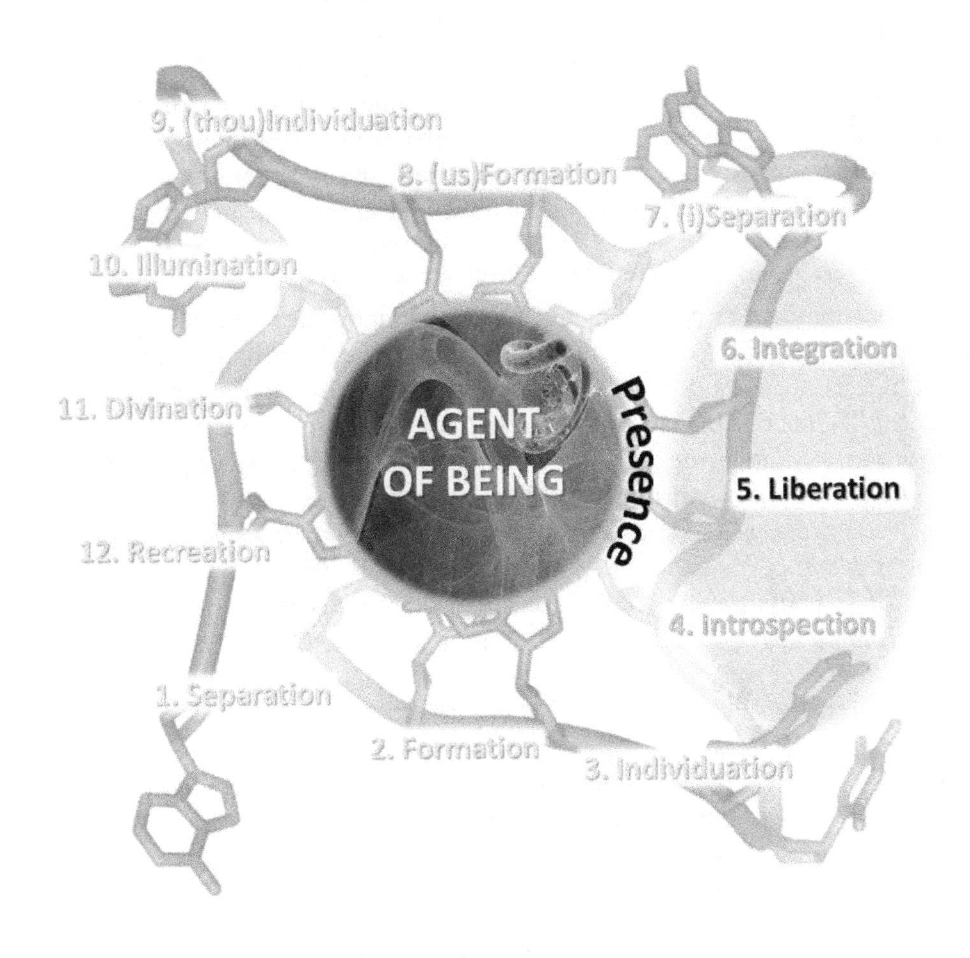

"Liberation exists . . . and You will never be liberated." — Ramana Maharshi

Liberation, the Fifth Phase of Presence is about awakening to being at Choice, self-aware and actively taking responsibility for the meanings we assign to our life's circumstances. Within the expansive space of *Liberation* we open to embracing the deeper flow of emotions and feelings moving within us, how they affect us and how they influence others. In this Phase, we're willing to risk our ego and self-image and tell the truth about our detrimental behaviors, and we're more dedicated to surrendering our need for self-importance than to protecting it. *Liberation* is also about letting go of our attachment to being at the effect of our circumstances, at the mercy of others, or victims of the world at large. There is a positive synergy that arises from *Liberation* in that it fosters exponential growth within us, and that growth inspires new curiosity and interest. In other words, the more we exercise Choice and take responsibility for our life, the more self-aware and fully realized we become.

"You" Will Never be Liberated

Liberation is about letting go of our need for self-importance and our ego's insistence on believing that it alone resides at the center of the universe, rather than the reality of being only a small part of the universe's expanse. Maharishi had it right when he wisely declared, *"You will never be liberated."* While this may be confusing at first, once we understand that *Liberation* is not the freeing *of* you, but rather the freeing *from* you, his declaration makes perfect sense.

Liberation is not a token reward or merit badge we somehow earn by working on ourselves. Rather, it's a very arduous and deeply humbling process of surrendering our ego-self; all that we thought we were, believe we are or hope we will someday be . . . and doing so with no expectations of something better or different replacing it. So rather than gaining something, *Liberation* is about letting something go. It's about ending the Hollywood movie storyline that permeates the character called "You."

Once we liberate ourselves from the final vestiges of who we have known ourselves to be, who we truly are, finally has the room within our psyche to become present. The ego-self is what I call a "space hog" in that it takes up all the empty "theater seats of Self" with its big rump, leaving nowhere for anyone other than itself to sit. If the chair reserved for our Agent of Being is occupied, the best it can do is stand patiently beside us and try to get our attention at some point during the movie.

The Ego-Self And Our Terrain of Mobility

I want to clarify that the *Liberation* process, the total surrender of "You" does not mean giving up your identity, or that all of your character traits will suddenly vanish. Nor will you be moved to give away all of your belongings, donate all of your money to charity, or take up residence in a cave. Rather, the surrender work has to do with freeing ourselves from the "ego-self" we have for so long been attached to so that we are able to gain access to our Higher Self and Agent of Being.

As aware as most dedicated personal growth travelers are, and as much time as we invest in ourselves, in our personal development, our physical well-being, spiritual maturity, in broadening our horizons, healing our past wounds, opening our minds and even accessing our hearts, there remains a fundamental aspect of *Liberation* that eludes many of us. This is so because it's too close in, so close in fact that we can't see how to deal with it because we are seeing from the very terrain we need to free ourselves from. Think about how a bird experiences the air they fly in, or how a fish might experience the water they swim in. For them, their terrain of mobility, their conscious environment is so close in that they are unable to distinguish themselves from it as they move through it. The same goes for liberating ourselves from the confines of our ego's terrain.

One might surmise that we humans, being so high up the species chain would have an edge over birds and fish; that possessing the higher faculty of Self-Awareness would somehow elevate our level of insight, but this proves not to be the case. In fact, Self-Awareness, (while remaining the main goal we are striving for within the *Stage of Presence)* if not carefully navigated, can actually add to the obscurity. This is so because the more aware we become of our "self," or who we think we are, what our ego-self wants and doesn't want, what we believe and don't believe, what we are willing or unwilling to experience, the core values we identify with, and the ways we see the world all contribute to the obscurity around the process of our *Liberation.*

Revisiting The Dynamics of Our "Box"

Our Primary Decision and its insidious structuring of our Box is the source of most of the obscurity as it's the culprit feeding our ego-self. As we've previously discussed, the Box is an all-encompassing emotionally-charged medium, much like turbulent air to the bird and tidal water to the fish. It's an automatic mechanism that imprisons us inside an invisible tomb-like structure that we can't see but surely can feel the effects of when our Box gets reactivated. As we've learned, our Box is designed to defend against any future incoming threats, be them real or merely perceived. The problem is that it not only reduces the likelihood of threats and abuses, it also restricts all life experiences, both negative and positive. The result is a well-protected, yet profoundly diminished capacity to be present to the spontaneous nature of life. Not only does the Box restrict our incoming life experiences, but it also diminishes our outward expressions, our creativity, capacity to love, share, be open to life, and most of all, to contribute who we really are into the world-at-large.

The process of *Liberation* is about engaging in an exodus of the ego-self in which we choose to vacate the lower terrain within our psyche that contains our "I, Me, My" based material. The experiences that arise as we make this epic migration are profound, challenging and liberating. So will you be able to succeed at this exodus and free yourself from the confines of your Box? To be honest, it's up to you. The work of *Liberation* is what I call "an inside job." You are the only one who can embrace yourself to your depths. And you are the only one who can face your inner terrain, your invisible conclusions, your fears, loves, joys, and losses. What I do know with certainty is that if you're willing to open yourself, feel into your heart, be willing to be vulnerable, curious and humble, you will indeed be able to do the needed work of *Liberation.*

My job is to be your guide, to assist you with ideas, principles, examples, questions, and encouragement so you can travel into the depths and migrate your way to your own inner heights. *(A/N: Because the author/reader relationship is a one-way process of me writing and you reading, there's no way to have an engaging dialogue. I can only influence you through this literary "menu" and hope that you will engage fully in the actual "meal" on your own. I'm going to trust that if you've stayed with it this long, you have the dedication and resolve needed to do the work. I have continued faith in you and trust that you will succeed.)*

As a way to provide you with more heart-opening experiences and insights, I'm going to recount three case studies from my public workshops for you. Each one illuminates a different Box, a different set of circumstances and a different *Liberation* process. My recounting will be just as these processes occurred, but a bit abbreviated because it would require a chapter per case study if I included all the details, wild goose chases, blind alleys, and nuances. Since most Boxes revolve around the three key issues of *control, abandonment, and violation,* I've selected examples from these three categories. *(A/N: You may want to refer back to chapter 3's Exploration And Integration Guide and review the Ten Box Categories I listed there as a way to further ground yourself before moving on.)*

Before we dive into the case studies, I want to point something out about the nature of the Box that may not have become fully apparent yet. Invariably there is a deep dilemma of dualistic oppositional forces, a "push/pull" dynamic woven into every Box, (except for the *"Non-Being"* Boxes which are unilaterally singular). This is so because those involved in the initial Box casting process are usually primary relationships in our lives, like our mother, father, siblings and other relatives and friends with whom we were initially bonded. This positive bond mixes with the negative energy of fear during our primary incidents to produce the dualisms I'm referring to. Let's review the case studies now and see how this dynamic plays out.

(A/N: This is a big section, so please remember to breathe, take frequent breaks and perhaps do some cathartic journaling as you venture into the most intimate and deeply stirring terrain of these three remarkable people. Throughout the years I have come to absolutely l-o-v-e the process work of Liberation, but at the same time, it can be terribly challenging because of the depth of tragedy, abuse, and neglect many children endure as they grow up within their families of origin. Bless all the children, and bless you for your willingness to venture in so intimately and deeply as you are about to do.)

Case Study #1 – The Control Box: "Go Away! / I Need You!"

Carol was in her late 40's, married twice previously and had three teenage children when she participated in the *LifeChoice Intensive.* Her two daughters were with her current husband, and her son was from a previous marriage. While her current marriage was stable, she and her husband were experiencing more frequent arguments, and the troubles between them were becoming more upsetting as time went on. Carol's husband refused to attend the program but promised that if he saw "big changes" in her he would consider it. While I suspected he had major control issues of his own to deal with, his biggest complaint about Carol was that she would "pick fights" when she didn't get things her way. She would then emotionally withdraw and punish him for days on end. Carol saw it differently of course, but for her, it was important to do something positive about a negative situation, so she chose to focus on her issues rather than on his.

Carol's goals were to get to the bottom of her controlling tendencies and her pattern of withdrawing and pushing those she loved away when she felt unappreciated or uncared for. She also wanted to re-experience the depth of love for her husband she once had and wanted a better relationship with her children, particularly with her son, whom she was having huge problems with because of his use of marijuana and bouts of anger towards family members.

Reviewing her pre-work it became clear that Carol's relationship with her mother appeared to be good, but her father was a different story. Her parents got divorced when she was five years old. Her father went on to start a whole new family, but her mother remained alone, raising her daughter on her own. Carol had been estranged from her father for years as an adult and kept her children away from him for most of their youth due to what she considered to be verbally abusive treatment towards them. Carol was an only child, and her mother was a stay-at-home-mom. During the first five years of her life, her father was a traveling salesman and was on the road during the week, coming home only on the weekends. According to Carol, when he was home, he spent more time drinking and watching sports than spending quality time with her or their family.

Just prior to doing her *Liberation* work, Carol confided in me that she was afraid she would not succeed in finding her Box because she had almost no memories of her early childhood, other than those her mother recounted to her. She also voiced that she didn't feel "damaged" and that perhaps this process was not for her, even though she saw some patterns in her life that needed to change. I assured her that she was in the right place, to "trust the process" and try and set her fears and doubts aside. This seemed to help, but she was still visibly anxious and her posture in the course room revealed that the closer she got to doing her work, the more anxious and guarded she became. That's not unusual, and not a problem as protective behaviors such as these are to be expected as part of the Box's evasive control mechanism. Keep in mind that the Box has been in control for many years and it isn't prone to being "liberated." It's like asking a dictator to kindly step down and relinquish their tyrannical command without a fight.

It was late in the evening, and everyone was exhausted from the previous Box work done by other participants. Carol raised her hand and announced that she was terrified and wanted to "get it over with." After some counsel that it wasn't about *getting over anything* but more *about getting under everything,* she calmed down and agreed to proceed. She closed her eyes and everyone shifted their bodies in their chairs, somehow knowing this wasn't going to be an easy process.

Two hours into the inner journey work Carol was no further along than when she started. She felt numb and could not seem to locate any incidents that might lead to her Primary Decision. The participants were feeling uneasy and her Box was closing in around her, forcing her controlling behaviors into exactly how they play out in her relationships when things get tight; withdrawn and closed up. We turned the overhead lights off as a way to ease the intensity of the process and I asked her what she was feeling in her body. *(A/N: This is a very good way to start identifying "fragments of memories" as our body holds the emotional charge of past events in various locations and within our Chakra centers. This is important for you to keep in mind as you do your own inner journeying and Uncasting work.)*

Carol suddenly keeled over as if to vomit. We got her a paper sack, and I asked her to feel her way into the center of the sickness in her body. (Using that specific word "sickness" was intentional on my part). "Where exactly in your body do you feel the sickness Carol?" "In my stomach." "Ok, now what have you been stomaching all these years that is making you so sick?" "My father, I'm sick of how he treated my mom and me!" "He doesn't care about us." "All he wants to do is drink and watch TV." "Alright Carol, please recall a time when he didn't care about you and you were sick about it." Silence, silence, "It was my birthday, I was going to be six and he said he would come to my party, but he didn't come!"

"Ok, now very slowly recall exactly where you were when you found out he wasn't coming." "I was sitting on the living room couch and Mom was next to me . . . she was on the phone with Daddy." "Mommy's face got very sad and she started crying." "What's wrong Mommy?" "Carol, your father isn't going to be here for your birthday tomorrow, I'm so sorry honey." Carol started crying uncontrollably in the workshop as well as in her memory image. "Carol, right there what did you decide?" Silence, silence, silence . . . and then out of her mouth came, "If you're not coming Daddy, then you just go away . . . forever!" Everyone in the workshop sighed with hope. And while it seemed like the right decision, something told me there was an earlier incident, especially since Carol's parents had divorced a year prior to her sixth birthday.

"Alright Carol, I'm so sorry your Daddy didn't come to your birthday party." "Now, I want to ask that you recall an earlier similar incident in which you wanted your Daddy to "just go away forever." "Take whatever comes to you and don't worry if nothing comes, it's alright." Silence, silence, silence . . . and then she started weeping uncontrollably, gasping for air. "Where are you Carol and how old are you?" "I'm in my bed listening to Mommy and Daddy yelling at each other, and I'm four, I think because I have my Teddy with me." "Ok hold onto your Teddy and tell me what happens next." "I get out of the bed and go to the doorway . . . Daddy has a suitcase and he's pointing his finger at Mommy saying he's leaving and never coming back!" "I run over to him and throw my arms around his legs . . . Daddy, please don't leave! We need you! We love you! Please, please!" "Get away from me and go to your mother, she will take care of you from now on!" Silence, silence, silence . . . and I probe for the decision, "What did you say to yourself Carol, right in that moment?" ***"Daddy just go away forever then . . . and I'll go away from you forever too!"*** There it was, Carol's initial Primary Decision in all its vivid intensity.

Carol wept for a time integrating what she had decided and then in a moment of *Liberation* she suddenly perked up in her chair, opened her eyes and declared, "So that's why I have been such a stinker all these years!" "I get it now!" "Every man in my life since my father has played right into my Box!" "Any time I felt unloved I would withdraw so I wouldn't get hurt by them leaving me." "And my son . . . oh my God, I can clearly see how I've pushed him away!" I gently suggested a slight adjustment . . . "No Carol, your Box pushed him away, who you are at your core loves your son, just like you love your husband . . . and even your father." *(A/N: This is a risky extension, but in this case, she broke into tears nodding in agreement and as she did, it delivered her to her Liberation. Carol opened her eyes and beamed with an inner light that had been missing since about her sixth Birthday.)*

After the program, Carol's life totally transformed, as did her relationship with her husband and her son. Her husband registered for the next workshop and is our next case study to explore. Carol's son was too young to attend, (our age requirement at the time was 20) but he entered counseling and last time I checked, he had stopped smoking pot and was making positive movement in therapy. Carol's relationship with her father didn't transform for some time, but within a few years I learned through correspondence that they had a loving reconciliation . . . at her fiftieth Birthday party.

Case Study #2 – The Abandonment Box: "You Left Me / No One Loves Me!"

Carol's husband, Mark sent in his pre-work and the challenges he faced were a perfect counterpart to his wife's issues. *(A/N: This is very common. In fact, the Box residing within most spouses unconsciously seeks out and finds a partner with a counter-Box that fits into its reactive dynamics like a hand in a glove, or like two adjacent jigsaw puzzle pieces. The "Couple's Box Clearing" sessions I do are a way for those who are dedicated to rising above the detrimental dynamics of their clashing Boxes to get some relief and healing.)*

In his pre-work, Mark listed a number of patterns that were recurring in his relationships and life. He had been married once prior to Carol, and it ended badly when he caught his then-wife having an affair. When Mark confronted her about it, she abruptly announced that she was leaving him, packed her bags and walked out of his life. This pattern was repeated numerous times in his earlier relationships. Whenever he would fall in love with a woman, she would somehow let him down, leave him or violate him in some painful way. And likewise, any time Carol withdrew from him, Mark would get triggered into his abandonment insecurities and would predictably act in kind by withdrawing himself as well. When he and Carol "went at it" he would always say, "You don't really love me, because if you did you wouldn't treat me this way!" This specific phrase was useful when it came time for his *Liberation* process. You can bet the reactive phrases we use in our present-day interactions can be traced back to an original time when we first cast our Box into existence.

The other important piece of information was about Carol's son Jason, Mark's step-son. Their relationship was bad right from the start. Jason was quick to remind Mark that he was not his father and to "butt out of his life." For Mark, this was a cutting rejection that triggered him into withdrawal in which he would not bother to seek common ground between them. And when it got really bad between them, Mark would pressure Carol to make Jason show respect . . . which triggered Carol, which triggered Jason, which triggered Mark . . . which triggered everybody's Box in the family.

It was Mark's turn to do his work, and to my delight, he was actually eager to engage. His whole attitude changed when Carol came home after her *Liberation* work and apologized for her behaviors and asked that they start anew and bring love back into their relationship. Observing Mark in the workshop as others did their work, I noticed that any time a participant felt all alone, or during their closed-eye process called out while in a memory sequence for someone to comfort them, he would get agitated and pull on his left thumb with the fingers and thumb of his right hand. *(A/N: While this may seem like nothing, it's actually a documented insecurity behavior infant's display when they are left alone for any period of time. The adult version is "wringing our hands.")*

Mark's *Liberation* process was in the morning so everyone was wide awake and ready to venture in. Within the first hour, we'd identified two childhood incidents that had to do with abandonment. One was in second-grade when Mark was accidentally left behind during a field trip to a local museum. He was eventually found and fortunately rejoined with his classmates before the bus left. While certainly concerning, the incident didn't carry enough charge to be the primary material. The other incident was closer to home having to do with Mark being dropped off at pre-school and him panicking when he realized his mother had left him with strangers. While the incident was frightening, again it wasn't primary material. *(A/N: How you will know you have reached the terrain in which your Box was first cast is that if you scan the images associated with the incident and your experience prior to it occurring is a sense of comfort and peace, you're there, if not, you still have deeper unsettling terrain to back your way into. Why this is so is that prior to the Box, peace, and ease is usually our native state.)*

Three hours into the closed-eye process we hit a roadblock, and it seemed like there was nowhere to go. We kept circling around the two secondary incidents and couldn't seem to venture deeper into Mark's psyche. The Box is responsible for these delays in that when it realizes it's about to be exposed, it pulls every trick it has to avoid it from happening. One of its best tricks is, "I don't know how or what to do, I'm trying as hard as I can, but I just can't do it." Copping incapability over unwillingness is a standard ploy for the Box, and anyone who buys it, including the occupant within it, is foolish. Who we are is far more capable than we let on to be. Why? Because if we acknowledged our capability we would no longer have a convenient excuse for remaining small, at the effect of, and ineffective in our lives. *(A/N: It's Bucky's "Trimtab" principle I shared with you in our Introduction chapter. I can't tell you how many hundreds of times I have relied on this deep wisdom, and it has always, always assisted those who have fooled themselves into being small and incapable to press themselves beyond their self-induced limitations.)*

In Mark's case, "not knowing what to do" was actually a key to accessing his deeper abandonment terrain. Infants who are neglected or abandoned feel helpless in that they don't know what to do as they struggle to survive in a confusing and ominous situation. *(A/N: Remember that infants always magnify everything and make every problem and fear they encounter all about them. Being left alone not only evokes helplessness for infants, but it also evokes self-judgment as in, "something must be wrong with me if no one is here with me." The only course of action to take with Mark was to head directly into the helplessness and magnify it to a deeper degree of hopelessness until the elevated concern motivated him to dive deeper.)*

"Mark, you feel helpless and don't know what to do, yes?" "Yes." "Ok, let's go with that .

. . perhaps there is nothing that can be done for you." "Perhaps we can't help you . . . could the Box have too tight a grip on you?" "You're giving up on me?" As he spoke it his body began to quiver. "No, we're here with you, but only you can do the work, it's an inside job, remember?" "Alright, but what can I do?" "Nothing . . . there is nothing you can do Mark, you are alone and even calling out is hopeless, isn't it?" Suddenly he curled up in his chair and began weeping and mumbling like a baby. "Mark, is anybody answering or coming?" "No, no one is coming, I'm all alone." "Where are you . . . look around you, what do you see?" "I'm in my crib wearing a blue jumpsuit . . . it's the one with bumpy bottoms on the feet." "Where is your mother?" "She's not here . . . where is she?" "Call out for her Mark . . . does she answer?" Silence, silence, silence . . . "No, she's gone!" ***"She left me . . . I'm all alone and she doesn't love me!"***

Mark suddenly opened his eyes, "Oh my God . . . my whole life I've been afraid of being left alone!" "That's incredible!" "Every relationship I've ever had fits this pattern, and every time I felt abandoned and couldn't understand what I had done wrong . . . but I did nothing wrong, I was just a baby!" "Yes, Mark and what about your mother?" "Did she do anything wrong?" "She was always there for me as a child, she was probably just busy and didn't realize I was so frightened . . . so no, she wasn't wrong either . . . but boy, every woman I've ever been with since sure as hell has been wrong!" The other participants in the course room burst out in laughter in response to that statement!

In putting this couple's two Boxes together, it became crystal clear why Carol and Mark had such a troubling marriage. Her Box being, ***"Daddy just go away forever then . . . and I'll go away from you forever too!"*** And his being, ***"She left me . . . I'm all alone and she doesn't love me!"*** It doesn't take a brain surgeon to figure out why they were at such odds with one another. *(A/N: For those in a marriage or a committed relationship you can bet that you and your mate have Boxes that fit together much like Carol and Mark's. While it's not actually funny, I call it the "Couple's Boxing Match," in which both partners invariably lose.)*

Violation And Molestation Background Information

Our last case study is one that is sadly very common, more so for young girls than young boys, but it unfortunately happens to children of both genders. Most people do not realize that over 30% of all children have endured some form of sexual violation. (I actually believe the statistic is higher, as molest often is unreported. My estimate, based on working with thousands of attendees over the years is that over half of all children are sexually violated in some way before they reach the age of 18.) It's also a statistical fact that 95% of all molesters were molested themselves, revealing the sad reality that it's a learned behavior. Furthermore, molestation is often a "family legacy dysfunction," meaning that acts of sexual violation are passed down from generation to generation. And finally, sexual violations always imprint a "molest marker" meaning that those who have been molested are easily identified by prospective perpetrators in that they appear like "deer in the headlights" of their radar screen.

There are three roles involved in the way molestation unfolds; the *Victim*, the *Perpetrator,* and the *Corroborator*. Let's examine each role in detail before we dive into the case study as it will help you understand the dynamics of sexual abuse within the family structure if you are not familiar with them.

The *Victims* are our innocent children. Not a single child who has ever been abused sexually or otherwise "deserved it." Children are totally innocent and play no part in the violation other than as targets. It's important to understand that sexual abuse at a young age results in "rips" and "tears" in the fabric of the psyche. Like torn clothing, the continuity of the fabric is interrupted and what is underneath becomes exposed. But also like a torn shirt can be mended, the psyche can recover and will function without dire consequences depending on the extent of the violation. In extreme cases, molestation can result in a portion of the terrain of the psyche to "split off" into islands of separate identity, a condition known as "multiple personality disorder." In less extreme cases, the identity is semi-divided into a public self and a more secretive private self; much like a watery moat surrounds and protects a castle from invaders. In all cases, *Liberation* is still a possibility, but it takes a little more work to reintegrate the ego-self before surrendering it up. This is so because if the ego-self is not in one piece prior to letting it go, "fragments" or "slivers" remain lodged within the psyche, much like how a shattered thumbnail might grow back in incongruent pieces rather than as a whole and healthy nail.

The *Perpetrators* are typically close family members such as fathers, step-fathers, grandfathers, uncles, older siblings, cousins, close friends, and family confidants. (Females can also be perpetrators but the statistics are quite low.) Perpetrators mark their targets by feelings of instability, self-doubt, self-criticism and weak boundaries on the part of their victim. While the tendency is to demonize these perpetrators, the reality is that most of them were victims of sexual abuse themselves and are driven to unconsciously act out similar violations that happened to them as children. There are some "professional perpetrators" who are truly evil, and while they too were most likely sexually abused as children, any degree of understanding or compassion is tough to offer up to them.

The *Corroborators* are almost always the mothers, step-mothers, and sometimes grandmothers or legal guardians of the victims. Their role is to leave the victim unprotected by "looking the other way" as the perpetrator sets up and carries out the violations. It's not that corroborators consciously expose their children to molest, but rather that they are driven by unconscious forces residing deep within a section of their own violated inner terrain. To understand this dynamic, it's important to realize that just as with the perpetrators, most corroborators were also sexually abused themselves as children, or they witnessed someone's boundaries being violated. Having been violated without ever "traveling within" to liberate oneself from abused inner terrain, the tendency is to avoid and deny any circumstances that carry the molestation marker. One of the most unfortunate outcomes of this mechanism of denial is that the victim will often hold a grudge against the corroborator for not believing them when they tried to expose the violation, as we will see in our final case study.

Case Study #3 – Violation And Molest Box: "I'm Bad / I Deserve To Be Hurt"

Theresa was in her mid-thirties when she participated in her *Liberation* work. She was a single mom, living alone and raising two boys who were ten and twelve years of age. In her pre-work, it was clear that Theresa had a rocky relationship with both her parents, more so however with her mother than with her father. She also had major issues of betrayal in her intimate relationships in which she played the role of both victim and perpetrator. Additionally, Theresa had very low self-esteem and as she put it, she felt like "damaged goods." Her divorce was due to having an affair with the long-time best friend of her ex-husband; a very painful end to an eight-year marriage. What comes around goes around showed up in two of her three rocky relationships after her divorce, when both partners were found to be unfaithful to her. The other more concerning pattern was that these men would verbally abuse her and then over time, escalate their abuse to threats and finally to physical violence. *(A/N: Theresa came to the workshop with a bruised left cheek, claiming it was "just an accident." It's understandable why women want to hide the abuse they endure but at the same time, as a professional I must say that it is unacceptable to not squarely address acts of violence and abuse.)*

"Alright Theresa, are you ready to do your work?" "Yes, I've learned so much from others so far." "But . . . everyone is so wonderful and so great that I feel kind of intimidated . . . like I'm not good enough to be part of this group." *(A/N: What not to do is to try and convince her that she is good enough, but rather to simply note her self-judgment and reflect it back to her so she can see it directly. The reason for this is that no matter how much we try to boost people up, their Box is totally invested in tearing it all down as a way to prove just how "bad" and "unworthy" they really are.)*

"Can you tell me what is 'not good' about you Theresa? You used the phrase, 'damaged goods' in your pre-work, remember?" "Yes, for longer than I can remember I've felt less than others, like I'm bad, a misfit and disconnected like some kind of alien." "I constantly compare myself to everyone, especially other women." "And how do you measure up to other women?" Theresa, put her hands over her face as she replied, "Not as pretty, not as thin, not as happy, not as smart, not as accomplished, and not with a handsome, well-to-do man . . . that's how."

"And how does that make you feel Theresa?" "Like shit!" she snapped back. "Alright, I'm going to ask you a personal question now and I want you to take your time answering, ok?" "Ok." "Do you have any memories of having been abused as a child?" "You don't mean sexually do you because I can't imagine it happened to me." *(A/N: This reaction is almost always a sign of defending some deeper violation that is lodged unconsciously in the psyche.)* "Not necessarily, but are you willing to explore with me what might have happened to you that could account for why you have such low self-esteem?" She nodded her head tentatively. "Ok, thank you . . . please recall a time when you felt like shit and were being bad . . . and take whatever image comes and try not to edit or force anything." Silence, silence, silence . . .

"I remember being with our next-door neighbor, Johnny at his house." "He said he wanted to show me something I would like in his basement." "I was eight then I think, and he was about ten." "Ok, so let's take it slowly, please recount the incident from the start . . . what's the first thing you remember?" "He told me to lay down on the wooden coffee table over in the corner . . . I did and then he lifted my dress and started touching me down there." "Alright, and was that uncomfortable for you, Theresa?" "No, It was ok . . . I was a little cold, but it was ok." *(A/N: Any time sexual explorations at a young age don't trigger fear, embarrassment or concern in the victim you can bet they've already acclimated their psyche to being violated and are emotionally numb to it in the future as a result.)*

"You are doing fine, so what happens next Theresa?" "I remember his mom catching us and her telling me I was a 'bad girl' and that I needed to go home." "And did you?" "Uh-huh, and I remember feeling bad like it was my fault that Johnny got into trouble." "Alright, let's go deeper now . . . please recall an earlier incident when someone was touching you down there and you felt bad like it was your fault."

Silence, silence, silence . . . "I don't see anything, just darkness." "That's alright Theresa, the way this works, especially around violations having to do with sex or violence is that the images will come in fragments, like broken shards of glass" "Why do they appear that way?" "Because this part of the psyche experienced trauma, much like dropping a mirror on a stone floor . . . so now peer into the darkness Theresa, look for a splinter of glass." "Oh, yes, I see something in the distance, but I have more of a feeling about it." "What kind of feeling do you have?" "I feel sick to my stomach." "Ok, stay with it Theresa and let's go right into the center of the sickness . . . where exactly is it in your stomach?" "It's lower, below my belly button . . . it feels hot and icky." "You're doing fine, now what images are associated with the hot icky feeling?" "I think I'm making this up, it can't be real!" "Theresa, it doesn't matter if it's real or not right now, it's just what's there, so please move into it and tell me what you see." She put her hands up and covered her mouth, "I feel a big rough hand between my legs and I see . . . I see a penis and it's so big . . . I'm scared!" "It's ok, breathe . . . now, where are you exactly?" "I'm in my bed at the house on 14th street and my stepdad is in my room . . . he's standing next to my bed with his pants down." "And how old are you Theresa?" "I'm small, about four I think." "Now stay present, keep breathing and slowly move the images forward like you are watching a film strip, one frame at a time."

Everyone in the course room was stunned and in horror . . . "What does he do next Theresa?" "His hand, his hand is on the back of my head pushing me forward . . . Oh noooo, don't do that Daddy!" "It's ok, you survived it then, you'll survive it now Theresa, you are doing fine . . . stay with it." "Ok, but did this really happen?" "No, it can't be . . . but I see him . . . I even see the scar where he had his appendix taken out . . . and I see what he's doing to me!" "Theresa, we don't make up these kinds of details . . . just tell me what happens next please." "I can't breathe!" "Take it out, it's too big . . . I'm choking!" "What is t-h-a-t . . . it's hot and slimy in my mouth, take it out!" "He tells me that 'I wanted it' and that if I tell Mommy I will be in big trouble." She breaks down in gut-wrenching tears and I immediately ask her, "Right there Theresa, what did you say to yourself?" . . . ***"I'm a really bad girl and it's all my fault!"*** "Alright Theresa, where are you now?" "It's all quiet . . . I'm up in the corner of the room looking down on myself." "Good, very good, you left your body as the molestation happened . . . that is exactly what you needed to do, do you know why?" "Yes, it protected me, I could get away from him." "Absolutely, you did just the right thing by getting yourself away from him . . . what it means is that only your body was molested and that you were untouched." "Who you are is pure just like you always were. It's only your Box that's bad." Suddenly Theresa popped out of her Box and everyone in the course room burst into joy. "Holy shit! I'm not damaged goods, and I never was damaged goods!" "That's right Theresa, you are pure, untouched and as beautiful as you were when you first arrived in this world." As this powerful revelation sunk in, Theresa covered her face with her hands and started crying uncontrollably. All the participants got up and ran to her and circled around her, holding her, and telling her how much they loved and admired her. There wasn't a dry eye in the room.

(A/N: Theresa's Liberation process took a bit more time to decompress the trauma she experienced, as well as to provide support for the other participants who got triggered during her work. How deeply sad these kinds of violations are! I've facilitated hundreds of them over the years, but every time I witness them it devastates me. If there is one issue alone that negatively impacts our well-being for years to come, it is definitely sexual abuse. It's a massive dysfunctional "secret" all across the world that needs to be addressed squarely. Also, it's very common that molestation victims or victims of extreme physical abuse will separate out from their bodies and find a safe place to hide. The inner terrain of the psyche actually splits into two or more segments much like an earthquake fault line divides the landscape. These splits or tears eventually heal, but the identity often gets trapped in two or more separate places causing a number of personality disorders . . . disorders that the victim can successfully liberate themselves from by doing the work I've illuminated in these case studies.)

Theresa came out of the workshop shaken, but free of her pattern of self-loathing. She also ended her abusive relationships and committed to never allow perpetrators into her life again. The one thing that posed the biggest challenge for her was confronting her mother. Shortly after the molestation, Theresa told her mother all the details of what happened. Basically, her mother said that her stepfather would "never do such a thing," and that she was "making it all up," (which is partially why she was so doubtful prior to and during her process). The violations continued until Theresa was old enough to be taken seriously, in which she threatened to tell her teachers at school if he didn't stop. To date Theresa's relationship with her mother remains distant, but not for lack of effort on her part; her mother remained in denial and refused to discuss it further.

This case study, along with the previous two examples illuminates some intense inner terrain. While your childhood circumstances may have been different and the threats you faced may have been less or more severe than Carol, Mark or Theresa's, the important takeaway is in gaining greater clarity about how to traverse the slippery slope of your Primary Decision. I have worked with cases much more severe than these three, and I can say with absolute certainty that no matter how challenging your history was, or how threatened you may have been, your human spirit and your Agent of Being is profoundly resilient and can rise up above any and all the abuse you may have ever endured, or ever will encounter in your life.

♦♦♦

Liberation From The Ego-Self And The Power of Choice

In each of the three case studies, we witnessed the *Liberation* process in action. For Carol, it was about freeing herself from the need to control her intimate relationships so she wouldn't get hurt. For Mark, it was about letting go of his insecurities regarding being abandoned. And Theresa liberated herself from the sickness of molest and self-loathing. In all cases, no matter what the circumstances may have been, the work is about ending the story called "You," and surrendering yourself up to a vaster space in which who you are is no longer ego-based but instead Agent-based. Our Agent of Being is orders of magnitude more vast than the familiar identity of "You/I." Even though "You/I," experiences *Liberation* when we emerge from the Box, as I've mentioned, the ego-self still exists as a permanent presence within our inner terrain, but through the *Liberation* process we no longer tend to wander into our "danger zones" or dramatize the decisions we've cast in our past.

What makes Primary Decisions so devastating is the combination of fear, negative emotions and the act of making a definitive decision that further dramatizes the dynamic of *Separation* dwelling at our core. The word *"decision"* comes from the French root, *"decider,"* or *"to kill the alternative."* Much like the French guillotines of old that separated the victim's head from their torso, so too does making a decision cut off our options . . . and in this case, the option to exercise our Power of Choice. Unlike a decision, Choice is about the ability to select freely and after consideration. Think of Choice as being an extraordinary capability belonging to your Agent of Being, and a decision as a detrimental ego-self artifact originating from the *First Stage of Emergence.*

It's important to understand that the Box is an ego-based decision-making machine invested in proving how powerless we are, gathering evidence at every turn so that we stay small and under its control. Here is *the* most crucial insight about the entire *Liberation* process - *Those who have concluded that they are powerless and at the effect of their negative circumstances forfeit their ability to transform their negative circumstances into powerful forward moving choices.*

Revisiting "Choosing To Be The Chooser"

If you recall, I introduced the notion of *"Choosing to be the Chooser"* in chapter one and promised to explore it in greater detail. As I previously mentioned, the "joining" process the self undergoes when we first cast our Primary Decision is one in which we lose the power to Choose from a place of freedom. This is so because once we join with a detrimental Box, it not only serves as a protective barrier that restricts all potential incoming threats, it also restricts all our outgoing intentions and expressions. Imagine being encased by a stone structure with high walls. Nothing can enter this fortress, but also nothing can escape it. And because the nature of whatever we chose during the *Stage of Emergence* is typically grounded in fear, it sends us careening into the terrain of *Separation*, thus disabling even further our ability to freely Choose.

If we had initially bonded with love rather than with fear, the outcome would be completely different. Why? Because love is infused with acceptance and recognition, two essential virtues for being the Chooser in our lives. We lose the ability to freely Choose because as a victim, our investment is in remaining at the effect of our circumstances rather than operating from a position of cause.

Rehabilitating our Power to Choose requires not only un-choosing the initial Primary Decision we cast as infants, but it also requires *"Choosing to be the Chooser"* in our adult lives. One does not simply say they are the Chooser, however. It requires making some very challenging lifestyle changes. We must dedicate ourselves to taking full responsibility for our lives, for what we experience, what we assume, and what we conclude and harbor within the heart of our hearts. *(A/N: This final point is of utmost importance as the entire developmental process of coming into accord with our Agent of Being depends on understanding and embracing this crucial distinction. As a way to become familiar with the ways of being a Chooser is brought about in one's life, I will provide you with a list of recommended lifestyle changes and "Agent of Being Practices" outlined in the Exploration And Integration Guide below.)*

Casting our Box for the first time was our initial use of our Power of Choice. While I call it a Primary "Decision," it's actually a Primary "Choice" a reactive choice, that once chosen, entrapped us into the illusion of powerlessness whereby our ability to freely choose gets disabled, until that is, as I mentioned above, we "un-choose" what we initially chose. This reverse action liberates us from the illusion of victimhood. In other words, the moment we stop dramatizing and denying that *we* were the ones who chose to decide what we decided, rather than blaming others or our circumstances, we regain the Power of Choice. *(A/N: Remember the identical twins who each chose something completely different while experiencing the very same tragic circumstances? This tells us that we are the ones who add the devastating meanings to our experiences and not that the circumstances are responsible for the resulting behaviors we act out for years on end.)*

It's important to realize that *Liberation* is just the beginning process of rehabilitating our Power of Choice and gaining access to our Agent of Being. Coming into accord with our Higher Self requires that we have the room within us for it to come about. Once we are "out of the way" as it were, the Power of Choice returns to us as one of our most vital and sacred higher faculties. This is an important distinction for all *Travelers Within* to integrate, one that will take time to fully grasp and live into. But make no mistake, once you *"Choose to be the Chooser"* you will indeed become fully present to the true liberating power of your Agent of Being.

Liberation's Linkage With The Fifth Chakra: Throat Energy

The Fifth Chakra is that of "Throat Energy" or "Vishuddha" which translates to "very pure." The Throat Chakra is located between your collarbone and it radiates down to the center of your heart and up to the center of your eyes. When our Throat Chakra is open and balanced, we become fully present and are free to express ourselves purely and authentically. Much like being "seen" is a key factor in elevating our level of *Presence*, so too is being "heard." The process of becoming present to our powerful faculty of verbal expression brings us one step closer to gaining access to our Agent of Being. When this Higher Self-expression center is closed or unbalanced, we lose access to our true voice and often will either remain silent and acquiesce, or dramatize its opposite by aggressively yelling as a way to overcome the deeper self-suppression that comes with not being liberated. In terms of the linkage with *Liberation*, it's clear that the freedom to speak our truth and let go of the suppression and confining energy of our Box is in alignment with the higher expressive capabilities embodied within our Throat Chakra.

Exploration And Integration Guide

As a way to support you in your *Liberation* process, I've listed below what I call the "Nine Agent of Being Practices." These powerful daily guides are designed to accelerate your ability to master the Power of Choice by experiencing yourself as the Chooser with respect to your daily circumstances. Some of the more advanced practices pertain to our next *Phase of Integration* and even reach into the *Stage of Transcendence,* so take on as many of the practices as you feel you can without getting overwhelmed. Don't worry about following them to the letter, in fact, what you want to be watching for is where you are *not* in alignment with them. For it's only by becoming humbly present to what we are not yet "stretching into" that we can strengthen our muscles of new insight and capability.

1. Developing Personal Impeccability – Being more committed to learning and growing than to protecting our ego's self-image. Impeccability means holding ourselves accountable for being authentic, real, and transparent and for being responsible for the effects we produce in ourselves and others. At its source, impeccability is about consistently demonstrating our espoused beliefs and spiritual aspirations through our tangible actions and behaviors. Impeccability also goes hand-in-hand with practicing being the Chooser in our daily lives.

2. Accepting 100% Responsibility – Our experience of the outer world is a reflection of our inner causality. There are two ways of living – dealing with life's challenges while being at cause, and being at the effect of life's challenges while denying being at cause. 100% causality begins by accepting full responsibility for what arises within our experience and within the circumstances of our daily lives. As we accept causality, we stop being a victim and start living at choice, knowing that we are 100% responsible for our experiences as well as for our outcomes and results.

3. Releasing Self-Importance – Surrendering our need for self-importance opens the way for us to embrace life's extraordinary movement. The more we release our ego-agendas, the need for control, and expectations of what we feel we deserve, the more we move in concert with life's majesty. Releasing Self-Importance is about maintaining a healthy identity, while at the same time surrendering our ego-identity so we can come into accord with our Agent of Being.

4. Embracing Life's Paradoxes – Rather than striving to transcend our humanity and escape into "spiritual bliss," let us embrace the paradox of being both Human and Divine, a way of being in which we are in acceptance of everything from our reverence to our irreverence. By embracing all of who we are, we free ourselves to be authentically Human as well as profoundly Divine.

5. Experiencing Our Experience – To experience life is to open to being fully alive and allowing life to move us, inspire us, humble us, give to us, take from us, and constantly redefine us. We remove ourselves from our experience, and from life's sacred movement when we rationalize, suppress, ignore, minimize, externalize or internalize. The challenge is to stay open to and fully feel the effects of our experience no matter what arises in our space and trust that by doing so we will be delivered to exactly where Spirit and life intend for us to go.

6. Opening And Opening Again – When we feel we've opened, let us open again and again and again. Only when we open to, and surrender to life moment-by-moment do we become a big enough space for life to freely move through us. Opening to our vulnerability is an intentional act that allows for our heart to remain open even during the most vulnerable or challenging of times. As we open to and embrace all that life gives and takes from us, our understandings of compassion, empathy and love exponentially grows and expands and the

Power of Choice becomes ever-more real for us. *(A/N: I want to clarify that opening again and again can include some closures along the way. By realizing that opening and closing is a natural rhythm, we are empowered to strive for an ever-greater capacity to open to all of life's experiences.)*

7. Reclaiming Our Life Energy – Each of us is given a limited amount of life force energy, which we either embrace responsibly or misdirect during the course of our lives. Misdirection of this energy occurs when we fail to act responsibly or avoid being at cause. Whereas reclaiming our life force energy occurs as we accept responsibility for being at cause. This includes coming to terms with, and opening to any and all the pain, sorrow, anger, loss and disconnections that was generated by closing our hearts and acting out the survival-based energies associated with the *Stage of Emergence.*

8. Cultivating Curiosity and Inquiry – Constantly surrendering our assumed reality for the possibility of learning and becoming anew moment-by-moment. This cultivation is about living into the mystery of life's infinite possibilities rather than defending our certainty or our familiar conclusions. The practice includes embracing a "beginner's mind and heart" through being genuinely interested in growing ourselves and opening to the full spectrum of life as well as to the diverse, and often-times contradictory perspectives of others.

9. Devoted To Being of Service – Giving up our personal agendas, selfishness, fears, ego-needs and agendas to a greater practice of servitude – a selfless space of giving that is bigger than our need for comfort, control or certainty. Being of service is a practice in which giving takes precedence over receiving, and offering acceptance and support takes precedence over being right, holding grudges or making others wrong. *(A/N: While the Nine Agent of Being Practices may seem overwhelming in terms of applying them in your daily life, the truth is that if you have done the work up to this point, many of them are already present within you and all you need to do is recognize them and nurture them along. Don't worry too much about how I specifically described the practices. What's important is to grasp the spirit of what each of them addresses and dedicated yourself to moving into them fully.)*

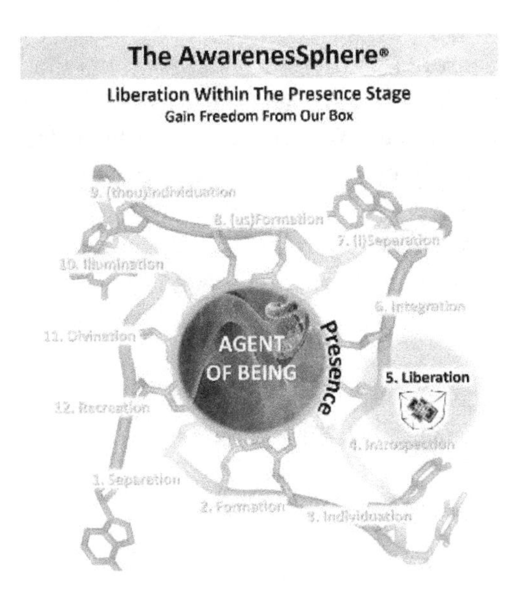

Let's move on by recapping *Liberation, Presence's Fifth Phase of Self-Awareness.* This Phase is about awakening to being at Choice, developing our higher faculty of Self-Awareness and actively taking responsibility for the meanings we assign to our daily life circumstances. *Liberation* is about embracing the deeper flow of emotions and feelings moving within our psyche, how they affect us and how they influence others. We "liberate" ourselves by being willing to risk our self-image, telling the truth about our detrimental behaviors and getting to the bottom of our Primary Decision and the Box it keeps us in.

Liberation is also about letting go of our need for self-importance and our ego's insistence on believing that it alone resides at the center of the universe rather than being a small part of the universe's expanse. Maharishi was right when he wisely declared, "*. . . You will never be liberated.*" Once we understand that *Liberation* is not the freeing *of* you, but rather the freeing *from* you, his quote makes perfect sense. The work to do is about freeing ourselves from the "me" we have for so long been attached to so we are free to access our Agent of Being.

What keeps our ego-self intact for so long is the presence of our Box, a highly structured mechanism that imprisons us inside its invisible tomb. Our Box is designed to defend against incoming threats, and the result is that we are well-protected, but are also left with a reduction in our capacity to be present to the fullness and magnificence of life. Not only does our Box restrict our incoming life experiences, but it also diminishes our outward expressions, our creativity, capacity to love, be open to life, be at Choice, and most of all, to contribute who we really are into the world-at-large.

I shared three case studies from my public workshops, and in each case we witnessed the *Liberation* process in action. For Carol, it was about freeing herself from the need to control her intimate relationships so she wouldn't get hurt. For Mark, it was about letting go of his insecurities regarding being abandoned. And Theresa liberated herself from the sickness of molest and self-loathing. In all cases what makes a Primary Decision so devastating is the combination of fear, negative emotions and the act of making a definitive conclusion that further dramatizes the existence of *Separation* dwelling at our core.

The Box is an ego-driven decision-making machine invested in proving how powerless we are, gathering evidence at every turn so that we stay small and under its control. As I mentioned *the* most crucial insight about the entire *Liberation* process is this . . . *Those who have concluded that they are powerless and at the effect of their negative circumstances forfeit their ability to transform their negative circumstances into powerful forward moving choices.* Our power to choose, and being a positive force in the world returns to us the moment we *"Choose to be the Chooser"* and end our investment in all the reasons why *we can't* choose. ~

In the next chapter, after the Q&A section, we will venture together into *Integration,* the final Phase of *Presence.* Within this sacred high ground, we're going to explore what I call *"The Two Sides of Wholeness,"* a condition in which our opposing Archetypal forces come face-to-face with one another and dance. It's also the Phase where we finally come into full accord with our Agent of Being . . . but only after ascending to a paradoxical plateau that hosts the entire spectrum of diverse characters, from the brightest light of angels to the darkest plight of demons. What an image . . . angels and demons locked arm-in-arm, dancing together high atop *Integration's* paradoxical plateau. Let's get a move on so we don't miss out on any of the festivities!

♦♦♦

Reader's Question & Answer Section (Chapter 5: Liberation)

Allison - Q: Sometimes there is confusion between taking 100% responsibility and those that have been abused, whether sexually or emotionally or physically. For example, someone is just jogging down a road and then gets attacked, or innocent children being molested, or a woman repeatedly attacked by her husband. I get that the choice of the Box is unique to all, but the idea of taking 100% responsibility and forgiving that abuser can be one of the greatest hurdles. Can you explain your process and beliefs around this more?

Val Jon - A: I believe the confusion arises around the definition of "responsibility." There are two main detrimental influencers I want to address. First, is the notion of guilt, blame, and obligation. True responsibility, (the ability to respond) has nothing at all to do with any of these three. Historically, and even still today, women were "responsible" for the sexual and physical abuses committed against them because "they were asking for it" based on the way they were dressed or how they acted. That's not responsibility, it's out-and-out patriarchal blame and abuse. Second, is the New Age hyperbola called "you created your abuse," or "you attracted it to you" in some way. What a huge disservice these misconceptions have been and continue to be.

While I do believe our Box can indeed open us up to repeated detrimental circumstances, compel us to choose partners who possess similar behavioral patterns as our early childhood abusers and blind our better judgment through the extremes of neediness or rigid pride, this does not mean an innocent child or adult has called abuse upon themselves. "100% responsibility" means that we completely and totally own our emotional reactions to what happens to us along with whatever meanings we assign to those happenings, but not that *we caused* them . . . unless we did evoke them as I mentioned above, by acting out unconscious behaviors arising from our inner "danger zones."

Allison - Q: I have found many challenges getting stuck in the feeling of grief and sadness around being violated. What steps support this emotional state? What can one choose to do to then be in the "Experiencing our Experience" and "Opening and Opening Again" if some particular emotion feels unable to change?

Val Jon - A: So many spiritual seekers and self-growth proponents make the mistake of trying to aspire to be open, unconditionally loving and trusting over the top of feelings of mistrust, anger and hurt. The only authentic choice is to open to and experience the unexpressed negative feelings lodged within you, not only those emotions associated with recent violations, but also with the initial similar violations you encountered as a child. There is, however, a very important way of going about resolving these unexpressed emotions.

"Getting stuck" in our feelings is symptomatic of either entertaining a "spiritual bypass," (lying to ourselves about what is really going on under our pretense of "angels and light"), or harboring two opposing emotions at the same time that pull us in opposing directions and cancel each other out, thus causing the "stuckness" we feel. In your case I believe, being violated by someone you trusted and loved, and the deeper feelings of anger and resentment lodged in your inner terrain is what is immobilizing you. Rather than collapsing the two opposing feelings, work with them both, but individually and one at a time. Either open fully to your love for this person all the way to your core until you "experience love's experience" completely . . . or open to your suppressed anger and hurt towards them all the way to your core until you "experience anger's experience totally. Beginning with either one works, and as long as you completely re-experience and express all the emotions associated with both, you will free up your movement forward into the light of height.

Allison - Chapter Statement: In taking responsibility for our lives along with opening to the expression of our authentic selves, becoming "heard," we can then feel liberated from the bond of our Box and how that has dictated our suffering. Embracing that this is part of the whole of the human journey, that everyone has this experience, has freed me from thinking the *"I'm the only one dealing with this kind of suffering"* and *"No one will ever really know me"* mentality.

Anna - Q: While working through the acceptance of responsibility I revisited many choices I made in the past, some out of self-preservation not realizing the impact they would have. How does one overcome the feelings of guilt and regret for circumstances long past with people who are no longer in your life?

Val Jon - A: One of the most fascinating aspects of the human psyche is that it doesn't function within the confines of time and space. In other words, what happened years ago between us and others in a distant location is continuing to happen right now, right here just as it happened then and there. This is why the strong emotions we felt for, or about someone in our past are often just as strong for us in our present experience. Not only this but people's Energetic Essence, (which I explain later on) also remains with us, a kind of pseudo-self-representation of the person we can actually interact with and complete things with. This is good news for Uncasting guilt and regret that we get stuck holding. The way to go about this is to work with a process I provide in chapter 9's *Exploration And Integration Guide* called *"The Empty Chair Exercise."* It's a Gestalt Therapy technique that if done correctly, will free you from all the negative bindings associated with those who are no longer in your life.

Anna - Q: As I integrate and define how my Primary Decision has impacted my life, I find myself feeling out of place within society, as well as people just thinking I'm plain weird. How does one find the balance of others expecting the "old you" and the "real you," which you are now being?

Val Jon - A: As you evolve who you are towards ever-greater dimensions of your authentic Self, your values, preferences, and lifestyle will evolve along with you. This will cause a change in who you bond with and choose to share your life, work and free time with. Those who judge you as being "weird" do not understand what attaining "higher ground" is about or the value of the inner journey. You have three choices, love them and be with them anyway, invite them to join you as a fellow *Traveler Within*, or disconnect from them and move on. I've participated in all three categories and found my groove with them. I'm sure you will as well.

Anna - Chapter Statement: My life has changed so much since reading this book. I've spent many years searching for answers and now I am finding them within me. Learning to accept myself for the person I am becoming and not be defined by my past. I realize that I have the personal choice and responsibility for my future and how I want to spend it. I don't have to remain in the past, reliving the traumas and recreating them because it is what's familiar. Each moment of my life brings me an opportunity for choice and personal responsibility. What pains me more today than ever before, however, is how wounded our collective society is and how much we all need this awareness to make the shift our society so desperately needs.

Antonio - Q: If I allow myself to revisit old traumas, can I use the tools applied here to safely return back into the loving embrace of the Divine?

Val Jon - A: While I can't guarantee your safe return, I can say with absolute conviction that the principles and practices provided in this body of work are about as supportive and effective as any I know of. And, if for some reason they fall short for you, I personally will be there to support you with all the love and care I can bring to bear.

Antonio - Q: Do I speak my authentic truth, or is it my truth for ego validation?

Val Jon - A: I love this question! Some questions are best left unanswered because there is more value that comes from the inquiry than from the answer. This is such a question. By constantly holding this query in your awareness I cannot help but think that your speaking will be more authentic and your authentic truth more self-evident.

Antonio - Chapter Statement: A wonderful reminder that we choose to be liberated or we choose to continue to remain in the cycle of suffering we self-created through our Primary Decision. Many years ago, I was going through a difficult passage revisiting old traumas. I realized, as my breathing was short and labored, that if I chose not to confront the shadow parts of my psyche and simply ignored the difficulty of being present with this painful aspect of myself, that I would be stunted in my own personal growth for many years to come. At that moment, I saw that I had a choice. I saw myself running and never stopping if I chose to ignore this difficult passage. In running, there is the notion of looking for an escape, any easy way out. Then I saw myself confronting this experience with mindfulness of breath, and heart-fullness of unconditional love. I chose to love myself enough to want to break the chains of the past that had kept me bound and fearful. It was difficult, indeed, but I broke through. This was a powerful lesson that empowered me to know that there is nothing the Divine will deliver that I cannot handle.

Cyn - Q: If we do not have a core group of trusted souls to take us down the journey of finding our Box, is there an "at-home" system beyond the 10-year segmenting to help push ourselves to those deep, dark and heart-pounding places of discovery?

Val Jon - A: Short of actually doing the work with a skilled facilitator the only other way to gain access to the incident in which you cast your Box into being is to revisit your early childhood inner terrain often and with a focused intention. Following the steps I have provided and feeling around for slivers of images, or fragments of memories much like shards of broken glass will often trigger more recollections. Also, your dream time can reveal material that may be still suppressed so pay close attention to your dream sequences and dream patterns. As for a group of "trusted souls," our reader membership, the *Traveler's Within Society* will be the perfect place to connect with others who are on the path to higher ground. You can find out more in the final section of this book.

Cyn - Q: I believe all of us have undercurrents and whirlpools in our lives. Is there an internal "life vest" we can choose to carry with us during these times that actually bring us closer to our Agent of Being? Sometimes I feel like we live, without intention, that game of *Chutes and Ladders.*

Val Jon - A: I remember that game! Unlike *Chutes and Ladders* in which the objective is to advance through the terrain as fast as possible, traveling through the terrain of our inner psyche is about taking our time and trusting the process. And just as you mention in your statement below, it is "trusting the process" that is your best "internal life vest." Knowing that no matter what arises, what you discover in your hidden terrain, and what you must face into, all will be well. You can't go wrong doing this work. You can't make a mistake, and you will not backslide once you take higher ground. The other thing to know is that no matter how embarrassing or unsightly some of the "chutes" residing within your psyche may appear, the "ladders" of your inner beauty and goodness are far greater than any of them.

Cyn - Chapter Statement: *Trust.* I think it is one of the most powerful words in our vocabulary and yet we so often do not give it the power it deserves. I have found in my life when I have been able to "get out of my own way" and trust the Universe, myself and the process, miracles have happened. Doors have opened, I could never have imagined. I am a true believer in the Nine Agent of Being Practices. Thank you, Val Jon, for leading us into a richer journey of discovery and release.

Elise - Q: The term "victim" is highly charged and can be easily misunderstood. How do I distinguish between someone who is, say, a victim of molest and someone who constantly complains about how the world is against them? Are the two related and if so, how?

Val Jon - A: Clearly we can be victimized in many ways, both as children and as adults. Whether we are victims of abuse, violence, theft or harassment, these are crimes committed against us, and in most cases, there was little or nothing we could have done to prevent them. (There are, however, some crimes we share a responsibility in by exposing ourselves to high-risk situations, by not paying attention, or by allowing our ego to dictate our choices.) Someone who is dramatizing victimhood, on the other hand, uses their unfortunate circumstances as an excuse for being powerless to do anything about them. While life can be extremely challenging at times, how we deal with the challenges we face is what matters. By taking a responsible stance we can navigate our challenges with greater effectiveness and ease, as well as minimize the chances of getting caught in detrimental situations that would tempt us into victimhood.

Elise - Q: How do we keep attaining a "beginner's mind," meaning how do we "open again and again" in our daily lives?

Val Jon - A: Opening again and again is not unlike the courage it takes to embrace pain on an ongoing basis and learn how to "be with it" rather than resist it. Constantly returning to a beginner's mind requires a willingness to ask ourselves questions and surrender up our assumed certainty to the process of discovering new possibilities. Opening again also means practicing the art of Intense Curiosity and reminding ourselves that *learning* is a higher order than *knowing* can ever be. In terms of the practice, when you think or feel you've opened as much as you can, open even more. Press yourself beyond your self-imposed limitations to love and accept with ever-greater capacity. By doing so you'll discover that your heart is capable of opening far more than you thought it was.

Elise - Chapter Statement: This was a huge chapter for me. Allowing the space for the aspects of the Nine Agent of Being Practices to grow after taking responsibility and becoming accountable is for me, a lifelong journey. My own healing and awakening is reliant upon learning to surrender to and being accountable for the choices I have made in my life. Reviewing and changing decisions to bring more integrity and impeccability into the space of being is a lifetime job, and one I'm up for.

Mindy - Q: I am admittedly relieved and grateful I was not violated as a child; my Liberation came in the form of relinquishing the need for constant approval from my mother. I still, however, cringe if I perceive a comment from her as critical. Have I not truly experienced Liberation? Do I need to continue my work in this Phase before I can truly journey on?

Val Jon - A: Think of your reaction to your mother like a "rock in your shoe" as you travel the ground of your inner terrain. It's best to remove it to minimize your discomfort, but it's not a requirement to traveling on. Some people wouldn't know what to do if their chronic irritations suddenly vanished. I'm not being irreverent, but rather straight-up about this point. The pain you still carry regarding your mother is woven into your core identity, much like how love gets intertwined with pain for many. In order to feel love, pain must also be present, because without it, the love feels incomplete. It doesn't make any sense, and it's a nauseating proposition, but it must be considered. I believe you will need to take additional passes at the early symbiotic relationship between you and your mother to get to the core issue. Do the work, like I know you can do it and you'll remove the rock in your shoe sooner than later. In the meantime, get a move on as we have much more terrain to cover!

Mindy - Q: Is "releasing self-importance" a factor in professional success? I've always thought driven, successful people needed a certain amount of ego and ambition, but as I work through the Stages and Phases of the AwarenesSphere, this practice along with Intentional Humility seems paramount. Do we need to factor these into our professional growth alongside our personal journey?

Val Jon - A: There are countless cases all down through the ages of egomaniacs and ambitious power mongers who've attained vast amounts of wealth, control and status . . . but are these outcomes examples of "professional success?" It depends on the meaning we apply to the notion I suppose. One can be a "professional" at scamming other people, and there are indeed many who are "successful" at it. And while the less virtuous traits of ego and ambition may be required to succeed in these "lower" career fields, I don't believe they are a prerequisite for being successful as a "higher ground" professional. It is true however that most career professions in today's world are highly competitive, which tends to evoke survival-oriented Emergence tactics, so accessing and applying one's greater virtues is more challenging but not impossible. There are many examples of successful professionals who bypass ego and ambition, and instead, draw their "grit" and drive from a higher source, namely their Agent of Being and their relationship with the Divine. The distinction to explore is, I believe, between *ego-based ambition* and *spirit-based dedication.* The place to look for clarity is in their root definitions. Ambition, from Latin *"ambitio"* means *"the act of soliciting for votes."* And *"ambire"* means *"to go around and solicit."* Essentially Ambition comes down to *"the ardent desire for rank, fame, or power."* Dedication, on the other hand, from Old French, "*dedicacioun,"* means *"the action of consecrating to a deity or sacred use."* And *"dicare,"* meaning *"to give oneself to a greater purpose."* Clearly, Ambition is about external control, whereas Dedication is about internal resolve. Success can come through either means, but engaging in a profession that is truly fulfilling and nurturing is, in my opinion, derived from employing the higher virtue of Dedication.

Mindy - Chapter Statement: I was feeling rather proud of myself until I read this chapter again. I am certain I did not properly apply the principles of this Phase and must work through Liberation again. I recommend a continual review of the Stages and Phases as one travels within.

Susie - Q: I'm curious as to whether and how other people in the world have discovered "true liberation" from their self-imposed Primary Decision and their insidious Box if they haven't attended your programs or read your books and done the exercises outlined in them?

Val Jon - A: I suspect it's not unlike the principles of any self-growth program. Those who've not experienced the specific work being presented by workshop facilitators probably will not have the exact distinctions within their awareness, but they may well have accessed the same understanding in other ways. There are many paths to the top of the mountain, and as far as I'm concerned as long as my fellow life travelers are gaining altitude, in my opinion, they're headed in the right direction.

Susie- Q: How can we begin to become aware of these challenges at a much younger age?

Val Jon - A: The good news is that younger generations are gaining Self-Awareness at astonishingly early ages. As each generation acquires greater insight into their higher nature, our children will follow suit and integrate higher awareness into their maturing identities. Also when parents have traveled their inner terrain in a way that elevates their own ways of being and behaviors, I believe their offspring will learn to navigate life's challenges much sooner and with greater ease and understanding. As Mahatma Gandhi once said, *"You must be the change you wish to see in the world."*

Susie - Chapter Statement: I truly had a magical childhood, with extremely loving and encouraging parents. I had to wrestle with finding my Primary Decision and the Box I created. Surprisingly, (to me) I found a little more access by starting backward and looking at where I've gotten repeatedly stopped or stuck in life and work backward from there. I have newly discovered that I stop being my powerful self, as soon as people start being aggressive, negative, yelling, and/or speaking over me. I experience that *"people are scary and they are not being fair, kind, respectful."* I totally shut down and get very judgmental of others, when it's truly just a reflection of how inadequate I feel about myself. I discovered that perhaps this stemmed from my birth experience. I was the oldest of 6 kids and for my mom's first 4 kids, she arrived at the hospital and was immediately given a drug that knocked her out. She then woke up several hours later to meet her new baby, all cleaned and wrapped in blankets. I know that was a terrifying time of separation for me, emerging into a loud, bright environment, being firmly, (but not necessarily lovingly) passed from one person to another and being cleaned and weighed, measured, wiped and wrapped in blankets without the loving mom I'd been with for so long from the inside. I suspect I made some decisions that the world was loud and scary, and that it wasn't fair to separate me from my mom. I can now see that throughout my life, I shut down in loud and scary situations. I haven't known how to stand up for myself, be articulate, or negotiate this landscape. After reading this chapter, I have some new access to Uncasting my decisions from the past and for stepping into the capable, powerful human being I am!

Victoria - Q: What if the Box holds within it humiliation, unimportance, and servitude and that any choice is really God's choice? For me, this is the Box I've had to liberate myself from in order to find and connect with my Agent of Being and any sense of self-value.

Val Jon - A: For those children who were raised under the "critical thumb of God," their Box is almost always forged within the negative forces of domination and judgment, and the outcome is almost always forced compliance which is disempowering for the child. (I want to be clear that the religion of a family's choice is not the problem, but how that religion gets shared within the family unit that produces the demeaning sense of self you speak about.) If God is indeed "good," then "God's children" surely ought to value and even celebrate the goodness that dwells within them.

Victoria - Q: Does the "opening and opening again" ever end or do you find that there are always new layers to open to?

Val Jon - A: Opening is an infinite process, but without closing occasionally it's not an "alive" process. What I mean by this is that the act of opening must include closing in order to be healthy and nurturing. The "opening again and again" I refer to isn't meant to be a linear process as if one were to inhale repeatedly until they turn blue and go unconscious. What it means is that we open, and we close, and we reopen and little more, and then maybe we close again . . . and then we reopen a little wider and then possibly close again . . . on and on this living process goes. In this way, we expand our capacity to open little by little, and at the same time, we safeguard our vulnerability by closing when closing is called for.

Victoria - Chapter Statement: I see personal Phase of Liberation as a four-part process; physical, mental, emotional and spiritual. My physical liberation came at 17 when I ran away from home. I began my mental liberation at 21 when the concepts of Choice and Self-Responsibility were introduced to me. I remember being angry at my parents for not teaching these to me, and then realized they could not teach me what they themselves did not know. My journey into the Phase of Liberation has been about letting go of the belittling beliefs of my childhood religion and finding my inner-voice of love and empowerment. Disbelieving can be painful and also well worth the effort to dismantle false assumptions and other people's beliefs from our own. This chapter was a great reminder for me of how difficult the beginning of this process was as I struggled to find my own identity and how rewarding and freeing it is to choose responsibility.

♦♦♦

CHAPTER SIX: INTEGRATION

The Two Sides of Wholeness

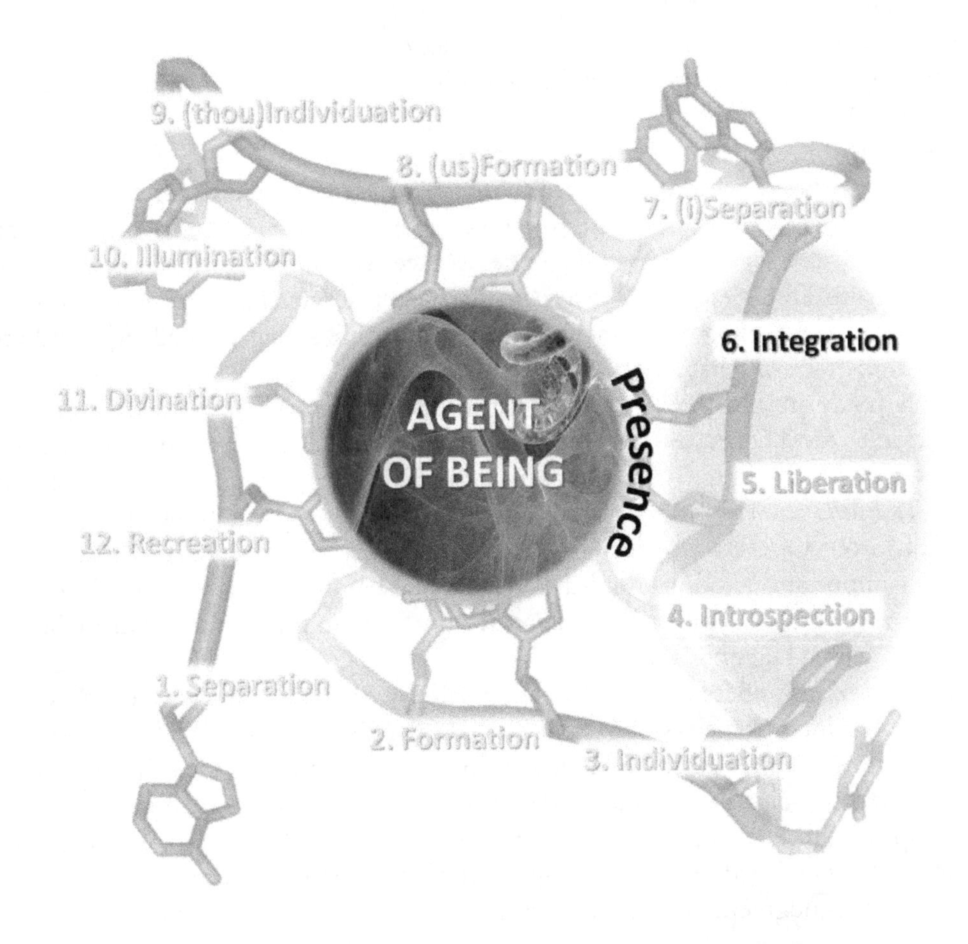

"Whoever believes in Me but does not believe that good and evil are by My preordainment, let them look for another Lord besides Me." — Allah

Integration, Presence's Sixth Phase of Self-Awareness is about embracing our shadow and light sides, a paradoxical coming together of the oppositional forces residing deep within our psyche, a reconciliation and existential acceptance of "what is, just as it is." Within this Phase, our higher faculty of Self-Awareness undergoes yet another major transformation in which we begin to integrate the paradoxical facets of our finite presence with our infinite nature. Said another way, we dare to embrace both the darkness of our primal forces and the light of our spiritual virtues.

This movement towards *Integration* is the beginning of a wave of powerful *Dharma Energy* [31], a divinely inspired paradoxical force that transcends even the experience of *Liberation.* The Dharma Energy of *Integration* is about embracing life's cyclical three-fold movement from nonexistence to existence and back into nonexistence. It's about coming to terms with our mortality and with life's paradoxical ways. In its higher service-based expression, it's about supporting others in opening to courageously embracing life's biggest challenges and growing themselves in the face of whatever they encounter.

From this point onward in our journey, we will need to traverse into ever-higher ground, and as a result, the challenges we must face will become ever-greater. *Integration* is the preparation phase for exiting the *Stage of Presence* and crossing the next evolutionary gap into the *Stage of Transcendence.* This migration will require surrendering everything we've achieved up to this point in our journey. The surrender includes emptying ourselves of all our remaining issues of self-importance, and even releasing any pride having to do with our developmental accomplishments up to this point. In essence, we must move forward into our higher ground empty-handed with a beginner's mind.

This journey of emptiness is called "walking the narrow path," and the reality is that only the most devoted inner travelers ever walk it in a way that delivers them to their Higher Self and into the arms of their Agent of Being. Why? Because moving into the energy flow of *Integration* is like entering an emotional vortex, it requires nothing less than absolute surrender and giving up our life as we've known it. Access to the terrain of *Integration* is only available to those who are fully engaged in relinquishing the need to dramatize their self-importance, their indulgences in self-judgment and the temptations that distract them from coming into accord with their Agent of Being. *(A/N: I want to emphasize that these prerequisites do not need to always be met by us in order to gain access to the terrain ahead. As long as we constantly elevate our intention and continue to free ourselves from our ego-based behaviors we can successfully continue on with our inner journey.)*

Reconciling Our "Good" And "Evil" Within

The Koran recounts that when Adam was first created, God commanded the angels to bow down before his Divine creation, manifest in human form before them. All the angels kneeled before Adam, except for Iblis, who remained standing because he believed Adam to be less than himself since Adam was created from clay and he was forged from fire. Iblis' blatant disobedience was a preordained behavior designed by God to force humans to integrate the dynamics of Good and Evil on their own, rather than through the assistance of the Divine. Iblis thus became the human symbol of Evil which acts out God's intended mortal detriments of ignorance, arrogance, pride, envy, violence, and hatred. In this context *"eviL"* is merely the mirrored reflection of *"Live,"* two sides of the same whole, affirming Allah's declaration of *"preordainment." (A/N: Notice the mirroring of "eviL / Live" which illuminates the paradox of life we are exploring in this chapter. Evil is a highly charged word and carries much baggage with it, so the discerning Traveler Within must release their history around the term and approach it from a fresh vantage point. It's not unlike hiking to the edge of a canyon to take in the view and then hiking to a second vista point to see the same canyon from a new perspective.)*

Every religion on Earth portrays their own unique precepts regarding the battle between Good and Evil, but buried beneath this age-old moralistic battlefield is the deeper subterranean truth of *Integration. Integration* is about opening to the reality that both Good and Evil arise from the same source within us, and that our fear of, and moralistic judgments about Evil are mere shadows cast from the flames of its own hellish conclusions. In other words, it is our own unacknowledged indwelling Evil that tempts us into rejecting and denying its presence or existence.

This is Evil's seductive reverse strategy to hook us into its two most coveted vices, *fear* and *judgment.* If Evil can get us to buy-in to its vices, we bond with Evil ourselves. The moment we choose to empower fear by *fearing it* rather than *accepting it*, it gains control over us. And the moment we judge those who are judgmental we become just like them. The deeper subterranean truth here is that Evil has no power over us other than the power we choose to give it. *(A/N: Remember the definition of "Self," which is that we are designed to "join," and the moment we empower fear, we join with it, and in so doing also join with Evil. I want to clarify that this does not mean we are an "evil person," but rather that we merely possess dark forces along with many other forces existing within our psyche.)*

The *Sixth Phase of Integration* is the final step in the *Presence Stage. Introspection* and its two key virtues of Intense Curiosity and Intentional Humility open the way for us to travel to the depths of our psyche and become present to the terrain of self-induced enslavement dwelling with us. *Liberation* then is the process by which we free ourselves from the enslavement of our Box and the grips of our ego-self. The result of these two vital pieces of work is a migration out of the terrain of our ego-self and into higher ground, the summit of our greatness where our Agent of Being resides. It is here at the base of this summit, and the ground of our humble greatness that we peer up into the thin air and bright light of our Higher Self and plan our ascent route. As we do, we know full well that our ascension is not away from being human, but rather towards both the deepest heart of our humanity and the highest pinnacle of our spirituality.

To reiterate, the *Integration* process is about traveling to the heights and depths within us at the same time and expanding our capacity to embrace them both fully. This is an essential paradoxical practice in that only when we have embraced the totality of our humanity will we mature into the fullness of our spirituality.

The Paradoxical Context of Wholeness

The thirteenth-century theologian and mystic Meister Eckhart, clarified the paradoxical process of *Integration* this way, *"The highest heights of exaltation lie precisely in the lowest depths of humiliation; for the deeper the valleys go, the loftier the heights that rise above them; the deeper the well, the higher too: for depth and height are the same thing."*

Depth and height are indeed the same things within the larger context of *Wholeness*[32]. For something to be "whole" it must not be missing any parts, and it is resoundingly clear that the "parts" must include the full spectrum of forces in existence, both shadow and light. Wholeness and our Agent of Being go hand in hand in that they are both paradoxical in nature and are vast enough to embrace all the contradictions and dilemmas that accompany being alive.

Until we open to this paradoxical reality and become present to the opposing forces moving deep within us, the passageway into the *Third Stage of Transcendence* remains closed to us. Just as there was an evolutionary leap between the Stages of *Emergence* and *Presence*, a similar leap exists between *Presence* and *Transcendence*. This transition, however, requires a profound leap of faith in that it's virtually invisible and dynamically changing in its form and structure. Much like Ramana Maharishi's quote in the last chapter that *"Liberation exists but 'You' will never be liberated,"* no one ever crosses this bridge into higher ground, because it isn't built for only one, it's built for everyone.

So what does this mean in practical terms? Initially, as we move into the terrain of *Integration* it points to a complete redefinition of what it means to be both "whole" and "spiritual." Ultimately as we cross the gap into *Transcendence* it will mean leaving the singular nature of our identity behind and taking a leap of faith into a vaster context of Wholeness, one that transcends individuality and opens the way for our shared identity to emerge. I want to recount with you a very personal and powerful experience I had a number of years ago in which I was faced with this expansion into Wholeness and the challenge of coming to terms with *Integration.* Join me now as I lead the way into some deadly, yet enlivening paradoxical terrain.

The Call of The Wild And Beyond

The familiar high-pitched ringing in my ears woke me from a deep slumber. I've encountered this mysterious otherworldly siren many times throughout my life, and each time I've felt compelled to drop everything and follow its calling. My experience with honoring this inner call has always proved to be extraordinary in that when I've allowed myself to surrender to it, I've been guided to destinations far beyond the bounds of normal reality. What I mean by "beyond the bounds" is essentially venturing off the edge of the obvious reality and into some wild and truly profound otherworldly terrain.

The very next day I responded to the call by gathering up my gear, jumping on my Harley-Davidson and riding off into the mystery of the morning. I had no idea where I was going, but it was south, which was a welcome direction because it was October and there was a bitter chill in the air. Somewhere between Lodi and Bakersfield, I realized where I was being called . . . to the Joshua Tree National Park in Southern California. The "Park" located near Palm Springs, is 790,000 acres of desert land scooped out by ancient glaciers. It is a truly magical place and one I had wanted to visit for many years. The giant Yuccas, or "Joshua trees" populating the Park got their name from a Biblical story in which Joshua, (Moses' main assistant) reaches his parched desert hands up to the sky in prayer. I can see why the name stuck because the otherworldly cacti trees literally look like a pair of prickly hands reaching for the heavens.

I pulled into Palm Springs in the late evening and checked into a motel for the night. I recall a "giddy" anxious sensation in my stomach as I lay down and closed my eyes. I was definitely sensing something unexpected and ominous that was about to happen. My dream time encounters that night were a confirmation of my anxiety and a premonition of what was soon to come. Let's now transition into the moment . . . My dream sequence begins in the midst of a desert wasteland. In the middle of a flat level area sits a king-sized bed . . . its four carved wooden posts spiraling up into the blackness above. Blood-red luminous streaks run through the low-hanging clouds, and off in the distance, bluish-white lightning bolts pierce through the mist, striking the shrouded desert floor. With each intense flash, the tops of the desert cacti ignite into a multitude of flaming dungeon torches, lighting the way to a glowing fracture in the distance, a gaping crevasse leading to the demonic depths of Hell itself.

Struggling to sit up in the bed, my attention becomes fixed on the ominous crevasse. From deep within it a faint yellow glow illuminates its jagged edges, casting shards of light straight up into the night sky. Suddenly a massive dark shadow emerges from the luminous crack and begins advancing towards me. As it sways back and forth in mid-air I realize it isn't just one entity, it's a pack of separate entities flying in tight formation. Head-on, all I can make out is dark snouts, flapping wings, and low-hanging claws. If ever there was a time when the gates of hell opened and released its wrath upon the Earth this was it! As these ominous dark forms begin circling me, their features become visible, they're fur-covered hybrid beasts, half wolf and half prehistoric pterodactyl!

To my dismay I am completely paralyzed and unable to get out of the bed and run for my life. With all my might I manage to cross my arms in front of my face. I attempt to fend off the flying beasts as they lunge and dive at me, their gnarly teeth and jaws snapping and nipping at my arms and hands. The dream is so vivid I can actually feel their matted fur brushing up against me, the sharpness of their teeth, and the smell of rotted flesh emanating from their demonic bodies. Just as the entire pack is about to devour me, I bolt awake in a cold sweat. Out of my mouth comes a prophetic catchy little poem, *"The demons without, are the demons within . . . you can fight them off, but you will never win."*

Whenever I have such powerful "night-events" I know I'm traversing near my psyche's dark crevasse, my own personal fractured terrain that leads to the depths of my humanity where my Archetypal demons and angels dwell. *(A/N: I'm not unique when it comes to having such a gateway into darkness. We all have such a portal residing deep within our psyche. While this might sound terribly ominous, it really isn't. Think of your portal into darkness much like how your "belly-button" is an umbilical portal leading to your internal organs. Press on the button with your fingernail and you'll feel a "tingle" deep within. Our inner demons and angels produce a similar tingle when we reach in and touch them . . . and just like we have control over how much tingle we are willing to experience, so too can we manage how much darkness we are willing to embrace. Remember, you are the Chooser, and as such you have command over your experience and over the meanings you assign to what you encounter in your life.)*

Reciting my little poem, *"the demons without are the demons within . . ."* I fall back into an uneventful sleep and awake the next morning refreshed and with a deeper enthusiasm for this extraordinary desert-bound adventure I'm about to embark on. Checking my gear, I do a methodical inventory of the supplies I'll be taking with me into the desert. In addition to my standard hiking attire and backpack, I have a large leather water pouch, a variety of dried fruit and nuts, a light rain parka, a flashlight, snakebite kit, and a large bowie knife. Traveling light for such adventures has always been my preference as being encumbered with too much gear is unwise and a waste of my available life force energy.

By around 8:00 o'clock in the morning, I'm on my bike headed for the Joshua Tree Visitor Center which is about a 45-minute ride. About an hour later I pull up to the one-story Visitor Center, enter the building and make my way to the huge map of the Park's three-quarters of a million acres posted on the lobby wall. Suddenly my eye catches a red marker which I investigate more closely. It's a section of the Park towards the Hexie Mountains that's off-limits to visitors. I take a closer look at the bulletin posted next to it and learn that the area was closed due to "mountain lion encounters." *"Hmm,"* I wonder to myself . . . *"Is that code for somebody got eaten?"* As I walk away, the call of the wild pulls me back to where the restricted zone bulletin is posted. *"Oh great . . ."* I muse to myself, *". . . like a moth to a flame, I get to be the moth or uh, in this case, the meal."* So the "restricted zone" it is then! That queasy tingling sensation in my stomach is back, but this time it's magnified tenfold.

Hopping on my bike I head south on the dusty dirt road leading towards the mountain range. The Sun is up and the sky is a pristine bright blue . . . as the wind rushes by my face I feel a deep sense of gratitude for being here and for being alive. Within an hour I'm miles from the Visitor Center out in the middle of nowhere. I pull up to a dilapidated parking area with a rusted barbed-wire fence bisecting it and winding its way in both directions as far as the eye can see. I park my bike, recheck my gear and hop over the old rusty restricted zone sign, and as I do, unbeknownst to me, I'm crossing over into the terrain of *Integration.*

All around me stand massive, otherworldly rock formations jutting out of the desert floor like the jagged teeth of a thousand lurking demons. Small stands of spidery ocotillo plants swaying in the breeze along with squatty cacti add a whimsical, angelic flare to the desolate landscape. My welcoming committee is out in force this fine morning; horny-toad lizards doing "push-ups" atop smooth flat rocks, golden-yellow centipedes creeping around the underbrush, and brown desert spiders clutching their webs within the prickly arms of the Joshua trees. Standing silently for a moment, I take in the sound of the wind blowing through the canyons as it merges with the call of the wild ringing in my ears. What a hypnotically soothing resonance these outer and inner sounds evoke within me. Looking up into the sky I see thin stratospheric clouds beginning to form, and upon their under surfaces, I can make out what looks to me like faint streaks of . . . red.

Around high-noon I come to a mesa where two ravines intersect, squatting down I spot paw tracks in the dirt and what looks like a fresh dung pile. Pushing my finger into the mound, its green mushy warmth sends a danger signal up my arm and into the center of my chest. It's fresh, and these are not rabbit droppings or coyote turds. From their size, and by the look of the tracks, this is a much larger animal and almost certainly feline. I instinctively stand up and scan the terrain around me. Across the deep ravine, I can see shadowed indentations in the cliff walls that appear to be cave entrances, perfect abodes for these pristine beasts. *(A/N: Being part Cherokee Indian I have a deep respect for the natural world and for wild animals. I consider animals to be my brothers and sisters in Spirit. And while they can be unpredictable siblings at times, they are nonetheless my revered kin.)*

All of a sudden I feel a strong "pull" in my abdomen, around my Third Chakra, the one that contains the energies of personal power and autonomy. I immediately realize there's a power source somewhere in the vicinity, a place where reality folds in on itself and opens into alternate dimensions. *(A/N: For those who are unfamiliar with the notion of "alternate dimensions" I ask that you reserve judgment until we cover the Essence Stage of the AwarenesSphere. Also, I want to address the internal dialogue I'll be sharing with you that began at the Visitor's Center . . . the "conversations" you are about to become privy too are not fantasy or embellishments, nor am I suffering from multiple personality disorder. Our Agent of Being is a very real force dwelling within us. Call it whatever you want, "good conscience," "intuition," "Divine guidance," or whatever, the fact is it offers wise counsel to those who heed it. I also want to stress that I'm not special or have some supernatural gift. Each of us possesses our own Agent of Being, a meta-resource we simply need to start asking to come forth and be present in our daily lives.)*

Turning a complete circle, I spot in the distance a huge cracked boulder standing at least thirty feet tall. I walk directly to it and investigate its front-facing surface. The crack runs nearly vertical and is wider at the top than at the bottom, and it looks to be a large enough opening to crawl into. I also notice that the two halves of the boulder are asymmetrical but fairly close in size and shape. A moment of insight flashes through me, *"This boulder is on its way to 'Dis-Integration,' but I'm on my way to 'Integration' . . . so is the calling here for me to enter or not?"* The dilemma is that on one hand, I could make the wrong decision by entering and put myself in grave danger. But on the other hand, it could be the right decision in that I'd be following the "call" I've come to so deeply respect throughout my life. What to do? At that moment my Agent of Being steps forward into my awareness, *"Val Jon, it's not about wrong or right, it's about trust and surrender." "And furthermore, you need to make a choice, not a decision."* Instantly I know what to do.

Turning sideways I work my body into the opening of the huge vertical crack and slowly insert myself into its massive stone jaws. The smell of sandstone and rock mixed with moisture fills my nostrils with a calming earthy fragrance. I say "calming" because the crack is narrowing substantially and I find myself lodged between a very real rock and a hard place. My chest is compressed and my breathing is shallow as I edge my way forward. I did indeed want to explore paradox, yes? Well, I've got a grand one right here, right now. It's too late to turn back as there's no way to change the position of my body, but it's too early to tell if there's a way out ahead. I'm wedged in tight and my feet are no longer touching the ground. I can't get any traction and the harder I try, the further down my body slides into the ever-narrowing stone jaws. It reminds me of the little bamboo "finger puzzles" I played with as a boy, the more I struggle, the more stuck I become . . . *"Ah-uh-huh, that's it VJ, relax into this bind just like you did with those finger puzzles."*

By surrendering my resistance and rigidity I was able to nudge my body forward, inching my way deeper into the stone split, but the sunlight fading behind me and the darkness intensifying before me triggers another bout of fear, and along with it comes a compelling insight. *"So this is what Integration feels like . . . two opposing forces coming face-to-face in the same moment of Now - light and dark, life and death. I never realized it before but fear actually expands the Now into a big enough space to hold multiple experiences and moments at the same time."* Then my inner Agent chimes in with, *"No Val Jon, your Now isn't expanded by fear, Now is always and forever . . . what fear does is temporarily interrupt the ego-self's control over altering your perception of reality to fit into its illusion of time."* *"Huh? Oh, I see, that's why time seems to 'slow down' during threatening situations, our ego-self is losing its grip and the illusion of time wanes."* *"But why does the ego-self want to perpetuate the illusion of time?"* Again my inner Agent responds, *"Because if it can make you believe that you are temporal rather than eternal then you are vulnerable, and if you are vulnerable you are susceptible, and if you are susceptible you are controllable."*

I mutter to myself, *"Eternal trust, surrender, staying out of the way and allowing life to lead."* All the right words and still I'm terrified! The reality is that I'm being controlled to the point of thinking I'm going to die. Then a realization dawns on me. I *am* going to die someday, just not this day. I sigh in relief as I surrender to this moment of Now . . . and low and behold, in the very next moment I spot a thin sliver of light ahead! What a relief to see light at the end of the tunnel! I manage to nudge forward, and soon the crack widens enough that I can regain my footing. Within a few moments, I step out of the crack and into an honest-to-goodness alternate dimension of reality. I can't believe what I'm seeing! It's a perfectly groomed meadow, circular in shape and approximately one hundred feet in diameter with a rock fire pit at its center. It's enclosed by high rock formations on three sides and opens to a high mesa on the far right. I'm literally miles from civilization in a remote part of the desert and yet this sacred place appears to be meticulously cared for.

I kneel down to examine the fire pit and notice faint traces of soot. It's not recent, but it's definitely the result of flames scorching the inner surfaces of the rocks at some time in the past. It *feels* indigenous to me, and while there are no Indian tribes currently living in the Park, in the 1700 and 1800's the Serrano, Cahuilla and Mojave Indians populated the area. I reach out and touch one of the larger rocks in the circle and suddenly see images of natives in full ceremonial dress, shaking feathered spears towards the heavens, dancing around a blazing fire pit to chanting and ritual drum beats.

Whether real or imagined, it's a powerful vision that humbles me deeply in that it represents an *Integration* of my Indian heritage of the past with my presence in the here and now. The only thing that separates us is the illusion of time. Their feet were right here where my feet are.

Their eyes gazing up into the heavens just like mine are. I wonder to myself if I could set aside the illusion of time would I be able to join with them in celebration. Immediately my inner Agent replies, *"You have already joined with them, Val Jon . . . they are your tribe and you are with them, as they are with you in your now, and they are with us in our forever."* Tears fill my eyes, a deep pang of sadness and a comforting joy wells up within me, like holding a thorny rose while at the same time smelling its sweet petals. Again, another invitation for me to embrace the paradox of *Integration*, to grow myself beyond the limitations of "Me" and into the grace of "Thou."

Still crouched down, turning on the balls of my feet, to my right I notice a large flat, vertical rock approximately eight feet high standing on the edge of the circular meadow. As I study it, I can just make out a faint image on its smooth front surface. I walk over to it and sure enough, there is an image . . . in the form of a "Cross." It's not a Christian Cross, but more like a "plus-sign" as in the Cross of Wotan, the Celtic and Coptic Crosses or the Pagan Sun Cross symbol dating back thousands of years before Christianity. And the symbol isn't carved into the stone, but rather folded into its surface as if it were created when the rock was molten hot magma. But the vertical and horizontal lines are perfectly straight and intersect in the very center of the Cross with the precision of a laser beam. How could this image have naturally come about so perfectly? Again my Agent of Being chimes in, *"Pay attention not to your mind's conclusions or your heart's wonderings, but rather to Spirit's knowingness. For this symbol's meaning transcends both the mind and the heart."*

Wonderful. I can't use my mind or my heart to figure this one out . . . so what am I supposed to use, my intuition? Or braille perhaps? Rather than heading down an irreverent path, however, I back up, quiet my mind and still my heart. I mumble to myself, *"Let's just go with what I'm being presented with . . . two perfectly straight lines, one running vertical and the other horizontal, and they are intersecting right in the center."* The nexus of the Cross suddenly awakens something in me . . . *"It's a perfect representation of Integration!"* I never thought of the Cross this way, perhaps because of my Christian upbringing. I always related it to the Crucifixion of Christ and to be a brutal backdrop of torture and death. Yes, I know it's supposed to represent "resurrection," but as a child, seeing blood dripping from Christ's palms and the agonizing look on his face, the holy meaning of the Cross was not even a remote possibility for me.

How remarkable to come across this mysterious *Integration* stone. I kneel down, close my eyes and thank it for its sacred message and then stand up and bid it farewell. Moving around its left side, I notice its long shadow being cast by the setting Sun. The shadow points directly to a high mesa off in the distance, perhaps an hour's hike away. I need to get a move on because that's where I'll need to find a secure location to spend the night. *(A/N: So my fellow traveler we're headed to that high plateau I mentioned where those otherworldly demons and angels dance together. Little do I know that before dawn I'll be doing a life and death two-step right along with them. You're still with me, right? Contrary to the nature of my Box, I'd prefer not to embark on this dance alone.)*

As I hike my way to the higher ground ahead I reflect on the symbol of the Cross and of the uncanny way the message of *Integration* was delivered to me. I wonder what the next message will be and get that sinking feeling in my stomach again as the underside of the thin cloud coverage above has turned crimson red. Within an hour or so I reach the high plateau just as the Earth's horizon is engulfing the Sun. To my left is a huge flat open mesa peppered with Joshua trees, shrubs and cacti, and to my right is a steep rocky slope that leads to yet another higher plateau. Instinctively, I hike up to the right to get some elevation and distance from the mesa floor, and from the myriad of creatures that I know populate it at night. About halfway up the slope, I find a small indentation to settle into for the night. I seldom travel with a tent or extra supplies as I find they encumber me and tend to buffer me from the natural elements which I love communing with. Sleeping under the stars is an ancient practice and one that I find expansive and inspiring. As a young boy, I used to camp out under the stars in my backyard and gaze up into the night sky in total awe of its vastness.

As night falls, the clouds have cleared and the blackness of space is ablaze with countless stars. My eyes drift down from the heavens, past the horizon line and into the shadowy desert floor below. Much like my dream time haunting the night before, phantom creatures swirl around jagged starlit crags, drawing me into a foreboding vortex of mystery. As my eyes adjust to the darkness of the desert floor, the threatening phantoms transform into benign cacti, rocks, and shrubs. With a sigh of relief, I settle back into the hillside and close my eyes for just a moment. Exhaustion gets the better of me however and I drift off into a very risky unplanned sleep.

I suddenly jolt awake, a wave of terror surging through my body! The musky smell of wild beast fills my nostrils. *"Damn it, I never should have allowed myself to doze off, especially in mountain lion country!"* The blinding darkness all around me yields no relief or certainty. Then, directly behind me, maybe fifteen or twenty feet up the slope, I hear the sliding of rocks and clicking claws. Bloody images of torn flesh and flailing body parts rip through my mind. Wedded in this eternal moment are predator and prey, engaged in the mortal question of, *who will make the first move?* My mind races to find a way out. Caught between a paradoxical embrace of mortal terror and Divine surrender, I have an epiphany. I purposefully came here to immerse myself in the natural world and to open myself to the mysteries of *Integration,* so I would be a coward and totally remiss if I bowed out now. I suddenly have the fleeting thought that if I'm dumb enough to place myself on a late-night dinner platter, I ought to not complain about being served up as a meal.

I slowly turn to face uphill and scan the darkness for any sign of movement. There it is! Just to my right and about twenty feet above me I can just barely make out a large feline silhouette against the blackness of the slope. I suddenly spot two luminescent green eyes peering straight back at me, piercing me to my very core. Locked in an eternal gaze, predator and prey dance together to the deadly tune of the survival of the fittest. There is no doubt in my mind that *she,* (and yes I could feel her energy as it was maternal and hungry) was the fittest in this particular dance. It was absolutely clear to me that my will, strength and even my trusted survival skills would be insufficient to extricate me from this deadly stand-off.

Loud and clear my Agent of Being intervenes, *"Surrender is your only choice, Val Jon."* It sure seems like it to me as well, and after a brief moment of doubt I make my choice . . . in a clear but calm voice I utter out loud, *"I surrender to you."* As my words ring out into the darkness, the rocks above me scatter and slide, and the feline lets loose with a blood-curdling growl. Like a blast of death-wind, the flesh on my face constricts back against my cheekbones. Terror is an intense experience, and fortunately, I learned a long time ago that fearing terror, rather than being with it immediately escalates it into panic . . . a result I *do not* want to evoke in this moment. Being with terror requires four key things, remembering to breathe, being willing to surrender your life, a massive amount of focused presence, and leveraging your heightened senses towards embracing the terror head-on.

In a vacuous eternal moment, I hang in the balance between life and death. And then, to my utter amazement, instead of pouncing on me, the feline turns and slowly walks away into the darkness. The pounding of my heart and rushing of blood through my temples is so intense I can barely breathe. The wind bristles across my sweat-soaked face and then, more terrifying than being eaten by the mountain lion, comes this message from my wise inner Agent, *"It's not the beast you must surrender to Val Jon, it's the Cross you must bow down before."*

Stunned, I gaze up into the night sky, and there at the zenith above me, I spot a dazzling cross-like constellation of stars. I count thirteen stars altogether, six on the horizontal axis and six on the vertical axis. Where the two axes intersect there is one additional star in the center, blazing with diamond-like intensity. Unbelievable! This constellation is an exact replica of the stone Cross I came across in the sacred meadow. I blurt out, *"You've got to be kidding me . . . I need to surrender to the Cross?"* To me, being a midnight meal is far more appealing than subordinating myself to any religion, be it Christianity or otherwise. It's not because I lack respect for the religions of the world, but the circumstances of my youth with a raging alcoholic father, Sunday school was more like a safe-house than a house of the Lord. "Surrender" to me meant having to believe something I felt would send me backward rather than forward in my life. But when in doubt, opting to be curious is the best course of action.

"What do you mean?" "Are you referring to Christianity or religion?" I query pointedly. There's no reply. Wonderful . . . my Agent of Being is either on its own dinner break or leaving me to work out this conundrum for myself. As I gaze up into the star constellation, the desert wind blasts me with a wave of frozen air, chilling me to the bone. *"Brrr . . . being trapped inside this frail mortal body certainly has its disadvantages." "Stars, on the other hand, can easily endure the frozen vacuum of space." "Wouldn't it be great if I could be like a star?"* Silence, silence, silence . . . *"That's it! I know what surrendering to the Cross means!"*

Suddenly a flood of insight about *Integration* comes rushing in from the *Beyond.* The first insight has to do with the symbolic meaning behind the Cross's horizontal and vertical axis. Like stars that are virtually immortal, the Cross's vertical aspect represents all things Divine, spiritual and eternal. The up-down position of its axis serves as a spiritual grounding rod connecting Heaven and Earth. This aspect of the Cross includes omnipotent qualities such as faith, grace, surrender, and unity. The horizontal aspect symbolizes the frail and mortal physical body, and all things human and temporal. Its left-right orientation represents our arms outstretched wide into the toils of mortality in which our human faculties of identity, emotion, intellect, and awareness resides.

My next insight is regarding the center star in the constellation. Using the theme of the two intersecting lines of the Cross as a foundation, I realize the nexus point of the central star represents the *Integration* of our Human and Divine aspects. I can easily see where I've achieved being Human in all its wonders and weaknesses. The Divine aspect is, however, more challenging. Although Divinity and its qualities of grace, sacredness, and reverence have indeed blessed my life, they don't always sustain, especially when things get rough. Reflecting on the practice of *Integration,* the importance of engaging in this paradoxical process must not be underestimated, for it is my devout belief that only when we have embraced the totality of our humanity that we will mature into the fullness of our spirituality.

Leaning back into the hillside and gazing up at the star constellation above it occurs to me that perhaps mastering this stellar paradox requires a symbolic death, kind of like a crucifixion of sorts. The notion triggers an intriguing question, *"What must I let go of in order to surrender to the Cross?"* The answer that comes floors me. *"Your mediocrity." "My mediocrity!"* To me, *mediocre* means blasé or pathetic, and I'm neither. So why would this insulting answer arise? Maybe it has to do with not staying in touch with my Divinity while I'm being Human. Again my inner Agent trues me up, *"Rather than being offended about being called 'mediocre,' what if you could remain humble while struggling with the possibility?"* I sometimes hate it when my Agent of Being is right. The definition of *"mediocre"* is *"of ordinary quality or ability"* and if I look at it this way, I can reluctantly accept that my ability to integrate my Human presence and my Divine nature has been somewhat mediocre. While the sobering news is that I need to get busy with the work of *Integration*, the more cheerful news is that I'll be exiting the desert on my Harley rather than in an ambulance, or worse yet, a hearse.

(A/N: I must admit that this assault on my ego disturbed me deeply. What I needed to face was that I coveted an image of myself as being a "bold adventurer" who may be a bit heedless perhaps, but not "mediocre" by any stretch of the imagination. Funny how some feedback we receive from those who love us or are far wiser than we are, sticks with us like an unwanted gift that keeps giving until we're willing to receive it. So do I now accept the notion that I'm "mediocre?" Uh . . . No.)

♦♦♦

The Integration Work Ahead

As I recounted my high desert adventure it's clear that *Integration* is the process of coming to terms with the opposing forces residing within us. When we finally realize that both demons and angels dwell within us, the work simply becomes about allowing these two opposing forces to co-exist and "dance together" within our psyche. Also, the insight of the central star in the constellation being the "nexus of the soul," our own personal bridge between our Humanity and Divinity is a revelation worth perusing and coming to terms with.

The implications of *Integration* are far-reaching for us *Travelers Within.* What it means is that we must acknowledge and take responsibility for every shadowed act we've ever committed against another or others, as well as stand up humbly into the light of every act of kindness and goodness we have ever done. It also requires ending the story of how others mistreated us and how *"we would never do such a thing."* Perhaps we *wouldn't* do such a thing, but we'd better be honest about the fact that *such a thing* exists within us as a possibility, and that under the right circumstances we may very well act on it. Anyone who tries to tell you that they've transcended the human condition, or is ultra-spiritual in some way, invite them into a decompression chamber and start removing all the air and watch how "holy" they truly are. *(A/N: Forgive me as I can be a bit sarcastic at times. I think I just need to entertain myself at times through my literary musings. Honestly, though, I don't relate to spirituality as a badge of purity, or as a means to puff up one's ego status.)*

I want to return to the wisdom and insight of Carl Jung for a moment. Jung put forth the powerful assertion that whatever shadow aspects we possess deep within our psyche that we fail to bring into our consciousness will appear as "fate" in our lives. He went on to state that we do not become enlightened through aspiring to symbols of light and goodness, but rather by bringing our inner darkness up into the light so we become present to it and integrate it into a healthy balance within us. Here is how he put the challenge of *Integration.*

"The meeting with oneself is, at first, the meeting with one's own shadow. The shadow is a tight passage, a narrow door, whose painful constriction no one is spared who goes down to the deep well. But one must learn to know oneself in order to know who one is." And when asked how to proceed with this ominous *Integration* task, he gave this advice, *"There is no generally effective technique for assimilating the shadow. It is more like diplomacy or statesmanship and it is always an individual matter. First one has to accept and take seriously the existence of the shadow. Second, one has to become aware of its qualities and intentions. This happens through conscientious attention to moods, fantasies, and impulses. Third, a long process of negotiation is unavoidable."*

(A/N: "Negotiation," what a wonderful way to put the work of Integration! Somehow it removes the ominous feel of doing the work, doesn't it? I'll list a few such negotiation tactics for you in the Exploration And Integration Guide before wrapping up this chapter. I'll also introduce you to the process of how to gain access to your own Agent of Being. But first, I'd like to share a little story with you that might give you a bit more clarity about the Integration work ahead.)

Jekyll And Hyde, A Match Made Deep Within

In Robert Louis Stevenson's classic story of *The Strange Case of Dr. Jekyll and Mr. Hyde,* rather than following Jung's advice, the good/bad doctor instead acts out the opposing forces dwelling within him in the form of the good doctor Jekyll and the very bad Mr. Hyde. The novel opens with the good doctor accidentally running over a girl in the street. Rather than admitting his mistake and guilt, he instead decides to cover up this tragedy by sending the unfortunate victim's family a bribe. The dark chasm within the good doctor begins to widen when he decides to concoct potions to ease his guilty conscience and the growing rift within his psyche, which in no uncertain terms magnifies the divide.

The situation is made even stranger when doctor Jekyll decides to bequeath his entire estate to his alternate personality, Mr. Hyde. Hyde now stands to inherit everything and in a celebratory drug-induced delirium, rather than a spending spree, he goes on a mad killing spree. As a result of his good side witnessing the acts of his bad side, eventually, doctor Jekyll shuts himself up inside his laboratory, mixes up a batch of deadly potions and commits suicide. His suicide note explains that he wanted to separate his good side from his bad side and that he thought he could control the diabolical split with drugs, which eventually cast him into a deep abyss of depression and despair. Seeing no other alternative, doctor Jekyll decided to take himself out, thus taking Mr. Hyde out with him.

It's a timeless novel, and unfortunately, one that is played out many times over with real people in the real world. Trying to separate ourselves from our shadow side and pretend like it isn't there is unwise and even risky. The human psyche is elastic, but it has a ripping point. Cross this point and even the best of us can find ourselves torn to shreds and smack in the middle of the darkest night of madness. There are degrees of denial no doubt, and the most extreme expression of madness most of us need not worry about. But it's important to understand that even a . . . dare I say it, *"mediocre"* degree of denial comes with a price tag. We may not end up like the good/bad doctor, but landing somewhere between the poles of these two characters results in merely living a mediocre life. The healthy alternative is to do the work of *Integration* so the opposing forces that reside within us stop struggling with one another and step out onto the dancefloor of life and celebrate moving together in perfect discordant harmony.

Integration's Linkage With The Sixth Chakra: Third Eye Energy

The Sixth Chakra is the "Third Eye Energy," or "Ajna" which translates to "beyond wisdom." This Chakra center is located between your eyebrows and extends down to your mouth and up to the crown of your head. The Third Eye is a "lens" or "meta-optical nerve" that transcends the mind, the material world and even the realm of our five senses. It is our visionary center that contains the powers of intuition, extra-sensory perception, ethereal insight, and psychic energy. It is also the "meta-visual" vantage-point from which we are able to see through the eyes of our Agent of Being and directly experience its wisdom.

When our Third Eye is open and balanced, we experience a deep sense of equanimity and peace and come into accord with the deepest and highest ground within us. Our five senses take on an infinite capability in which we are able to see more, hear more, feel more and know far more than what we glean from our finite senses.

When our Third Eye is blocked and unbalanced we lose our connection with the Divine, resulting in feeling uselessness or purposeless, which triggers us into temptations, distractions and activities that further blind our higher knowing and vision. In terms of the linkage to *Integration*, because this Sixth Chakra is the departure from the physical reality and entrance into the metaphysical reality, there is a huge pull to drift in one direction or the other. Just as *Integration* requires us to master the paradox of our shadows and light and bring *Presence* to our deepest oppositional forces, so too does the Third Eye present us with a similar challenge in terms of which direction we channel our life-force energy to flow within us.

Exploration And Integration Guide

Now for some "negotiation" tactics as Jung calls them that will assist you in your personal *Integration* work. Because everyone's journey into Wholeness is different, and each of us has our own unique "shadow-self" to bring to light, you'll need to engage with my suggestions in a manner that meets your specific needs. This exercise is multi-purposed in that it's also designed to assist you in completing your Box work so you can prepare yourself to cross the great divide between *Presence* and *Transcendence.* Only from this expansive space can you begin your *Integration* work. If you have not gotten clarity on your Box yet, I suggest returning to the previous chapters and taking another pass at it. To be honest, liberating ourselves from our Box is a formidable task as it has many ways to remain in control. For this work to be successful, you at least need to have your Box identified and have in place a practice of catching yourself whenever it gets reactivated and shows up in your relationships and life. Let me be clear, you do not need to always be out of your Box, but you must bring forth a sustaining curiosity and humility in order to gain forward movement into higher ground. Ok, on with the negotiation tactics for doing the work of *Integration.*

1. The "Life Recapitulation" process I introduced in chapter five is the perfect medium to use in order to illuminate your darkest shadows. The added clarity required here is to be more rigorous with yourself in terms of identifying violations, betrayals and other dark acts you yourself may have committed, were exposed to, or allowed to occur in your personal space.

2. For every shadow you call up I advise you to "be with it" until the shame, blame, self-judgment, and regret dissipates and drops to zero. You'll know when that is because your compulsion to justify, defend or deny what you did or experienced will begin to fade and you'll be able to simply "be with" the issues without your ego-self making a fuss about them.

3. As soon as you call up a shadow, act upon and complete the step above. I suggest that you also find a positive act you committed and engage in the same process, but with a positive spin on it as a way to balance the dynamics of this exercise. Calling up too many shadows in a row will cause you to implode, and you'll find yourself paying a visit to the good/bad doctor.

4. Do a journaling process of listing all the "Basic Assumptions" you may be holding about God, Spirit, Religion, Faith and any other deep-seated moralistic beliefs residing within your psyche. As you identify each one, ask yourself if you are willing to release it, let it go, and essentially disconnect your identity from it. (Don't panic, if the specific belief you release is truly authentic to you it will naturally return on its own. If on the other hand, it does not return, you'll know it was not truly yours to begin with.)

5. Do a journaling process on your fears and judgments of humanity's "dark side," such as acts of brutality, violence, war, murder, rape, torture, molest, etc. List them one by one and what specifically they pertain to. Be intentional, authentic and rigorous with yourself in this exercise, as it's easy to gloss over the prejudices we harbor that have been lodged within us for many years. What you are looking for is the arrogant denial of *"I would never do that."* Maybe you as an individual never would do it, but "you" are more than an individual, you are also part of the human race, and as such you do indeed share in humanity's atrocities. Undoubtedly resistance will arise, so expect it and be with your shadows until you can accept them fully and actually dance a light-hearted "two-step" with them.

6. Do a journaling process on the virtues and values that inspire you, the ways of being that represents your Higher Self and Agent of Being. List all those mentors and leaders current and past who inspire you, and dive into what exactly inspires you about them. Then work with the reality that if you value and admire these individuals, you must possess some of the same virtues within you, else you wouldn't value them. Find these virtues within, honor them and bring them into your consciousness right along with the shadows dwelling within you. After all the more "dance partners" the better, so be courageous and outrageous!

7. Open a dialogue with your Inner Agent of Being. Yes, finally we are here! In your own private space with no one else around, somewhere that is sacred and special to you, call forth your Agent of Being and ask for its guidance. You must do so with no expectations and no willfulness. It is a *request you are making,* not an *order you are giving.* The form in which your inner Agent will manifest will be unique to you and will not match up with my inner Agent, so please don't compare. You may have already had access to your Agent of Being prior to reading this book. If that's the case, great, stay with it and perhaps deepen your connection. Maybe the notion of an inner Agent is totally new for you, in which case you want to let go of the opinion that you are at a disadvantage because you are new to the notion. Instead, I recommend assuming that you have as much access capability as anybody else, regardless of their tenure.

(A/N: Before we move on, I want to take this opportunity to thank you for all the hard work you are doing and for being courageous enough to traverse the challenging paradoxical material within the Presence Stage. I honor you and want you to know that it's a privilege for me to be traveling with you and providing whatever guidance I can regarding your journey. I'm only as good a guide as is the Traveler who accepts my guidance. Bless you and the goodness and greatness within you!)

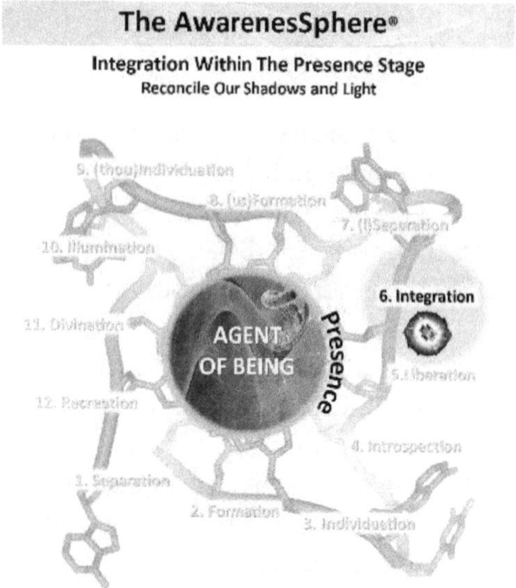

The AwarenesSphere®
Integration Within The Presence Stage
Reconcile Our Shadows and Light

Let's move on by recapping *Integration, Presence's Sixth Phase of Self-Awareness.* This Phase is about embracing our shadow and light sides, a paradoxical coming together of the oppositional forces dwelling within our psyche. The "integrating" to be done has to do with reconciliation and acceptance of the diverse behavior traits and energies moving deep within us. It's also about being with and accepting "what is" even if what is, is not pretty, pleasant, or socially acceptable.

Within *Integration* our higher faculty of Self-Awareness undergoes yet another transformation in which we begin to come to terms with the paradoxical facets of our human presence and spiritual nature. This journey is called "walking the narrow path," and only the most devoted travelers walk it in a way that delivers them to their Higher Self and Agent of Being. This is so because moving into the energy flow of *Integration* is like entering an emotional vortex, it requires nothing less than absolute surrender and giving up our life as we've known it.

Every religion on Earth portrays their own unique beliefs about the battle between Good and Evil, with most emphasizing Good winning over Evil. But *Integration* is about opening to the reality that both Good and Evil arise from the same source within us, and that our fear of, and moralistic judgments about Evil are mere shadows. I shared the story of Dr. Jekyll and Mr. Hyde for the purpose of illuminating not only the battle, but also the importance of integrating our darker forces in a way that enables us to possess them, but not dramatize them or act them out. Once we realize that both demons and angels dwell within us, we can end the battle and simply allow them to co-exist and "dance together" within our psyche.

Until we open to and accept the opposing forces moving deep within us, the gateway into the *Third Stage of Transcendence* remains closed to us. Just as there was a bridge of curiosity and humility that needed to be crossed between *Emergence* and *Presence,* a similar bridge must be traversed between *Presence* and *Transcendence.* This bridge, however, requires a profound leap of faith in that it's virtually invisible and dynamically changing in its form and structure.

I shared the story of my sojourn into the Joshua Tree Desert and the profound awakening I had encountering the mountain lion and the star constellation. These life-changing experiences drew me into the vortex of *Integration* in which I came face-to-face with the opposing forces residing within me. I came to accept that both demons and angels dwell within me rather than trying to convert my demons into angels. This deep-seated acceptance was a powerful revelation for me. The implications of *Integration* are far-reaching. What it means is that we must acknowledge and take responsibility for every shadowed act we've ever committed against others, as well as stand up humbly into the light of every act of kindness and goodness we have ever done. It also requires ending the story of how others mistreated us and how *"we would never do such a thing."* As that story ends, a new one begins. And the new story is one of Interconnectedness, Wholeness, and Transcendence. ~

Other than the Q&A and Member Resources sections below, this completes *Volume 1* along with the introduction to the *AwarenesSphere* and its first two Stages of *Emergence* and *Presence.* In *Volume 2,* we will continue our journey upward around the spiraling terrain of the *AwarenesSphere* and on to the Stages of *Transcendence, Essence* and *Beyond. (A/N: You will find Volume 2 on Amazon.com. Also, if you found this first book in the series valuable, I ask that you post a review on my Amazon page, as well as share this book with your friends and family. It would mean a lot to me as your support will encourage others to begin their journey within. In both cases you can simply search for "Travelers Within" on the Amazon.com* URL *and both Volumes 1 and 2 will display.)*

In the first chapter of *Volume 2,* we'll crossover the mysterious divide between the *Second Stage of Presence* and into the *Third Stage of Transcendence.* Once you review the Q&A section, I'll be your guide once again in *Volume 2* into some ominously inspiring jungle terrain, so sharpen up your machete and pack your mosquito repellent, because we're heading into a shamanic paradise of terror I call, *"The Inner Jungle of Come, Stay, Go!"*

♦♦♦

Reader's Question & Answer Section (Chapter 6: Integration)

Allison - Q: In integrating our shadow self, I find it easier to accept and integrate what others did to me, but harder to integrate and accept some poor choices I might have done in the past where I possibly hurt others. In this Integration process, are there more tips for the process of undoing guilt or shame? I have sat with them so many times and the part of my ego that wants to punish myself always comes back.

Val Jon – A: I can empathize with you totally. When I was a boy of no more than 12 my father took me deer hunting and I made the unfortunate mistake of shooting a baby fawn rather than a buck. The bullet paralyzed its back legs, and once it went down, it dragged itself along the ground with its front hooves. My father made me follow it and put it out of its misery. I'll never forget the cries it made and how it looked at me just before I killed it. While its suffering ended in that moment, mine just began. What I did that fateful day has haunted me my whole life, and even as experienced as I am with this wonderful inner work, there is a part of me that feels deep shame and remorse, awful visual images that never go away, no matter how much processing I do. And, at the same time, I believe Spirit *wants me* to retain this deep shame so I am reminded of the sacredness of life and motivated to never ever again cause harm to others, be them animals or humans. While what I did can never be undone, I have come to a place of "paradoxical peace" about it knowing that it is a cross I must bear for maintaining a deep devotion to the sacredness of life. You too can do the same. Find peace in what Spirit wants for you with regard to your own poor choices and rise up into being the good and great human being you are, and bear what you must with a healthy humility as you travel on.

Allison - Q: Can you explain a bit more about the connection between integrating our shadow and becoming balanced in the 6th Chakra? Are you saying that to have that Chakra come into alignment do we need to heal all of our shadow work?

Val Jon – A: The Third Eye Chakra is the sacred center in which our spiritual vision comes into focus and we attain not only the ability to see more deeply into the Divine movement of Spirit and life but also develop the ability to actually manifest our visions into reality. This action of manifestation requires a fine balance between accessing and moving with both our Human presence and our Divine nature. Without embracing and integrating our shadow aspects the Human side of this balance is under-represented causing a "blurred vision." Imagine wearing a pair of glasses in which one lens has ten times less magnification than the other lens. Not only would your ability to manifest what you envision be disabled, but you also wouldn't even be able to stand up and walk in a straight line. Does this mean we need to do *all* our shadow Integration work before we can move on? No, but we must have embraced enough of the dark material and forces dwelling within us to be able to breathe easy into the darkness. Without this ease, we'd be spending way too much energy in watching our back for a self-imposed shadow-attack.

Allison - Chapter Statement: I have been working on my shadow aspects for some time now in my life and although I still feel suffering attached there, I am stepping into the "personal bridge" between my "Humanity and Divinity." I can do this very easily for others, but still hold an almost misbelief at some of my past unconscious actions, especially when I was a teenager and felt very lost after an extreme experience with sexual violation. This chapter has my heart right there with it, and my prayer and devotion to self-growth and evolution know that it is here where I am ready to integrate fully into my wholeness.

Anna - Q: I might need to borrow some Faerie dust from Tinkerbell if I'm going to chase down my shadows! I've discovered some of them are quite dark and scary and it surprised me that I could hold such evil in my heart, even though I would never act upon them. I could never bring myself to inflict the type of suffering I've endured in the past on another or others. Yet, when I really looked hard at others, I began to imagine what was in their Box that has them so trapped that they would even consider being evil in the first place. How does one become reintegrated with a society that is so trapped within its individuality?

Val Jon – A: As we journey into our higher inner ground, the disparity between where we are and where the masses are with respect to traveling within increases exponentially. There are two paths we can take with respect to this disparity. The first path, which I do not recommend, is to live inside a "bubble of clarity." Essentially you go about your life experiencing your inner travels, growing yourself and simply tolerating the gap between you and others. The second path, which I highly recommend, is to put yourself right in the midst of the "individuality" you experience people being trapped in and be a light in the darkness for them. To be of service and assistance by walking with others on the path and gently showing the way around the upward spiral of the AwarenesSphere is the best course to take. What you'll find is that your virtuous service along with a super large sack of "Faerie dust" helps keep your path forward both doable and magical.

Anna - Q: How do we find a fulcrum point between the two opposing forces within?

Val Jon – A: A "fulcrum point" implies "balance," but that is not the objective of the work of Integration. The goal is not to balance or equalize the opposing forces that dwell within us, but rather to enable them to coexist within our psyche regardless of their diversity or imbalances. What we want to be establishing within is a clean and clear space that empowers us to be with our paradoxical energies in a way that we can acknowledge the darker side of them without going into reaction, dramatizing, or acting them out.

Anna - Chapter Statement: Learning to integrate both dynamics within has been a real struggle. I found myself accepting actions that have been done to me because I believed that was just how it was. Yet it wasn't that way for any others. Coming into awareness for me means accepting life as a woman versus how a man might go about doing so, and considering what is acceptable behavior for each gender. Also, it includes being aware of how conditioned we are to accept abuse in a myriad of forms and how unconsciously we participate in their perpetuation. Be it, parenting, community, culture, religion, education, entertainment, the list can go on as to how they all influence our development as a human being. I have come to the conclusion that the battle is between Human Being and Being Human as Val Jon suggested in the introduction.

Antonio - Q: If I remove all judgment from my actions of "right" or "wrong," I am left with only what is. Can I see that this was/is, is all part of the Divine play, and that every situation I find myself in is created for this process of self-discovery and Integration?

Val Jon – A: The poet Rumi once said, *"Out beyond ideas of wrong-doing and right-doing there is a field. I'll meet you there. When the soul lies down in that grass the world is too full to talk about."* I can't help but say to myself, "yes," and at the same time, if I suddenly woke up, looked in the mirror and noticed that all my judgments, worries and doubts were missing, I'd probably think I was somebody else. There's no doubt that we humans love to make stuff up and then place ourselves in what we made up, forget we placed ourselves there, and proceed to find ways out of it, only to make up a whole new level of stuff. So yes, it's all for our process of self-discovery . . . and perhaps also for our perpetual entertainment.

Antonio - Q: If I don't surrender to Spirit and move into a space of allowing instead of integrating the shadow and light aspects of the self, will my psyche remain fractured and at the effect? Will I and my relationships be in a constant state of "disintegration," without me even being aware of it?

Val Jon - A: Our natural state is to evolve and integrate, so even if we ignore the work of Integration or choose not to surrender to Spirit, we'll still grow in spite of ourselves. This isn't necessarily the case for everyone, however. There are some people who are their own worst enemies, and their unchecked detriments send them into disintegration. But it must be understood that for some, the "darkness comes before the dawn" so even they are included in the evolutionary process we are all blessed with. On a more practical note, there's an old Chinese proverb that addresses the issue of complacency and denial. It goes like this, *"If we don't change the course we are on we're going to end up where we are headed."*

Antonio - Chapter Statement: A great reminder that with humility comes the ability to surrender to something infinitely larger than myself. With surrender enters the possibility of transformation. When I allow myself to move into a space of being, and specifically, becoming the silent witness to the stillness in my thoughts, the rise, and fall of my breath, I have the presence of mind needed to not overthink things, a valued awareness that lessens my mental suffering. Only when I can let my trust unfold within me, can I learn to listen to the inner guidance of my Agent of Being. The power is always within. Sometimes we just need gentle reminders.

Cyn - Q: How do I discern the spirit of my Agent of Being and know to follow the intuitive call versus that from an "internal imposter" from my darker side?

Val Jon - A: Your inner Agent will always, always offer you advice that is not only for your own benefit but for the betterment of everyone involved. "Imposters within" are as easy to spot as flashing red lights in that they always have a selfish agenda or a temptation that plays into the shallowness of the ego. Besides, if you happen to get duped you'll know it almost instantly because of the detriment you soon find yourself in. The encouraging news is that as the Chooser, you can, (as you mention in your chapter statement below) simply *"tap your heels together three times"* and get yourself back to Kansas, where you can pay closer attention the next go-round.

Cyn - Q: How do I know when I am in my truth? Do we have physical reactions to truth?

Val Jon - A: The one absolutely fool-proof way to know is to listen to your internal chatter. If you find yourself having to justify your "truth" to yourself, make excuses for it, or try to convince yourself of its merits, it's not your truth, but rather your ego's attempt to control your better conscience. The physical reactions are not quite as trustworthy because we tend to have pockets of unconsciousness throughout our bodies that act as blinders to the truths we hold.

Cyn - Chapter Statement: My mind immediately jumps to the Wizard of Oz. I believe I saw that film when, at age 6 or 7, we moved to Illinois and within the first week were running down into the ground beneath two rather flimsy pieces of wood as shouts of "tornado" rang loud and clear. But that movie of good and evil has stayed with me and struck me as a lesson in love and the heart-wrenching tragedy of so many who desperately need to be loved. I love in this chapter the opportunity to say to oneself, *"loving yourself is a journey,"* and when we take time to discover who we are, warts and all, all the doors of loving are opened. There is no doubt in my mind the tango of good and evil exists in each of us, acknowledging the fact that we even harbor dark thoughts and are sometimes compelled to act on those thoughts knowing someone will be hurt or reap the consequences of our actions is not something to be proud of, but I do think it is a part of the human condition, and wonder where the line of Integration exists. Unique for each of us, I presume. It is the power of the stars for me, the only consistencies in my life were my mother and Orion, yes, the star constellation, and I thank you for adding a dimension to my life which rings so true–the now, the eternal, the life cycles and the power of the Universe–the vastness of our individual space if we can just allow our outstretched arms/wings to catch wind!

Elise - Q: What is the difference between "Am" and "Be?"

Val Jon - A: They are both two sides of the same hand. "Am" is our sustained presence appearing *outside* the illusion of time. While "Be" is the insertion of our presence *into* the illusion of time with the intent to have it persist. To "Be" is the tangible fulfillment of "Am." A simple analogy is of a fireworks skyrocket being sent up into the air. Before it explodes into a dazzling light show it's "Am-ing," but the moment it explodes into a burst of color, it is "Being."

Elise - Q: The good/bad choice gives us patterns for our lives, so is an idea of "bad" what always needs to be undone, or does the "good" need undoing as well?

Val Jon - A: Good and bad are "navigational markers for the psyche," much like the painted lines on a highway that designate lanes. Whether staying within them is "good" or "bad" is situational and depends on the context. For example, it's "good" to cross the lines when turning left or right, but "bad" to do so when there are other vehicles in our immediate path. For this reason, in order to answer your question, I need to take the liberty of shifting the context from "good/bad" to "loving/fearful." That which is loving requires no undoing, as it's Spirit's essential nature and the core of our deepest human virtues. Fear, on the other hand, does require undoing because it creates a distraction that keeps us from recognizing and manifesting our deeper loving nature.

Elise - Chapter Statement: My physical illness placed me in the space of "crucifixion" due to the extraordinary physical pain that even morphine did not relieve. My understandings are similar and this chapter validated my experiences.

Mindy - Q: Is it outlandish that my shadow and dark side are something of a comfort to me? In my quest for perfection, am I embracing that side as a place I can be myself, with myself, for myself?

Val Jon - A: Giving ourselves permission to be fully human, (rather than half-human) is perhaps the greatest gift we can ever give ourselves. Opening to and the action of wholeheartedly embracing our shadow and dark side is a major cornerstone of mental health. What is "outlandish" in my opinion is to limit our access to only our good side and cut off our connection with our darker attributes. Imagine removing one each of your ears, eyes, arms, and legs, (yes view the image for a moment to get the reality of how well, happy and fulfilled you would feel without all these "sides" of yourself). As for a "quest for perfection," while I'm sure you mean it in the sense of being as fulfilled and as whole as possible, our "flaws" are part of our wholeness, so I don't recommend pursuing perfection unless you want to perpetuate inner frustration and self-judgment. And finally, the "comfort" you speak about is very important to understand. While getting familiar with, and accepting of our dark side is a healthy process, getting too "comfortable" with it can open the way for it to find ways of manifesting in our behaviors, which we do not want to encourage. I am totally accepting of my dark side . . . and completely vigilant with it so as to keep it "dancing" with my goodness rather than giving it enough leeway to kidnap me.

Mindy - Q: As we integrate, can we slip up and "dis-integrate?" And then, so we have to run to catch up with ourselves, so to speak? Do we completely lose momentum? (And yes, I'm using the Christian philosophy of "backsliding" here.)

Val Jon - A: Backsliding is an important learning process regardless of our religious or philosophical preferences. What few people understand is that reverting to old patterns and backsliding into depression, chaos, upset or even apathy at times is absolutely essential for successfully reaching higher ground within. What backsliding provides us is a means for becoming aware of what was missing all along our journey through life as we were making forward progress. This failure to notice what we are missing can set us up for massive breakdowns in the future if we fail to discover them in a timely manner. Let me give you an example. You are going on a cross country trip, you pack up your vehicle, plan your route and off you go. Your journey includes crossing valleys, mountains, and deserts. A few hundred miles into your trip you get a flat tire and pull off the roadway. You proceed to change the tire, but you discover that you have all the needed equipment except that your spare tire is . . . also flat. You have no cell service to call for help so you need to "backslide" into the little town you passed a few miles back to get the flat tire repaired. Now imagine if you didn't discover what was missing until you were stranded in a blizzard atop the mountains looming ahead or in the parched desert that stretches for hundreds of miles on their far side. The same goes for our emotional and behavioral backsliding. We need to revisit our inner "danger zones" enough times until we've checked all our human equipment and made sure it's up for the "journey into being human and beyond."

Mindy - Chapter Statement: This chapter had a profound impact on me. As a Christian, the concepts of Good vs. Evil and Dark vs. Light have been part of my daily life always. Before beginning my journey through the AwarenesSphere I felt compelled to hide the dark side. I now know I can fully experience Integration with all parts of my psyche, and I purposefully visit my shadows. I need to go there as a release. I would encourage my fellow inner travelers to take the time to focus and really work through each step of the *Exploration and Integration Guide.* These tactics will provide an extraordinary insight into full Integration.

Susie - Q: Is it possible that there is no "Evil" per se, but rather, just automatic negative reactions from our Primary Decision and Box?

Val Jon - A: I believe we humans make up the personifications of Evil, such as the "Devil," "Satan," and other dark aberrations. However, because Evil is defined as the "antithesis of life," (that which destroys rather than creates) I believe it exists as a real force. A black hole for instance tears worlds apart. The day one approaches Earth, (or the arrival of any other cataclysmic event) you and I will know that Evil indeed exists. On a more down to earth level, cancer is Evil in the sense that it takes life rather than gives life. But the nature of its Evil is not personified, it is merely a dark aspect of the life and death cycle we must come to appreciate. I personally had to face the Evil of cancer within my own body as I was writing *Travelers Within.* Rather than negating it and fearing it, I embraced it and redirected its negative energy into supporting my well-being rather than detracting from it.

Susie - Q: Is Integration about "being with?" Being with all aspects of our psyche?

Val Jon - A: Integration is a "functional" process, much as if you stirred an egg into a pancake batter. The more you whip it, the more integrated the egg becomes with the batter. Being with, on the other hand, is an "observational" process in which you watch as the batter becomes breakfast. The outcome of the Integration process definitely prepares us to "be with" all the diverse challenges our psyche encounters in our daily lives.

Susie - Chapter Statement: I have a lot to learn and practice as I have no experience of connecting with my Agent of Being, intuition or divine forces. I am a newborn baby in this arena. What I got from this chapter is that *it does* indeed exist, and a lot of people have had direct experience, so I am assuming that I can also. I have begun my conversations today.

Victoria - Q: When in the spiral of making one poor choice after another, even knowing and accepting self-responsibility, how does one pull themselves out of self-judgment?

Val Jon - A: Whenever we find ourselves repeating the same mistakes over and over again it's an indicator that we've not yet gotten to the core issue, nor the essential lesson that underlies our poor choices. There are degrees of "accepting self-responsibility" and in order to end detrimental patterns, we must engage at the highest degree in order to liberate ourselves. If you find yourself in a "spiral," (and it isn't heading towards higher ground) you are not being fully responsible or making contemplative choices. It is more likely that you are instead engaging in impulsive reactive decisions. As hard as it is to stop ourselves from reacting, we must intervene in our behaviors in order to free ourselves from our downward spiral. The crucial distinction is to not resist our self-judgments, but rather to embrace them just as we would comfort a wounded child. By being compassionate with ourselves and by surrendering up our impulsive willfulness, we are able to stop our downward spiral just long enough to turn ourselves around and face in an uphill direction.

Victoria - Q: As a child, I was called rebellious, yet for me, it wasn't rebellion. I just didn't feel right about the very tight confines of my parent's belief systems, and I pushed at the edges wanting to participate in a bigger world. Why do some of us seem to be more inclined to push the limits and break the rules more than others?

Val Jon - A: The inclinations we have are the result of how our core identity was organized and what behavior sets and values we took on during our development in the Emergence Stage. I recall you mentioning early on that your life has been made up of complete opposites and that you have always had as you put it, "an inner-truth" acting as your guide. These two traits should answer why you were, (and probably still are) a rule-breaker. Now the deeper question here I believe is how is it that some beings who arrive in life possess these two confounding traits? I don't have an answer for it other than to surmise that there must be a "thread of unbridled Spirit" that gets woven into the genetic makeup and destiny of some of us. I say "welcome to the weave," and consider yourself fortunate to be part of the, uh . . . "rebellious travelers" tapestry.

Victoria - Chapter Statement: This Phase for me was a long, hard road making poor choices, some of which nearly destroyed me. While I knew I was responsible for my choices and the potential outcomes, I had not yet learned to communicate with my inner Agent beyond basic intuition. I had begun the journey into knowing myself and letting go of old beliefs, however, my poor choices led to putting on new layers of self-belief I would later need to shed. At times my thirst for adventure and success overrode my gut feelings and inner moral compass. Other times my inner voice spoke loud enough to bail me out. Having children helped me to be at peace with myself as it showed me my best and worst self.

♦♦♦

TRAVELERS WITHIN SOCIETY AND MEMBER RESOURCES

The *Travelers Within Society, (TWS)* is a network of experienced life travelers, *"Agents of Being on the move"* if you like who share the common interests of personal growth, inner explorations and the challenge and opportunity of being "Trimtabs" in the world. Those who've traveled the inner terrain of the *AwarenesSphere* and done the work of reaching higher ground within are invited to join *TWS*. Our Society is made up of the *Travelers Within* reader audience, alliance partners and experts in the world of personal growth. The online resources we make available include but are not limited to articles, videos, website and Facebook links, bibliographies, event calendars, support forums, and specific personal development opportunities.

To join us, log on to www.travelerswithin.com. You will find an abundance of resources including the following pages available on our website:

Travelers Within Books Online
Travelers Facebook Group
YouTube Channel
Articles and Publications
Recommended Reading
Submit A Book Review On My Website
Programs and Retreats
Planned Global Expeditions
VIP Mentoring Programs
Corporate Leadership Programs
Professional Speaking Engagements
LinkedIn, Val Jon Farris
Contact Author, Val Jon Farris

Special *Travelers Within* Preceptorship Program Invitation to Mental Health Professionals, Personal Growth Practitioners, and Community Leaders:

I will be hosting a special training program for those interested in facilitating the principles and practices I've outlined in *Travelers Within*. The *AwarenesSphere* and all the developmental materials associated with its Four Stages and Twelve Phases will be made available under a formal preceptorship and licensing agreement. Graduates of this advanced facilitator program will be certified to host *Traveling Within* sessions in their hometowns. For more information, contact me via the website. Please add *"Leader Preceptorship Program Inquiry"* in the title and I will send you more detailed information. —Val Jon Farris

GLOSSARY OF TERMS

[1] **Higher Self** – An aspect of our identity that operates beyond the predictable limitations of the ego. "Higher" refers to a spiritual elevation associated with our greater human virtues of love, compassion, humility, faith, and devotion. It also suggests the higher faculty of Self-Awareness, or the ability to observe our behaviors and actions and calibrate them towards wiser, more virtuous interactions and outcomes.

[2] **Character Modeling** – Influencing our core values and behavior traits through exposure to mentors, teachers and role models. Human character traits are malleable and can be shaped both for the better or worse. Inspiration is the initial modeling activity and must be reinforced through sustained practices to ensure permanent character changes.

[3] **Trimtab** – A term coined by the late R. Buckminster Fuller describing a unique leveraging mechanism that enables a small intervention to produce a large result. This leveraging principle can be transferred to human behavior as well. Just as Trimtabs attached to the rudders of the "great ships of state" can facilitate massive navigational maneuvers with minimal power usage. Likewise, thinking of ourselves as Trimtabs empowers us to realize that we can make huge differences in our world.

[4] **Inner Terrain** – A descriptive term referring to the content of the human psyche and particularly the psychological areas of emotion, memory, history, belief and mental constructs having to do with the nature of one's personal identity and character.

[5] **Psyche** – In addition to representing all the aspects of our identity and personality, in Greek mythology, "Psyche" was a beautiful princess who fell in love with Eros (Cupid), the god of love, and went through devastating trials before being allowed to marry him. The story is often understood to be about the soul redeeming itself through love. In-kind, the Self redeems itself through the self-loving act of traveling through the *AwarenesSphere*.

[6] **Being** – The quality or state of having existence or existing. Being is the essence of all life and the source behind all that presences itself. It can also be understood as Spirit's gift of life force energy infused into living matter.

[7] **Agent of Being** – The existence of our higher spiritual nature as it arises within our field of awareness. Our Agent of Being is our omnipotent representative, a lifelong mentor and role model that resides within our psyche, and it serves as a sacred resource that we can call upon to make wise choices in our daily lives.

---

[8] **Intentional Choice** – To "choose" is to consider the alternatives and then make a selection freely and unattached to all of the alternatives. In other words, we accept our choices unconditionally rather than getting caught in a mental debate over whether they were good or bad, right or wrong selections. Making choices with clear intention means focusing on the outcome we desire and placing our positive energy and full conviction into embracing the "inner-tension" until we achieve what we are intending.

[9] **Self-Awareness** – The ability to be aware of our awareness. To be aware is to be sentient, but mere sentience lacks the "elevation of consciousness" needed to observe our behaviors, reflect on them as we act on them, and modify them as needed in order to produce the most optimal outcomes for ourselves and others. The higher faculty of Self-Awareness enables us to witness and choose our responses rather than automatically and directly reacting to them.

[10] **AwarenesSphere** – A psychological and behavioral model or "roadmap" developed by the author as a means for charting the developmental journey of the human psyche into higher levels of awareness. The *AwarenesSphere* documents the pathways, principles and practices required for accelerating our evolution into fully realized, fully alive and fulfilled "Humans Being."

[11] **Archetypal** – Defines an original model of a person, ideal example, or a prototype upon which others are copied or emulated. In philosophy, Archetypes refer to ideal forms of perceived or sensible things or types. The use of Archetypes to illuminate personality was advanced by Carl Jung early in the 20th century, who suggested the existence of universal energetic forces dwelling deep within the psyche that channel experiences and emotions, resulting in recognizable patterns of behavior with certain probable outcomes.

[12] **Divine** – A spiritual connotation referring to being connected to, and a part of God, Spirit or the Universe. The Latin root, *Di* means "Two" and *Vin* means "God." This dual nature of the omnipotent can be interpreted as "God within" and "God without," or "God above" and "God below." Rather than suggesting "Unity," the Divine can be understood as its deeper and more revealing meaning of "Sacred Division."

[13] **Basic Assumptions** – Emotionally charged conclusions and beliefs which we inherit from others or fabricate on our own. Once accepted as valid, we integrate these assumptions into our unconscious mindset where they automatically dictate our behaviors and actions without our conscious consent. At a deeper and more concerning level, Basic Assumptions also take control over shaping our values and preferences, as well as limiting or restricting what we are willing to experience, engage in and accept.

[14] **Primary Decisions** – Powerful emotionally charged conclusions and decisions we create during the *Emergence Stage* about ourselves, others and the world in general. We literally "join"

with these decisions and become them to the point of losing our sense of Self. More detrimental than Basic Assumptions, these early childhood reactions to either real or perceived threats shape our newly forming identity and act as rigid structures to inhibit or stop future invasions. Like being in a "Box," while we gain protection from future threats, our outward choices, expressions and liberties also become inhibited.

[15] **Casting** – The act of creating, declaring or bringing into existence some value-based conclusion, decision or belief about one's self or about one's abilities. The simple act of declaring *"I'm angry"* is a casting in which one does not simply express anger, but actually *becomes* the anger they are expressing. Casting is an unconscious choice to give over our power to choose and become a victim of our circumstances.

[16] **Infantile Introjection** – A young child's tendency to blame themselves for whatever negative circumstances arise during their upbringing. Introjection is a psychological assimilation mechanism that occurs when a child (or adult) internalizes the ideas, actions or voices of other people. This behavior is associated with the internalization of authority figures such as parents, grandparents or early childhood mentors.

[17] **Self** – Greater than the "identity" or the "personality," the Self is our essential being-ness and personal expression within the context of our own life. For purposes of *Travelers Within,* the Self is a "joiner," or bonding agent. The definition of Self is, *"the agent that of itself, acts in a manner implied by the word with which it is joined."* Because life itself, and our being alive is an interconnected process, there is a tendency for us to merge with other living beings and aspects of life. An inorganic example is two droplets of water that naturally join into one droplet. An organic example is mating, procreating and the bonding that naturally arises within couples, families, groups, and cultures.

[18] **Power of Choice** – To be able to choose freely and after consideration. A "choice" is different from a "decision," in that to decide literally means "to kill the alternative." Rather than denying alternatives, making a choice is about including all the alternatives, recognizing that they are not separate from what we choose, but rather are part of an interconnected whole. Possessing the Power of Choice means taking responsibility for the outcomes we produce, rather than blaming our circumstances for what arises in our lives. A "Chooser" also has the power to "uncast" detrimental assumptions and decisions.

[19] **Energetic Disposition** – Core identity genetics passed along to us by our family of origin and ancestors in the form of inherited behavior and emotional material. Just as physical traits are passed from generation to generation, so too are behavioral and emotional traits. This inherited genetic material "predisposes" infants to cast a very specific Primary Decision, one that is influenced by the behavior traits of their ancestors.

[20] **Chakra** – One of twelve metaphysical energy centers located within, below and above the human body. "Chakra," in Sanskrit means "wheel," which represents the cycling of Kundalini life-force energy within the Twelve Chakra centers. Each of the Twelve Chakras correlates with the Twelve Phases of the *AwarenesSphere*. There is a linkage between what occurs within each Chakra and what occurs developmentally for us within each Phase.

[21] **Uncasting** – The healing process of essentially "un-doing" whatever trauma we may have endured as infants. By intentionally opening to, focusing on and re-experiencing every moment of the traumatic incident, our psyche naturally releases the negative charge associated with it, and the result is that we free ourselves from its detrimental grip.

[22] **Symbiosis** – A pre and post womb bonding phenomenon in which mother and fetus, or mother and infant share the same life-force energy and are interconnected at a physical and/or emotional level. Symbiosis usually extends from pre-birth until one or two years of age. An example of the power of Symbiosis is that when a mother smiles at her baby, her baby also smiles. If that same mother frowns or displays anger, her baby will become immediately upset.

[23] **Assimilation** – The cognitive process of fitting new information into existing cognitive structures, perceptions, and understanding. This means that when we are faced with new data, we make sense of it by referring to information we already possess that may be similar. Assimilation continues throughout our lives but is most influential for infants between the ages of one and four. Infants "mouth" objects as a way to assimilate and integrate the information about their presence into their newly forming psyche.

[24] **Adaptation** – An early childhood development process that refers to an infant's ability to accept new information and adjust their internal understanding accordingly. Adaptation helps children with their identity formation, and with growing increasingly more mentally and emotionally capable, Adaptations that contribute their capabilities, personality and character traits as they mature.

[25] **Reactive Formation** – A defense mechanism in which a person acts in a manner opposite from his or her espoused beliefs. An example is declaring that we would never treat our children the way our parents treated us, and then when we become parents ourselves we find ourselves acting out the very same parental behaviors that our parents displayed. Why this happens is that the investment we place in resisting being like someone places their detrimental characteristics in our consciousness for an extended period of time. This has the effect of us assimilating those traits at an unconscious level. A simple example is staring at the Sun for too long, then when we look away, we're left with an imprint of its intense light in our field of vision.

---

[26] **False Validation** – The reaffirmation of a Basic Assumption or Primary Decision based on a similar threat or act of abuse we encountered when we first cast our assumptions and decisions. Why it's a "false" validation is that while the threat or abuse may be real, the conclusion we validate about it is only true within the confines of our Box, and not necessarily true in reality. With each False Validation we conclude, our Box gains greater control over our beliefs, behaviors, and actions.

[27] **The Box** – Otherwise known as a "Primary Decision," this emotionally charged structure gets cast into our psyche early on during our identity development. The "decision" we formulate is in reaction to a real or perceived threat in which we withdraw and defended ourselves in the only way we knew how as infants, to shut down and cut ourselves off from the circumstances and/or persons threatening us. While our Box was an initial solution to dealing with our childhood threats and abuses, as we mature, its presence within our psyche restricts our aliveness and produces adult behaviors that negatively impact our sense of self and our relationships with others.

[28] **Spirit** – Derived from the Latin root *"Spiritus,"* which means "breath of life," Spirit is the source and origin of all life and the animating force within all living things. From a philosophical perspective, Spirit can be understood as the non-personified version of God. Rather than being an entity modeled upon the human form, Spirit is a vast omnipotent force responsible for the persistence of all that exists, both animate and inanimate. Like the process of breathing, Spirit breathes life into existence, sustains the life it creates, and then "exhales" its creations back into nonexistence. Another way of describing this omnipotent process is [G]eneration, [O]rganization and [D]estruction.

[29] **Intense Curiosity** – This means to exercise a profoundly curious nature by placing greater importance on self-reflection than on self-gratification. Curiosity requires that we engage in a continuous inquiry process, calling into question our previously assumed "truths" and re-examining them to determine if they are still relevant for us. It also includes placing ourselves in uncomfortable learning situations in which we accelerate our growth and development, sacrificing our ego-self's vanity for our Higher Self's capabilities.

[30] **Intentional Humility** – The act of consciously setting our ego aside and bowing down to the reality that we are an infinitesimally small part of life, and doing so with a clear conscience and joyful heart. Being "humbled" and being "humiliated" are not the same thing. Humiliation is the ego's way of taking things personally, whereas humility is our Higher Self's way of taking things divinely and not being demeaned, but actually enriched. Additionally, from a position of humility we realize that what we've not yet mastered isn't evidence for self-invalidation, but rather proof of our good intentions to grow and better ourselves. Humiliation, on the other hand, the result of our ego being bruised and going into a self-pity tantrum over it.

---

[31] **Dharma Energy** – A Hindu term following the teachings of Buddha that signifies behaviors considered to be in alignment with the omnipotent force responsible for making all of life and the universe possible. At a granular level, Dharma includes all the duties, rights, laws, conduct, virtues and behaviors needed for us to come into accord with "cosmic law and order" as it's defined within the religious context of Buddhism.

[32] **Wholeness** – The state of being complete, having intact integrity with nothing missing or lacking. Wholeness also includes the experience of being in full accord with the Divine and experiencing a sense of interconnectedness within ourselves, with others and with all of life as a whole. Wholeness incorporates a sense of well-being and fulfillment within us both on a human as well as a spiritual level.

CPSIA information can be obtained
at www.ICGtesting.com
Printed in the USA
LVHW101955041119
636283LV00008B/468/P